Crossing B(l)ack

Mixed-Race Identity in Modern American Fiction and Culture

Sika A. Dagbovie-Mullins

The University of Tennessee Press
Knoxville

First Edition.

The paper in this book meets the requirements of American National Standards Institute / National Information Standards Organization specification Z39.48-1-992 (Permanence of Paper). It contains 30 percent post-consumer waste and is certified by the Forest Stewardship Council.

A section of chapter 3 was previously published as "Fading to White, Fading Away: Biracial Bodies in Michelle Cliff's *Abeng* and Danzy Senna's *Caucasia*" in *African American Review* 40.1 (Spring 2006). Parts of chapter 5 were published in "Star-Light, Star-Bright, Star Damn Near White: Mixed Race Superstars" in *The Journal of Popular Culture* 40.2 (April 2007).

Library of Congress Cataloging-in-Publication Data

Dagbovie-Mullins, Sika A.
Crossing b(l)ack: mixed-race identity in modern American fiction and culture / Sika A. Dagbovie-Mullins. — 1st ed.
p. cm.
Includes bibliographical references and index.
ISBN-13: 978-1-57233-932-3 (hardcover)
ISBN-10: 1-57233-932-2 (hardcover)
1. American fiction—20th century—History and criticism.
2. American fiction—21st century—History and criticism.
3. African Americans—Race identity.
4. Racially mixed people in literature.
5. Racially mixed people—Race identity—United States.
6. Passing (Identity) in literature.
I. Title.

PS374.N4D34 2013
813'.5409896073—dc23
2012020592

For my parents, Prospero and Frances Dagbovie

Contents

Acknowledgments	ix
1. What's Old Is New Again, or the Brand New Fetish: Black/White Bodies in American Racial Discourse	1
2. From Naxos to Copenhagen: Helga Crane's Mixed-Race Aspirations in Nella Larsen's *Quicksand*	27
3. Homeward Bound: Negotiating Borders in Lucinda Roy's *Lady Moses* and Danzy Senna's *Caucasia*	51
4. "This Is How Memory Works": Boundary Crossing, Belonging, and Blackness in Mixed-Race Autobiographies	77
5. B(l)ack to Last Drop? Mariah Carey, Halle Berry, and the Complexities of Racial Identity in Popular Culture	105
Conclusion	121
Notes	129
Bibliography	141
Index	161

Acknowledgments

One of my most vivid memories from elementary school occurred in some fourth grade festivities. Toward the end of the game "Red Rover," instead of calling out individual students' names, the teacher began calling students by various descriptors. As one of the last members of our team, I was excited when I heard "Red Rover, Red Rover, send everyone Italian right over." I ran and broke through two students holding hands but was promptly chastised by another teacher for running out of turn. Through tears, I explained that my mother was Italian (my childhood simplification of her ethnicity), but the teacher shook her head "no" at me.

In a small way, this memory highlights some of the critical questions I approach in this book. First, how do blackness and mixed race get defined? The United States has a complicated and inconsistent history with regard to racial categorization. The fact that, at least for some time, I could be nothing other than black to this teacher points to a second, related issue I take up in this project: the political and social will in America to define blackness as something static, set, and monolithic. This project considers a mixed-race identity that does not align with the practice of denying a black presence when it is not advantageous, while at the same time it challenges racial categories in the first place.

There is a box in my parents' basement filled with nearly every paper I ever wrote in high school and college. A quick survey of them reveals a preoccupation with identity, ancestry, and race: an embarrassingly clichéd poem titled "colors"; an article I wrote for my college newsletter titled "Black, White or Other?"; a cringe-worthy undergraduate freshman seminar paper, "Growing Up with Okra and Oregano"; and so on. As a young person, I struggled with expressing what seemed then like competing loyalties. I was thinking about some of the ideas in this project long before I knew what I wanted to say.

I would like to thank teachers, motivators, and mentors who, perhaps unbeknownst to them, encouraged my individuality and stirred my imagination, curiosity, and critical thinking from an early age onward—in particular, Dee Appleman, Wendy Geohegan, Jessica Sinclair, Charles Shaw, David and

Connie Robinson, Judy Gebre-Hewitt, Leon Forrest, Charles M. Payne, and Madhu Dubey. I am grateful for my extraordinary graduate professors and dissertation committee members, including Kwaku Korang, Zine Magubane, Ramona Curry, and William Maxwell. I am particularly indebted to my dissertation advisor, Robert Dale Parker, who continues to inspire me to be a better teacher and scholar. His classes, thoughtful comments, and sage advice have been invaluable.

This project received support from many sources and individuals. I would especially like to thank my colleague-friends: Marina Bachetti, Clevis Headley, Derek White, Jane Caputi, Andy Furman, Elena Machado Saez, Raphael Dalleo, Papatya Bucak, Eric Berlatsky, Taylor Hagood, and Patricia Saunders. It was a pleasure to work with the staff at the University of Tennessee Press. Thank you to my editor, Kerry Webb, for her steady encouragement and support from the beginning. I am so happy and appreciative that my new friend, artist Agnès Poitevin-Navarre, has graciously allowed me to use her compelling work for the cover. Deepest gratitude goes to my mother, Frances Dagbovie, who generously read, edited, and offered suggestions and insights to each draft of every chapter.

Friends and family have provided advice, encouragement, and affirmation. Special thanks go to my sister (chica) and kindred spirit, Summer Joy Poole, and my closest friends whose conversations, support, and love have sustained me through the years: Pascale Burns, Miyoshi Brown, Annie Campbell, Liza Colimon, Charifa Smith, and Nghana Lewis.

Whenever my brother or I had any kind of academic success, my father would reminisce and remind us that our Togolese grandfather would be beaming. We both knew the story well: Our grandfather would tell our father, then attending college in the States, "I don't know what they teach you at those universities but keep learning!" I hope I have made my grandparents (Peter Gaglo Dagbovie, Félicia Nuagnon Dagbovie, Charles Formosa, and Ruth Formosa) proud.

This book is dedicated to my immediate family: my beloved and deeply missed sister-in-law, TShaka, who was always one of my biggest cheerleaders; my incredible and loving nephews, Perovi, Kokou, and Agbelé; my brother, Pero, who has always been my role model, best friend, and champion; my mother and confidant, Frances, whose love of books transferred to me and whose compassion for others, immeasurable support, and healing powers are an inspiration; and my father, Prospero, whose life principles and unwavering optimism and pride have provided guidance, comfort, and assurance.

Finally, I would like to thank the amazing love of my life, Chris Mullins, who taught me good things come to those who wait.

Chapter One

What's Old Is New Again, or the Brand New Fetish: Black/White Bodies in American Racial Discourse

> As the multiracial men, women, and families profiled in "Mix It Up!" . . . remind us, beauty is in the blend.
>
> —*O, the Oprah Magazine,* April 2006 (251)

> [W]e're the poster children for globalism, hybridization, humanism, and a dozen other cultural products predicated on transcending boundaries—and you can't help but conclude: It's more than cool to be mixed, it's downright relevant.
>
> —Rebecca Walker
>
> *Mixed: An Anthology of Short Fiction on the Multiracial Experience* (14)

Americans have long been fascinated with racial crossings, imagining multiple freedoms associated with blurring racial boundaries. In the fashion world, fashionistas call new styles, particularly new color trends, the "new black," establishing black as vogue, at once classic and chic. In popular culture, especially since the 1990s, mixed race has literally and symbolically become the "new black," both replacing and continuing a preoccupation with the racial "Other." Thus while the sexual allure of and curiosity about mixed race had never gone away, it became even more pronounced in the late twentieth century, coinciding with the popularity of multiculturalism as both a buzzword and an ideal. For example, the cover of a 2003 *Parade* magazine shows seven ambiguously racially mixed children above the heading "The Changing Faces of America," a caption that closely resembles the title of a 2002 anthology of essays, *New Faces in a Changing America: Multiracial Identity in the Twenty-First Century.* The language in these titles mirrors that used in the current multicultural movement which celebrates multicultural children as America's future.[1] Multiracial organizations such as the MAVIN Foundation, established in 2000, consider media coverage like the *Parade* article instrumental to their objective. In response to the article (which offers a quotation from and picture of MAVIN founder Matt Kelley), the MAVIN website reads, "The popularity of our story has helped to increase mainstream society's understanding of the mixed race experience."

Much of the media attention on mixed race focuses on beauty and "blending." The April 2006 *Oprah Magazine* article "Harmonic Convergences" displays several mixed-race men and women, their ethnicities elaborated alongside their pictures (such as a model who is "German Indian African American"). In addition, pictures of five interracial families are featured under the headline: "Take one parent (Asian? African-American? Hungarian? Native American?). Mix it with another parent (Colombian? Caribbean? German-American? Pakistani Muslim?). And watch something beautiful happen" (274). A November 2009 article in *Allure,* "Face of the Future," featuring photos of five multiracial models, echoes this fascination with mixed race: "More than ever before, beauty is reflected in a blend of ethnicities and colors" (145). The articles in *Parade, Oprah,* and *Allure* continue a familiar theme in popular magazines, beginning with *Time*'s 1993 cover "The New Face of America" featuring a computer-generated image of a woman morphed from several racial backgrounds and *Newsweek*'s 1995 cover "What Color Is Black?" displaying over a dozen "black" faces of diverse shades, eye color, and facial features. Such articles in widely read periodicals illustrate America's obsession with describing, naming, exoticizing, and questioning mixed race. In many ways, racially speaking, "what's old is new," meaning the long-time fascination of mixed-race bodies in American history has recurred in contemporary popular culture.

Following the last two decades' steady increase of biracial discourse in fiction, memoir, and theory, this book contributes to ongoing debate and dialogue regarding what it means to be multiracial by recognizing a black/white mixed-race identity that I am calling black-sentient mixed-race identity. Sentience typically describes one's sensory capacity, ability, or experience.[2] I draw on this meaning to elucidate a black-sentient mixed-race identity, but I emphasize sentience as awareness and "sensitivity in perception or feeling."[3] Black sentience intimates a mixed-race subjectivity that includes a particular awareness of the world, a perception rooted in blackness. It suggests a connection to a black consciousness that does not overdetermine one's racial identification but still plays a large role in it. The emergence of multiracial organizations that promote multiple-race classification options on census and other forms promotes and politicizes a multiracial identity that, I argue, tends to diminish blackness.[4] Many black/white mixed-race people who reject multiracial classification advance a black subjectivity—a black-sentient consciousness, skeptical of what they see as elitism associated with projecting a biracial identity. A black-sentient mixed-race identity reconciles the widening separation between black/white mixed race and blackness that has been encouraged by contemporary mixed-race politics and popular culture. Television news stories, talk shows, and other media discussions frequently position "black" against "biracial," escalating this "us vs. them" mentality.[5] My study examines a mixed-race subjectivity that remains ascribed to a black historical and social past. The intention is not an anachronistic return to "one-drop" racist thinking but rather an effort to recognize that racism and racialized thinking has shaped how Americans regard and invest in mixed-race identity, an investment foregrounded by a historic repulsion and attraction to blackness. Frequently, black/white mixed-race individuals are labeled black, regardless of their assertions or objections. Instead of contributing to such one-dimensional thinking, *Crossing B(l)ack: Mixed-Race Identity in Modern American Literature and Culture* recognizes and examines assertions of racial identity that do not divorce a premodern racial identity from a postmodern racial fluidity.

In her essay "Anti-Essentialism and Intersectionality: Tools to Dismantle the Master's House," Trina Grill asks, "Is it possible to create a Black-identified biracial identity? Can one be biracial or multiracial and also be Black?" (124).[6] This book is an effort to answer this question by examining mixed-race subjects who attempt to both identify with blackness and embrace a postmodern racial identity. As David L. Brunsma asserts, "'race' is not something one *is*, but rather an elaborate, lived experience and cultural ritual of what one *does*" (5). I argue that this "doing" includes cultural memory, experience, and consciousness. A black-sentient identity is not a separate racial category, nor does it advance an additional classification for forms and documents. Instead, it merges one's multiracial personal outlook with a black vista. While black/white subjects would seem to have their proverbial cake and eat it too, such an identification does not advocate racial opportunism or celebrate uncritical racial fluidity. Generally, any distancing from blackness seems separatist and antiblack. However, a black-sentient mixed-race identity opens up possibilities for black consciousness.

There are some important parallels between a black-sentient mixed-race identity and vernacular cosmopolitanism, which Pnina Werbner defines as "an oxymoron that joins contradictory notions of local specificity and universal enlightenment" (496).[7] Indeed, cosmopolitanism is a term that has often been used to characterize our mixed-race president. Suzanne W. Jones states that supporters of Barack Obama viewed "his cosmopolitan multicultural background as essential for the new century" (131) while Michele Elam contends that Obama's inauguration ushered in what can be called his "mixed race cosmopolitan[ism]" (7).[8] In contrast, Linda Selzer argues that Obama represents "cosmopolitan blackness": "Through his political speeches and two books, Obama joins in this larger effort by articulating a form of world citizenship that recognizes multiple obligations and rights" (15, 28). Similarly, several characters and writers examined in this study travel abroad and claim a kind of kinship with people outside their communities, culture, or country. This is most clearly apparent in Rebecca Walker's aphorisms or James McBride's contention that he belongs to "one people" (McBride 104). In "Double Blood," Rebecca Walker explains, "The pliability of racial and cultural identity can be a tremendous gift. In Kenya, Mexico, Thailand, Egypt, Morocco, and several countries in between, I am embraced as a daughter, sister, mother, or potential wife. Rarely, if ever am I perceived as a foreigner." Being welcomed as a native creates cross-cultural mutuality. She continues:

> "Ah," the shopkeeper, teacher, or taxi driver will say, "you come from America? But you are like us!" I will laugh and shake my head. "No matter," the person will say, "now you are home." And I will feel at home, too. Even if I cannot speak the language, I easily absorb the mannerisms and rhythm of daily life. ("Double Blood" 130)

Several of the fictional characters I examine also subscribe to a subtle or more impassioned kind of global citizenship or universalism. When a fellow airplane passenger mistakes *Caucasia*'s protagonist Birdie Lee for Indian or Pakistani, Birdie initially corrects him, explaining, "I'm American." When the passenger presses her with "No, but where are you really from? Your ancestors. Where are they from?" Birdie's response is both local and transnational: "Everywhere. I mean, before they got here, I guess they were from England and Africa. My mom's white. Dad's black" (377, 378–39). Although Birdie's response reveals an adolescent acknowledgment of transnational connections, it symbolizes notable similarities between a universalist outlook and recognition of racial roots.

In the final chapter of his memoir, *The Color of Water: A Black Man's Tribute to His White Mother,* James McBride admits that he "felt frustrated to live in world that considers the color of your face an immediate political statement whether you like it or not" (262). Rebecca Walker registers a related complaint, asserting, "The not-so-fabulous part of being multiracial is the tremendous anxiety often felt as a result of belonging to several racial and cultural groups, each demanding almost lockstep allegiance" ("Double Blood" 130). Ross Posnock's discussion of cosmopolitanism in *Color and Culture: Black Writers and the Making of the Modern Intellectual* (1998) focuses less on allegiance and more on "the effort made to lift the burden of being a group representative or exemplar." He explains:

> To escape the pressure to conform to the familiar and recognizable, to stereotypes, is to be free to delete the first word or to accent the second in the phrase *black intellectual* or to vary one's inflections at will or as circumstance dictates. To impart something of this lability and this ambition to interrogate the very category of race, I use the term *antirace race man or woman.* (5)

In a similar sense, a black-sentient mixed-race identity interrogates the construction of race and challenges accepted societal racial delineations. However, black is not subject to erasure but instead grounds a more expansive identity politics.

In this work, I use "black/white" to describe the children of one white parent and one black parent; however, it can also describe those with less "recent" mixture. Oftentimes, biracial people repeat a common sentiment regarding why they define themselves multiracially: they do not want to deny or disrespect their (usually) white parent. Although not restricted to mixed-race people, a black-sentient identity specifically speaks to this dilemma and other issues concerning historical and personal racial ties. I use the terms "biracial" and "mixed race" interchangeably, recognizing that these descriptions can reinforce the idea that race is a stable or essential category. In this project, "multiracial" refers to people with many race mixtures or with racial mixture generations back. Using the term black-sentient identity urges a more directed vision of how some black/white mixed-race people identify.

Barack Obama: The New Racial Frontier?

Racial discourse surrounding Barack Obama and his own statements about his ethnicity speak to two of the major concerns of this project: (1) the contradictory ways in which mixed race is understood and perceived in American society and (2) a black-sentient identity that claims blackness without neglecting the specific nuances that shape a biracial subjectivity. When Obama gained notoriety for his speech at the 2004 Democratic National Convention and three years later when he first announced his candidacy for president, much attention was paid to his race and racial authenticity (or supposed lack thereof). On the one hand, some celebrated Obama's unique background as an ideal symbol of America's racial and ethnic diversity. On the other hand, others maintained that Obama was "too white" and thus unable to relate to the black masses. In this sense, Obama faced a situation similar to what Danzy Senna describes in "Passing and the Problematic of Multiracial Pride (or, Why One Mixed Girl Still Answers to Black)": "I faced a conundrum that many mixed people face: the black community of those heady times [the late 1970s] told me that I'd better identify as black, but that I would never be black enough. It was the ultimate double bind" (84). Obama has received similar criticism in the media by liberals and conservatives and blacks and whites alike. In the February 2007 NPR *Talk of the Nation* segment "Can Barack Obama Win the Black Vote?" journalist Clarence Page claims, "It was the media that raised this question because it's a great little headline: Is Barack Black Enough?" The racial catch-22s implicit in such questions and discussions—too black or not black enough—demonstrate that despite many people's efforts to self identify as they wish, the race or racial authenticity of others is still in the eye of the beholder. According to conservative black author Debra Dickerson, "Obama isn't black" because "by virtue of his white American mom and his Kenyan dad who abandoned him and America, he is an American of African immigrant extraction."[9] Racially opinionated comments about just who (or "what," racially speaking) Obama is came from blacks and whites, and notably from the political opposition. Rush Limbaugh jokes about the authenticity of a biracial identity: "Hey, Barack Obama has picked up another endorsement: Halfrican American actress Halle Berry. As a Halfrican American, I am honored to have Ms. Berry's support, as well as the support of other Halfrican Americans" ("Limbaugh on Obama"). Whether in jokes, news articles, interview questions, or internet discussions, Barack Obama's racial background invites speculation, interest, opinion, and criticism.

Celebrations of Obama's mixedness indirectly confirm his assumed "diluted" black identity. Hayward Derrick Horton contends that Obama "is perceived as acceptable as a neo-mulatto" (120) or someone who acts "as a buffer between blacks and whites" and has access to what Horton describes as "whitespace": "physical and social places that have been culturally defined as being designed primarily as being appropriate for the dominant population" (118). In some ways, the initial attention surrounding Obama's racial background repeats the attention given to Tiger Woods during his ascent to popularity and celebrity. While Woods was heralded as a symbol of the diversity in our nation's future, Obama's political positioning and rhetoric often advance him as a symbol of the nation itself. When Obama won the 2008 presidential election, Tiger Woods himself described Obama in similar terms: "He represents America. He's multiracial. I was hoping it would happen in my lifetime" ("Woods Calls Obama's Election 'Absolutely Incredible'").[10] As writer William Powers affirms in an interview, "[W]e feel better about ourselves because he is of mixed race and because he seems to represent this principle of the kind of country we'd like to live in" ("Obamapalooza"). Cartoonist John Cole's political cartoon featuring Obama's face as an ink Rorschach test parodies the excitement about Obama's biraciality. The cartoon asks, "Do you see," and offers, among four other possibilities, "The Multi-racial second coming of John Edwards?" This particular multiple-choice option and the cartoon itself reveal the racial appeal of Obama. Obama himself admits, "I am like a Rorschach test. . . . Even if people find me disappointing ultimately, they might gain something" (Powell). Many people see Obama as "the literal embodiment of our cultural hybridity" (Terry) and, as a *New York Times* article maintains, "Much of Mr. Obama's success as a politician has come from walking a fine line . . . as a biracial American whose political ambitions require that he appeal to whites while still satisfying the hopes and expectations of blacks" (Scott). Yet interest in Obama's racial background also elicited conflicting conclusions about racial naming. In a 2004 interview with Obama, CNN anchor Paula Zahn stated, "Given your mixed race, I'm still fascinated that you still identify yourself as black . . . in spite of your mother having been white." Similarly, in a 2008 *New Republic* article, "Invisible Man: How Ralph Ellison explains Barack Obama," David Samuels expresses surprise about Obama's racial identification.[11] He maintains that despite some thematic and structural similarities between Ellison's *Invisible Man* and Obama's autobiography,

> Obama believes in the old-fashioned, unabashedly romantic . . . quite weird idea of racial authenticity that Ellison rejected. He embraces his racial identity despite his mixed parentage through a kind of Kierkegaardian leap into blackness, through which he hopes to become a whole, untroubled person. (22)

Such comments reveal the contradictory nature of contemporary racial expectations in the United States. While many people, white and black, consciously or subconsciously subscribe to the one-drop-or-more rule, others continue to see black/white mixed race as separate from or even incompatible with blackness. Given Obama's identification as a black man, exploring the media and public receptions of him is thus fitting in terms of this project's discussion of a black-sentient identity. Asserting a black/white identity does not ignore blackness in favor of a more sanitized racial identification yet still resists racial classification. Similarly, Obama's assertions of blackness present another face not projected on *Time* magazine's 1993 cover "The New Face of America," whose computer-generated face, unattributable to any ethnicity, seemed devoid of racial connections and responsibility.

Once Obama's presidential aspirations became realistic, his blackness spoke louder than his benign or more palatable biraciality.[12] Instead of asking whether Obama was black enough, the media launched discussions about Obama being a historic black "first." Thus, when people realized that Obama actually had a chance of securing the nomination and possibly becoming president, major discussions about Obama's being mixed race lessened considerably.[13] When the media celebrated Obama as the first African American to win the Democratic nomination, the abandoning of one racial label to adopt another reflects the contradictory love/hate relationship American culture has with blackness and biraciality. As journalist Alex Cohen asserts in "Why Obama Chooses 'Black' Over 'Biracial,'" a January 2008 NPR segment: "What you don't hear is Barack Obama could be the first biracial president, nor do you hear the candidate refer to himself that way." Still, now that Obama has been elected president, some people are urging others to recognize his biraciality.[14] Changes in terms of how mixed-race people are perceived, exemplified by Obama's shift in the media from biracial to black, mirror the historical and contemporary inconstancy in the legal and social position of mixed-race people in American racial discourse.

In general, expectations surrounding Obama's racial identification and classification simultaneously demonstrate that while some racial rules seemed fixed, there are always exceptions. Presumptions about Obama's race also highlight the interconnectedness of "nation" and "race." How will America find his symbolic new face, one that seemingly won't "give up" blackness and wear a mask of racelessness even though multiraciality is increasingly seen as progressive and desirable? If Obama represents America, a self-described "skinny kid with a funny name who believes that America has a place for him," and a crucial political place at that, then he also makes us question who we are as a nation and why race still matters (*Dreams from My Father* 452). His 2004 declaration at the Democratic National Convention that "[t]here is not a Black America and White America and Latino America and Asian America—there's the United States of America" proposes a racial utopian vision perhaps complicated by his black identification (451). In contrast, for some, Obama's publicly professed racial identity complicates an image of him as a biracial candidate. Author Joy Zarembka maintains, "Friends of mine who are sort of part of the multiracial community very much feel like he should come out and be sort of a proud biracial America" (qtd. in "Why Obama Chooses").[15]

Obama thus provides an intriguing example of an expression of a black-sentient identity. In his autobiography, *Dreams from My Father: A Story of Race and Inheritance* (1995), he confides that addressing the complexities of racial identity and authenticity as a teenager was difficult: "I learned to slip back and forth between my black and white worlds, understanding that each possessed its own language and customs and structures of meaning, convinced that with a bit of translation on my part the two worlds would eventually cohere" (Obama 82). The experience of being mixed helped, Obama asserts, "strengthen" him: "[Y]ou're in a unique position, because you can communicate with the majority, but you also have insight into what it means to be on the outside" (interview with Paula Zahn). When asked by a journalist about a book reviewer's assumption that Obama's life emblematized the neither/nor dilemma, Obama offered, "If I were to write the review, I'd describe myself as coming from several cultures and feel I belong to all of them" (Terry). Yet Obama is also quick to point out that he self-identifies as black, explaining, "I've always viewed the African-American community and African-American culture as a hybrid culture by definition" (interview with Paula Zahn). This recognition of African Americans as already "hybrid" parallels statements from writers such as Danzy Senna, who maintains that she does not see her black identification "in contradiction with my white or Mexican ancestry." She continues, "Nor does it negate these other parts of myself. I have come to understand that my multiplicity is inherent in my blackness, not opposed to it" ("Passing and the Problematic of Multiracial Pride" 85).[16] Thus, Obama's view of himself echoes the assertions of many of the writers and characters in this study regarding their racial backgrounds, namely that being biracial or even multiracial and black not only is *not* contradictory but is also essential to their identity. As Rebecca Walker maintains, "Of course Obama is black. And he's not black, too. . . He's white and he's not white too. Obama is whatever people project onto him . . . he's a lot of things, and neither of them necessarily exclude the other" (qtd. in Washington, "Obama's True Colors").

Understanding mixed-race identity as encompassing multiple racial and cultural identities while being specifically, even undeniably, black, proposes a black/white mixed-race identity that sees race as both fluid and adjoining. In a world that is supposedly becoming "post-race," such identifications challenge racial constructs as much as they reaffirm blackness in terms of cultural memory and social, political, and economic relations.[17] James Olney describes personal memory as an "adaptive function" that turns back "to the past so as to position itself and us for what is to be dealt with in the future" (343). Rebecca Walker frequently makes reference to memory, beginning her autobiography, *Black, White, and Jewish: Autobiography of a Shifting Self,* by stating, "I don't remember things" (Walker 1). She continues, "without a memory that invests in information retention, without a memory that can remind me at all times of who I definitively am, I feel amorphous" (2). This causes her problems of identity as she feels lost, racially and otherwise, without memory. Cultural memory, as an "adaptive function," is equally important to one's identity, particularly a black-sentient mixed-race identity that never breaks away from an understanding of a black consciousness. This identity encourages the dismantling of racial categories while recognizing the challenge of dealing with racial categories that have created identifications and connections that do not disappear despite the acceptance of race as a social construction. *Crossing B(l)ack* examines particular ways in which characters merge the political and the social in an identity that is neither self-serving nor ahistorical or apolitical.

American (Racial) Idol: Contemporary Mixed-Race Hype

When Obama referred to himself as a mutt in a press conference held after his presidential win, most people viewed his comment as a lighthearted joke. Explaining that his family wanted to get a shelter dog to take to the White House, he said, "a lot of shelter dogs are mutts like me" (Rhee). However, rapper Kayne West's use of the term two years earlier was seen as less humorous. In a December 2006 *Essence* magazine article, West is quoted as saying, "If it wasn't for race mixing there'd be no video girls. Me and most of my friends like mutts a lot. Yeah, in the 'hood they call 'em mutts" ("Say *What?*" 72).[18] His statement reveals the mix of descriptions, names, and meanings inscribed on mixed-race bodies, both insulting and complimentary, belittling and approving. As the West quote intimates, despite the negative connotations of the term "mutt," racial ambiguity holds a certain amount of social cachet that is actively promoted by the media and advertisers.[19] Danzy Senna jokes, "Strange to wake up and realize you're in style. That's what happened to me just the other morning. It was the first day of the new millennium and I woke to find that mulattos had taken over. They were everywhere. Playing golf, running the airwaves, opening their own restaurants, modeling clothes, starring in musicals with names like *Show Me the Miscegenation!*" ("The Mulatto Millennium" 12).

The new surge of interest in multiracial Americans parallels a steady increase in the number of interracial marriages in the United States and reveals a national desire to be biracial, at least in a social sense. Despite anxieties over race mixing, multiracial organizations such as the Association of Multi-Ethnic Americans (est. 1988) and Project Race (est. 1991) attempt to cast aside conventional notions of race by renaming and reclaiming race. In this vein, some multiracial organizations such as *MixedFolks.com* have reclaimed the word "mixed" as a positive description rather than a disparaging label. Increasingly, multiracial individuals have renamed themselves, the most famous being Tiger Woods, who has self-identified as "Cablinasian" (referring to his Caucasian, Black, Indian, and Asian ancestry).[20]

White Americans often desire, emulate, and fetishize the modish new black identity of multiracialism. Since the early twentieth century, appropriating "blackness" has equaled "cool." Donnell Alexander aptly proclaims, "[W]hen mainstream America looks for cool we look to black culture" (368). At the same time, however, Americans still fear and loathe blackness, marginalizing and criminalizing black bodies. As Cheryl Harris, David Roediger, and Theodore Allen have already argued, whiteness is achieved through a distancing from blackness.[21] In thinking about biraciality, particularly in terms of the multiracial movement, I would like to suggest that black/white biracial subjectivity is achieved through a similar distancing. In other words, black/white biracial subjects often rely on their "difference" from blackness since black/white mixed-race identity and black identity frequently get collapsed. However, unlike white subjects, biracial subjects still retain a fragile connection to the "Other." This positioning allows them a special "space" in the American lexicon of race; however, the linkage contradictorily affirms both their affinity towards whiteness via blackness *and* their inescapable proximity to the darker "Other." The fascination with mixed-race bodies is metaphorically synonymous to racial slumming in the late 1920s. Kevin Mumford explains, "[T]he influx of white mainstream urbanites . . . temporarily participated in the interzones [black/white sex districts], usually for pleasure, and then returned to their homes and lives apart from the black/white vice districts" (133). Similarly, whites' obsession with black/white mixed-race bodies permits "consumption" of a more palatable form of blackness while allowing whites to return "home" or stay distanced from the supposedly less "attractive" aspects of black identity. Mixed-race identity remains exotic and "other," yet still safer and less threatening than blackness. The beginning of a 2001 *Mademoiselle* article perpetuates the fetishization of biracial women:

> You've seen her. She's beautiful—but in an unfamiliar, can't-quite-put-your-finger-on-it way that makes you want to look twice. You've considered tapping her on the shoulder to ask about her

> ethnic background, but . . . wouldn't that be rude? The four women we interviewed have all dealt with the curiosity that mixed-race beauty triggers. (Beland 61)

The term "mixed-race beauty" conjures images of octoroon balls and stereotypes of mixed-race women as exotic, erotic, and sexually inviting and available.[22] However, the term also highlights the media's fascination with multiracial identity in general. Americans stereotype mixed-race people as alluring, mysterious, and "different," marking them as "other." Stuart Hall explains, "Marking 'difference' leads us, symbolically, to close ranks, shore up culture and to stigmatize and expel anything which is defined as impure, abnormal." Hall continues, "[P]aradoxically, it also makes 'difference' powerful, strangely attractive precisely because it is forbidden, taboo, threatening to cultural order" (237). Images of mixed-race individuals attract media attention because they animate interracial relationships, which are less taboo today but still excite and threaten social order.

The current "hype" over mixed-race identity has reinscribed reductionist ideologies about race. For example, Erika Harold, Miss America 2003, whose mother is black and father is white, told *Jet* magazine, "If I had to choose, I would identify myself as African-American," suggesting her desire not to subscribe to racial labels. Two paragraphs later, *Jet* continues, "Harold is the sixth *Black* woman crowned Miss America" (10, emphasis added). Despite Harold's efforts to jettison racial descriptions, she still gets defined as black. A similar dynamic plays out in more general discussions of race. Although popular cultural discussions of mixed race are obsessively reproduced on television and in magazines, mixed-race identity remains exotic and "other." Michel Foucault's hypothesis about sexuality is helpful in understanding this contradiction. "As if in order to gain mastery over it [sex] in reality," Foucault writes, "it had first been necessary to subjugate it at the level of language, control its free circulation in speech" (17). Yet, despite Victorians' obsessive determination to regulate sex, Foucault asserts, there was "a veritable discursive explosion" (17). Similarly, despite efforts of multiracial groups and others to familiarize Americans with diverse racial expressions, magazine articles often sensationalize mixed race, reinforcing and producing our fascination and curiosity. For example, the photos of mixed-race people and descriptions of their ethnicities in *Parade* and *Mademoiselle* subtly work against the articles' supposed intention to demystify mixed race. The first two pages of *Mademoiselle*'s "Meet the Parents" article feature four mixed-race young women juxtaposed with four sets of parents on the other page. Though the article prints each woman's full name, only the first names of the parents appear. Because the seating order of the women purposely does not correspond with the arrangement of the parents, the article encourages readers to guess who belongs with whom. The reader's voyeuristic gaze at these bodies provokes the question "What is she?" and contradicts what the article partly criticizes, namely, the obtrusive scrutiny of mixed-race bodies. The remaining pages of the article then group each set of parents with their daughter, satisfying our curiosity and completing the racial puzzle.

Parade's piece, "A New Generation Is Leading the Way," sets up a similar dichotomy with a cover photo and an article discussing how racial labels confine mixed-race teenagers. At the bottom of the first page, each child's specific racial background follows the child's name—for example, "Maxwell Zaslower, 5 (Jewish Caucasian and Latino); Elizabeth Budhai, 8 (Latino and Indian)" (4). In the last section of the article, Donna Nakazawa writes, "Multihued and multiethnic, these young men and women are leading the way toward a society in which race may simply become an interesting background note to a person's identity" (5). Again, the process of guessing each child's racial background on the cover does not demystify biracialism; instead, it whets our curiosity, making us less likely to someday recognize race as just "an interesting background note."[23] Popular publications like *Parade,* along with melodramatic talk shows and other cultural public discourses, act as America's careless multicultural group discussion leader, ushering in and provoking our secret longings, fascinations, and misconceptions.

In Search of Nelly: Historicizing a Mixed-Race Presence in America

In Zora Neale Hurston's *Their Eyes Were Watching God* (1937), Janie's grandmother admonishes, "De nigger woman is de mule uh de world so far as Ah can see" (29). Her statement reflects the specific hardships of black women, who struggle simultaneously with racism and sexism. Yet, as Julie Haurykiewicz notes, Nanny's assertion also ironically speaks directly to Janie, a "quadroon," the child conceived after a white man raped her mother. Since Janie's mother was conceived the same way, the term "mule" takes on a particular racial significance.[24] Janie and her mother are symbolic mules by virtue of their low racial and gendered position *and* because they represent the supposedly unnatural merging of black and white. The image of the mule and the term mulatto as a metaphor for mixed-race persons emerged in the late eighteenth century, perhaps in part due to its linguistic origin from the Latin word "mulus," meaning mule and from the Spanish word for "young mule."[25] Charles White, an

English doctor, supported the polygenist theory of the origin of races (the belief that different races came from distinct species with separate origins) in his *An Account of the Regular Gradation in Man* (1799). Thomas Gossett writes, "To the argument that Negroes and Europeans are able to interbreed successfully . . . White replies that mulattoes—like mules—tend to be barren" (49). Some fifty years later, Robert Knox's *The Races of Men* (1850) affirms, "Nature produces no mules; no hybrids neither in man nor animals. When they accidentally appear they soon cease to be, for they are either non-productive, or one or other of the pure breeds seedily predominates, and the weaker disappears" (38). The idea of the mulatto as an unnatural hybrid fueled antimiscegenation sentiments. Joel Williamson explains, "That mules had no ancestors that were mules and no descendents at all was common knowledge, and many jokes were built upon that theme" (96). Hurston's use of the mule metaphor resonates in a novel whose protagonist is multiracial but whose mixedness plays no central role. This irony reflects the history of mixed-race people in American racial society, because America ignores the details of a multiracial presence just as critics have overlooked Janie's mixedness in the context of the substantial feminist themes in the novel. In other words, throughout American history, hardly anyone challenges the location of multiracial people as black. Still, mulattos have been frequently singled out for certain putative characteristics (beauty and intelligence or immorality and malevolence) and have similarly estranged themselves, particularly in southern communities in New Orleans and Charleston.[26] The views of William Hannibal Thomas represent an extreme example of this kind of mulatto separatist thinking. Not only did he distinguish between mulattos and blacks, but he also thought only "elite" mulattoes like himself (of "high" character) deserved high esteem. At the same time, Thomas's efforts failed in that his racist book, *The American Negro* (1901), only further alienated him from all "races." John David Smith writes:

> His plea for greater recognition of mulattoes, really just the recognition of one mulatto—William Hannibal Thomas—appeared at the very moment when African Americans of every shade were under severe attack. White American society defined Thomas not as he would have preferred, as a mulatto, but rather as a Negro. (276)

While both whites and blacks subsumed mixedness into blackness, both also considered mixed-race a distinctive racial "other."

Particularly since the nineteenth century, racial contradictions pervaded popular thinking and legal discourse in the United States. Legally, what constituted "white" and "black" varied according to place and circumstance.[27] Contrary to popular thinking, the "one-drop" rule was never consistently applied and racial taxonomy classifications differed from state to state, changing over time and subject to inconsistencies and contradictions.[28] Numerous cases involving miscegenation and racial taxonomy reached the U.S. Supreme Court including *Pace v. Alabama* in 1882. In *Pace*, the court rejected the constitutional challenge to the Alabama's miscegenation statutes that forbade adultery and fornication between blacks and whites. Although Alabama's statutes had more severe punishments for interracial unions as opposed to intraracial unions, the state won. Such rulings reinforced the conviction that intermingling between blacks and whites was abnormal and immoral. By extension, the offspring of such unions would be equally unnatural. The *Pace* case is important because it was "both a rehearsal and an important symbolic antecedent for the separate but equal rhetoric" of the *Plessy v. Ferguson* Supreme Court ruling in 1896 (Saks 12). The disposition of the *Plessy* case confirmed that mixed-race individuals were legally black, regardless of their ethnic makeup. Homer Plessy, a mixed-race man who looked white, was used by a New Orleans Creole group, Comité des Citoyens (or the Citizens Committee to Test the Constitutionality of the Separate Car Law), to prove that separate-but-equal laws violated the 14th Amendment. Jailed for sitting in the white section of an East Louisiana railroad car, the judge ruled that Louisiana could manage and set rules for railroad companies that solely operated in their state. Plessy appealed to the state Supreme Court and then took the case to the U.S. Supreme Court, which also found Plessy guilty, legalizing segregation.[29] In terms of mixed-race jurisprudence, the *Plessy* case both continued and rejected many cultural and legal convictions about "blackness" and "mixedness." The ruling indirectly confirmed Plessy as black, despite being seven-eighths "white." Although the purpose of the case was not to decide what constituted "black," it foretold the treatment of mixed-race issues in terms of how mixed race would be indirectly confronted, even if only to be overlooked, in American culture.[30]

Despite thinking of mulattos as black, many whites did make distinctions between "mulattos" and "blacks." After reconstruction, many writers and "scientists" viewed mulattos as immoral, criminal, and violent, some even suggesting that mulattos were the majority of rapists and murderers.[31] Ironically, most whites attributed these same characteristics to all blacks, regardless of their "degree" of blackness. George M. Fredrickson contends that "for many the distinction between violent mulattoes and docile purebloods was less important than a concept of the basic Negro or African character which supposedly accounted for extremes of submissiveness and violent audacity" (278). After slavery, the lynching of black men flourished as a form of socioeconomic control. It should also be noted that while some whites thought that mulattos inherited the worst of the races, others thought they benefited from the mixture. In *Testimonies Concerning Slavery* (1864), abolitionist Moncure Daniel Conway writes: "I, for one, am firmly persuaded that the mixture of blacks and whites is good; that the person so produced is . . . healthy, handsome, and intelligent. . . . I believe that such a combination would evolve a more complete character than the unmitigated Anglo-Saxon" (76). Others, such as sociologist Charles A. Ellwood, expressed optimism in his 1906 "Review of *The Color Line: A Brief in Behalf of the Unborn*" that the "gradual diffusion of white blood throughout the Negro race would lead to a general improvement of the race as a whole" (Mencke 74).[32] The point here is that whites held inconstant, often contradictory attitudes about black people but relied on these same inconsistencies to continue to oppress and control them. For example, while most whites agreed that mulattos were intellectually superior to "pure" blacks, many still believed in the moral and physical inferiority of mulattos.

In the early 1900s, many whites deemed "mulattos" psychologically unstable. Williamson reveals how early-twentieth-century neurologists performed "tests" that supposedly demonstrated how electrical signals controlled the body in one direction in whites and in an opposite direction in blacks. Williamson explains that these biological experiments would show "Mulattos . . . to be a highly confused people" (96). Scientists concluded that the "signals" of mixed-race people "were hopelessly mixed, and the slightest mixture—even one drop—was enough to upset the system and jangle the nerves" (96). These kinds of "experiments" increased fervor over ideas of white "purity." The trial of Alice and Leonard Rhinelander in 1925 highlights the hysteria about maintaining whiteness in American culture. Alice Jones was a mixed-race waitress who was married to Kip Rhinelander, son of a wealthy white family. The Rhinelanders insisted that their son end his marriage, claiming that Alice deceived him about her race. The court case was a sensation in many ways: it filled New York newspapers and had its salacious moments, such as when the defense showed the all-white male jury Jones's naked body to prove Kip must have known she was black (and thus that she could not have been dishonest about her race). The jury concluded Alice did not deceive, a ruling which implies that blackness is both real and detectable.[33] Blackness as visible is a belief that has pervaded popular thought, although racial passing subverts that belief. Yet, subscribing to the notion that race can be detected by the naked eye fuels the belief of whiteness as pure because it suggests that any "impurities" will reveal themselves (thus spoiling the integrity of whiteness).

Up until the middle to late twentieth century, legally sanctioned segregation continued to be a method to keep the races separate and prevent racial mixing. Despite state laws, however, some interracial couples did socialize and even married. Then one federal landmark case assured that interracial married couples would no longer be prosecuted. In 1967, the *Loving v. Commonwealth of Virginia* decision ruled that antimiscegenation laws were unconstitutional. Although the case was not involved with dictating whether or not the wife, Mildred Loving, was black, it indirectly had some bearing on mixed-race individuals. In 1958, Perry Loving and his wife, residents of Central Point, Virginia, were arrested by Virginia officials after they traveled to the District of Columbia, where there were no miscegenation laws, to get married. After their arrest, the judge said that their one-year jail sentence could be lifted if they did not remain in Virginia for at least twenty-five years. The Lovings appealed the decision and the case eventually went to the U.S. Supreme Court, which declared that miscegenation laws violated the Fourteenth Amendment and were thereby unconstitutional.[34] By legitimizing such marriages, the ruling indirectly legitimized mixed-race children produced from those unions.

This book investigates twentieth- and twenty-first-century representations of mixed-race identity in literature (and popular culture) as figured through six primary literary texts and two popular-culture figures: Nella Larsen's *Quicksand* (1928), Lucinda Roy's *Lady Moses* (1998), Danzy Senna's *Caucasia* (1998), Barack Obama's *Dreams from My Father: A Story of Race and Inheritance* (1995), James McBride's *The Color of Water: A Black Man's Tribute to His White Mother* (1996), Rebecca Walker's *Black, White and Jewish: Autobiography of a Shifting Self* (2001), singer Mariah Carey, and actress Halle Berry. Throughout, I detail the ways in which biracial subjects who negotiate racial borders claim multiple identities while remaining especially connected to blackness. I argue that neither the obsessive interest in nor the current debates about biracialism have facilitated healthy discussions about mixed-race identity. Rather, these discourses (as on talk shows, in popular magazines, and in the popularity of celebrities such as Tiger Woods) have elided the intricacies of mixed-race identity politics in preference for easy racial oppositions or romantic stereotypes about what mixed race represents while fueling America's obsession and desire to be mixed race.

Before theorizing about mixed-race identity, it is crucial to discuss the ways in which scholars think about blackness and whiteness in contemporary discourse. Michael Omi and Howard Winant's frequently referenced *Racial Formations in the United States* traces how the notion of race has shaped American society. According to Omi and Winant:

> There is a continuous temptation to think of race as an essence, as something fixed, concrete, and objective. And there is also an opposite temptation: to imagine race as a mere illusion, a purely ideological construct which some ideal non-racist social order would eliminate. It is necessary to challenge both these positions, to disrupt and reframe the rigid and bipolar manner in which they are posed and debated, and to transcend the presumably irreconcilable relationship between them. (54)

Omi and Winant's assertions explain how race both *is* and *is not* crucial to understanding the concept of a black-sentient identity that does not subscribe to biological notions of race but still recognizes how a black consciousness can shape black/white mixed-race identities.[35] Like *Racial Formations,* Paul Gilroy's *The Black Atlantic* attempts to come to terms with the contradictory assumptions that race (blackness) is either an illusion or a biological condition. Gilroy defines the black Atlantic world as the "stereophonic, bilingual, or bifocal cultural forms originated by, but no longer the exclusive property of, blacks dispersed within the structures of feeling, producing, communicating, and remembering" (3). Certainly, there is no biologically "pure" anything, black or otherwise. And yet, Gilroy points to the "Black Atlantic" as a nongenetic, unifying connection of black diasporic peoples around the world, who share a history and experience of exile, displacement, and migration. In other words, a shared history and social past bind people of African descent, particularly within America. Similarly, in autobiographies, fiction, and popular culture, biracial subjects negotiate notions of blackness and whiteness while often projecting a black/white identity. As Lisa Jones explains, "I'm a writer whose work is dedicated to exploring the hybridity of African-American culture and of American culture in general. . . . I don't deny my white forebears, but I call myself African American, which means, to me, a person of African and Native American, Latin or European descent. . . . I feel comfortable and historically grounded in this identity" (*Bulletproof Diva* 31). Though Jones seems to assert a black identity, her concept of blackness suggests a vision of a mixed-race identity rooted in African American culture. Jones's assertion speaks to Gilroy's "black Atlantic" endeavor in that Jones, despite her multiethnic/racial/historical background, recognizes her shared black diasporic racial past. *Crossing B(l)ack* examines a black/white intermix identity that remains connected to Gilroy's concept of "blacks dispersed within the structures of feeling, producing, communicating, and remembering" while resisting racial scripts.

Various scholars have theorized about the promise of embracing a mixed-race identity. In her seminal text *Borderlands/La Frontera,* Gloria Anzaldua finds possibilities, not limitations, in mixedness: "[T]he new *mestiza* copes by developing a tolerance for contradictions, a tolerance for ambiguity. . . . [S]he learns to juggle cultures" (79). For the mestiza, Anzaldua advocates relying on the strengths of multiple cultures and backgrounds to avoid struggling to belong, insisting that this cultural hybridity will create a mestiza consciousness. Since *Borderlands,* others have argued for the dismantling of race and for the recognition of a multiracial or mixed-race identity. In the 1990s, a number of anthologies and books discussing mixed race appeared, including *Racially Mixed People in America* (1992), *Race and Mixed Race* (1993), *American Mixed Race: The Culture of Microdiversity* (1995), *The Multiracial Experience: Racial Borders as the New Frontier* (1996), and *What Are You? Voices of Mixed Race Young People* (1999). In the introduction to *The Multiracial Experience,* editor Maria P. P. Root echoes Anzaldua's assertion that border crossing can be empowering, suggesting that such crossings will force the breakdown of racial categories. However we also need to remember that in a nation that marginalizes black, "language of mixed race" almost guarantees the devaluation of blackness so that such discussions must address the privileging of whiteness. Kerry Ann Rockquemore, David L. Brunsma, and Daniel J. Delgado describe social science researchers writing in the mid-1980s–1990s (including Root) whose work, they say, represents a "variant approach": "Theoretically, these new researchers . . . sought to explain psychologically, clinically, and developmentally how mixed-race people actively and consciously construct a 'biracial' or 'multiracial' identity and how they could maintain a healthy, integrated sense of their multiple racial ancestries, culture, and social location" (18).

In critical race studies, arguments skeptical of the mixed-race movement tend to focus on the political, legal, and economic ramifications of racism that biraciality cannot "fix." For example, in a 1998 essay, "'Multiracial Discourse: Racial Classifications in an Era of Color-Blind Jurisprudence," Tanya Kateri Hernandez argues that the official acknowledgment of mixed-race individuals inevitably privileges mixed-race people as a group. Lewis Gordon makes similar claims in his chapter, "Race, Biraciality, and Mixed Race—In Theory," in which he warns against ignoring racism in favor of mixed race and discusses how contemporary biracial discourse evades blackness.[36] In terms of theorizing about black/white mixed-race identity, the challenge is to resist the tendency to subsume mixed race into blackness or completely separate it from blackness. At the same time, it is important to recognize the complexities and nuances of black/white mixedness and the variables that shape racial subjectivity.[37] My work asserts that a mixed-race identity need not privilege whiteness; in fact, a black-sentient identity demonstrates the extent to which one's cultural history and social past can shape political and social identities.

Tragic Representations in Literature and Film

Traditionally, literary and cinematic portrayals of mixed race have produced one kind of representation: tragic. Werner Sollors credits poet and critic Sterling Brown for first using the term "tragic mulatto" in a literary sense.[38] According to Brown, several elements define the tragic mulatto: "[T]he mulatto is a victim of divided inheritance and therefore miserable; he is a 'man without a race' worshipping the whites and despised by them, despising and despised by Negroes, perplexed by his struggle to unite a white intellect with black sensuousness" (195–96). In addition, Brown claims that antislavery writers frequently used the archetype. Berzon similarly describes the tragic mulatto as "an outcast, a wanderer, one alone." Often "ambivalent toward the two castes," the tragic mulatto "is the fictional symbol of marginality. Rejected out of fear and hatred by the dominant group, he is often rejected out of envy and hatred by the lower caste as well" (100). In *Negro Poetry and Drama,* Sterling Brown suggests that male mixed-race literary characters, "merely because they were nearer white, were more intelligent and militant, and therefore more tragic in their enslavement" than "unmixed" blacks (Sollors 224). For the most part, Judith Berzon agrees with Brown's observations, claiming that male mulatto characters are "brave, honest, intelligent, and rebellious," yet that "few male mixed-blood characters are tragic mulattoes in the traditional sense" (74). Tragic mulattas are often characterized as exceedingly beautiful but destined to live tragic lives. Late-nineteenth- and turn-of-the-century writers use the tragic mulatto archetype for multiple ends: to denounce slavery, to critique the paradox of race, to condemn miscegenation through disturbing characterizations, or simply to foster an already destructive stereotype. Recent criticism has attempted to reclaim late-nineteenth- and early-twentieth-century mixed-race characters as biracial feminists and boundary-challenging women.[39] Since the mid-twentieth century, the term tragic mulatto has come to represent more generally a mixed-race character whose racial confusion and marginalization cause her or him personal despair and inner turmoil.

Generally speaking, nineteenth- and early-twentieth-century mulatta characters shared sad, pitiable, and unfortunate endings. Lydia Maria Child, the white writer and abolitionist, first used the tragic mulatta characterization in "The Quadroons" (1842), which established a familiar character type for many abolitionist novels: the beautiful white-looking slave. William Wells Brown's *Clotel: Or, the President's Daughter, A Narrative of Slave Life in the United States* (1853) follows three generations of mixed-race women who face the auction block because of their black blood. Each of these women die tragically: both Clotel and her niece commit suicide while her other niece dies of a broken heart. Similarly, in Charles Chesnutt's *The House Behind the Cedars* (1900), Rena Walden dies from illness and heartache. Rena decides to pass for white and falls in love with a rich white southerner. Her lover rejects her when he finds out her secret, and Rena's deep anguish over his rejection prompts her failing health. Like many tragic mulattos before and after, Rena thinks of herself as dual, repressing one "race" and bringing the other forward. John Warwick, though not as tragic as his sister, completely rejects his black ancestry and passes, tragic in his hatred of blackness. Passing continues as a theme in *The Autobiography of an Ex-Colored Man* (1912), in which the mixed-race, unnamed narrator admits he sold his "birthright for a mess of pottage" (154).

In the literature of the Harlem Renaissance, the popular theme of passing featured mixed-race women entangled in the complex world of racial masquerade. In Nella Larsen's *Passing* (1929), Clare Kendry accidentally runs into an old friend, Irene, while both are passing for white in a hotel. After seeing Irene (who only occasionally passes), Clare regrets her life decision to pass as white and begins a kind of reverse "racial slumming," passing for white at home but cavorting with blacks at dinners, dances, and teas. In the novel's dramatic ending, Clare's white husband unexpectedly shows up at a black party Clare secretly attends. Though the novel leaves it ambiguous as to whether Clare jumps to her death or is pushed, one thing is clear: the mixed-race character is unable to live in her "white" (or "black") body. Though twentieth-century literature continued to focus on the plight of mulattas, not mixed-race men, mixed-race male characters such as Joe Christmas in *Light in August* (1932) and Kabnis and Paul in *Cane* (1923) perpetuated tragic qualities attributed to their mixedness.

Most recently, a number of novels and short stories have specifically addressed issues of black/white mixed-race identity, including Danzy Senna's *Symptomatic* (2004), Emily Raboteau's *The Professor's Daughter* (2005), various stories in *Mixed: An Anthology of Short Fiction on the Multiracial Experience* (2006), and Heidi W. Durrow's *The Girl Who Fell from the Sky* (2009). Such texts suggest that "mulatto" archetypes are slowly being critically examined or rewritten in American fiction; they reflect the diversity of biracial expressions. For example, *Symptomatic* plays on the tragic mulatto archetype by complicating racial myths about mixed race. In the novel, Greta is a biracial woman who attaches herself to another mixed-race coworker who shares her phenotypically white features. Yet Greta's attachment soon becomes obsessive. When the narrator tries to end their friendship, Greta turns into a psychopath. When asked to speak to the ways in which Greta's character is reminiscent of the tragic mulatto, Senna responds, "I really wanted to take on the tragic mulatto stereotype in many ways, but not simply through creating a character for whom none of this [difficulties of being mixed race and appearing white] is an issue." She further suggests that academia uses the tragic mulatto

> to dismiss something, to not actually grapple with what the author is talking about. Greta falls into that stereotype in many ways, but the main character is much more complicated. I think Greta is the horror of what the main character could become should she let these experiences seep into her and become a part of her. I don't even see Greta as being, in some ways, a real character. I see her in many ways as a ghost, a reminder of the past and all these images we have to consume in this culture. So for me, that's precisely what the main character has to fight against. ("The Africana QA: Danzy Senna")

In some ways, Greta becomes a parody of the stereotype she embodies. Senna's characterization shows that the archetype of the tragic mulatta haunts contemporary mixed-race characters, including *Caucasia*'s protagonist, who is reminded by her white grandmother that she is tragic because of her racial mix.

Historically, cinematic representations of mixed-race characters have followed literary representations, meaning that many mixed-race characters on film have lacked diversity.[40] While laws attempted to prevent interracial unions, cinema tried to pretend they did not exist. Between 1930 and 1956, the Production Administrative Code forbade scenes depicting miscegenation. The absence of any interracial relationships no doubt contributed to viewers' disgust or disdain for the progeny of any such unions. At the height of the civil rights movement, the mulatto film archetype lost its popularity, yet tragedy continued to befall mixed-race characters. For example, *Devil in a Blue Dress* (1995) continues a familiar theme with its mixed-race character, Daphne Monet. Based on Walter Mosley's novel of the same name, *Devil in a Blue Dress* uncovers a mystery regarding the enigmatic girlfriend of a white politician. Mosley places his narrative in the 1940s, and his mulatta character reflects the same clichéd themes. Audiences learn that Daphne is a black woman passing for white. Again, the movie ends with a sad and teary-eyed mixed-race female character whose life seems full of misfortune. Despite independent shorts and films such as Julie Dash's *Illusions* (1983), which visually hints at mixed race and explores issues of representation and identity, and *The Corndog Man* (1999), which tells the revenge story of a mixed-race son of a white man, most characterizations remain clichéd and simplistic.[41] Though there has been an increase in the number of mixed-race or ethnically ambiguous actors, their roles often satisfy naïve expectations about a raceless American future or confirm recycled stereotypes.

Mixed Race: The Remix?

A 2003 *New York Times* article titled "Generation E.A.: Ethnically Ambiguous" examines marketers' increasing use of racially ambiguous models to sell their products. A twenty-six-year-old artist of French, Mexican, and Spanish heritage proudly proclaims in the article, "We [mixed-race young Americans] are the remix" (La Ferla 9). His statement alludes to the hip-hop term which describes a song that has been redone or remade, sometimes allegedly improving on the original. The remix is a black art form, emblematic of Black America's ability to reinvent itself. Has black/white biraciality become the new remix? More glitz, more glitter, more pizzazz, but ultimately more contrived? The concept of a black-sentient identity demystifies the social glitz and glimmer and remembers the original "track." In other words, black/white identity attempts to dismiss the valorization of mixedness, opting instead to recognize a more radical racial definition of a multiracial self connected to blackness.

American music provides a compelling metaphor for thinking about how blackness foregrounds a black-sentient mixed-race identity. American musical traditions such as rock, pop, rhythm and blues, and country have black musical roots. Despite their diverse cultural influences, all these musical forms owe a debt to blues (or jazz), which borrowed from African musical traditions. As Slash, the biracial former lead guitarist for rock group Guns N' Roses, confirms, "[T]he funny thing about white music, especially in rock, was that it was all influenced by black musicians" (qtd. in Greenfield-Sanders and Mitchell 13). Although these musical genres depart in their own ways from traditional African American expressive culture, the influence of blues is undeniable. *Crossing B(l)ack* reads characters who acknowledge the foundation of their black heritage born of racial struggle, at the same time that they recognize and even defend the other elements and influences that inform their lives. Chapter 2 examines Nella Larsen's *Quicksand,* a novel that marks a shift away from the tragic mulatto stereotype that was created out of fear and anxiety about miscegenation, yet used in abolitionist struggles for black freedom. Helga Crane reveals the conflict between self-identification and racial identity that typifies

America's confused and wavering relationship with blackness. She transcends mulatta stereotypes described earlier in this chapter and serves as a prototype of a black/white identity that other characters in this study appropriate. I argue that Helga Crane's unsteady yet sustained connection to "blackness" lays a foundation for literary works, including Lucinda Roy's *Lady Moses* and Danzy Senna's *Caucasia*, that follow on *Quicksand*'s engagement with black-sentient mixed-race subjectivity.

Jacinta Moses and Birdie Lee, the protagonists in *Lady Moses* and *Caucasia* respectively, exhibit conflicts with their racial subjectivity in manners akin to *Quicksand*'s Helga Crane. Chapter 3 investigates the concept of home as it relates to race. I explore how Jacinta and Birdie blur boundaries of class, gender, and sexuality, mirroring their circumvention of restrictive racial categories. Yet, their desire for racial fluidity does not erase their understanding of their blackness. Despite rejecting phenotypic or restrictive notions of race, they still want others to recognize them as people of color. Clare and Birdie map their identities through the cultural and racial assumptions they also resist.

Chapter 4 focuses on identity formation in James McBride's *The Color of Water: A Black Man's Tribute to His White Mother* and Rebecca Walker's *Black, White, and Jewish: Autobiography of a Shifting Self,* memoirs by "writer-activists" who redefine racial allegiance and biracial identification. I examine parallels between McBride and Walker and Barack Obama's *Dreams from My Father: A Story of Race and Inheritance,* a memoir that recounts Obama's identity formation. Recently, American readers have been drawn to mixed-race memoirs, an indication of the intrigue associated with boundary crossing.[42] From memoirs that attract readers interested in public figures such as *Dear Senator: A Memoir by the Daughter of Strom Thurmond* (2005), to hilarious reads such as sitcom writer Angela Nissel's *Mixed: My Life in Black and White* (2006), these memoirs animate the complexities of race in America. In particular, McBride's and Walker's autobiographies stand out from the recent influx of biracial memoirs and autobiographies for their lucid and in-depth narratives, which trace the emergence of a mixed-race politic connected to a black aesthetic. These life stories often relate the dilemma of racial belonging in a culture that demands people "wear" their race. McBride and Walker assert identities that are not solely black, biracial, or tragic. Yet, claiming a biracial identity does not suffice for McBride and Walker, who represent a cluster of biracial writers more interested in "doing" than "being" or satisfying other people's need for racial identification. The memoirs of Obama, McBride, and Walker speak to the fictional texts examined in *Crossing B(l)ack* in that they all question and challenge racial expectations and conventional notions of blackness and whiteness. This chapter demonstrates black/white identity in its variations, intimating the relationship between a biracial subjectivity and a black history and social past. Mixed-race autobiographies connect racial identity and political identity, revealing the foundations of black/white identity. In this book, both character and celebrity function as representations of black/white possibilities and sociopolitical debates about race. In popular culture, the images of mixed-race celebrities coincide with common perceptions of mixed-race people. Chapter 5 explores how the images of Mariah Carey and Halle Berry alternately represent blackness and "mixedness." I argue that the way they are presented via publicity and other mediums *and* the way the public and media receive them mirrors larger national inconsistencies regarding race and racial difference.

This book analyzes literary discourses on biracial subjectivity that speak to current political policies and social questions, even crises, regarding race identification requirements, racial solidarity in the black community, and racial loyalty. Considering the popularity and commercial success of books such as *The Color of Water: A Black Man's Tribute to His White Mother* and *Caucasia,* biracial literature presents a growing forum for these issues, offering alternatives to conventional racial identification and dispelling myths about "blackness" and biraciality. In the introduction to *Mixed: An Anthology of Short Fiction on the Multiracial Experience,* Rebecca Walker questions Americans' acceptance of mixed race in the "American story" we tell ourselves: "Which multiracial narrative fits our ethos of triumph over great odds? Which affirms our hopeful belief that our country really is a place everyone can call home?" (14). The fictional and personal narratives by Larsen, Roy, Senna, Walker, McBride, and Obama challenge readers to reconsider "home." Many of the characters may never find "home," if that home would exclude them or any part of who they are. While home is refuge, acceptance, comfort, and belonging, home is also consciousness, a "place" where self-awareness, self-knowledge, and self-acceptance offer comfort.

Chapter Two

From Naxos to Copenhagen: Helga Crane's Mixed-Race Aspirations in Nella Larsen's *Quicksand*

> "They always come back. I've seen it happen time and time again."
> "But why?" Irene wanted to know. "Why?"
> "If I knew that, I'd know what race is."
>
> —Nella Larsen, *Passing* (185)

In a 2008 National Public Radio (NPR) *News & Views* segment called "In Character: Who Would You Talk to?" one internet post proposes *Quicksand*'s protagonist, Helga Crane, in response to the question posed by the program's title. The post then asks, "Do Helga's perceptions of racial identity presage our post-modern, anti-essentialist notions of race, or does she allow the binary opposition, 'either-or' attitudes forged in the U.S. since the 16th century [to] annilihate [*sic*] her sense of self?" (Chideya). The question testifies that Helga's early-twentieth-century "mixed-race aspirations" continue to provoke readers' intellectual interrogations in the twenty-first century and astutely describes Helga's actions and assertions. In short, the answer to both of the post's questions is yes: Helga's problems with race and her efforts to subvert racial essentialism emanate not from a split sense of self but from other people's narrow-minded attitudes. Quicksand, a shifting mass of sand and water that can entrap, is a critical symbol for *Quicksand*'s mixed-race protagonist. Like the unpredictable nature of yielding sand, Helga's racial identifications and experiences are always turning and shifting. At the center of Helga's struggles is her mixed-race identity, made difficult because of other people's reluctance to view themselves and others multiracially. Helga Crane is not a tragic mulatto:

the novel follows her efforts to shape what George Hutchinson calls a "biracial subjectivity," a concept foreign to both Americans and Europeans. For Helga, a biracial identity means having the freedom to avoid restrictive racial labels. Contrary to what many critics have suggested, this does not mean Helga rejects her "blackness" or "whiteness"; nor does it suggest Helga's racial "split." Instead, it registers a self-formation process—how Helga comes to see herself in relation to others—that rejects conventional definitions of race and racial difference. Helga is highly self-conscious of her racial sensibilities and negotiations throughout the novel. Rather than being a "product" of racial uncertainty, however, Helga steadily authors more of her own racial story. Her biracial identity never completely strays away from an understanding of a black consciousness even though her relationship to blackness at times grows weak. Through Helga's frequent moves and changes, the narrative suggests that she desires a life unrestricted by racial burdens and classifications. At the very least, the novel indicates that Helga wants to create physical and cultural spaces that will allow for such freedom without breaking from a racial awareness that she describes as "something deep down inside of me" (Larsen 91). Helga thus asserts not just a biracial identity but a black-sentient mixed-race identity, one that refuses to abide by racial scripts but still acknowledges and honors a black connection.

The purpose of Helga's mental and physical journey is to find a place that neither accentuates nor negates her difference. But social forces and class hierarchies, which mandate specific social places for everyone, do not allow for Helga's cultural movements. Despite her attempts to flee, fight, or manipulate these forces, she is never completely successful. The novel implies that Helga's transitory success depends upon the boldness and unforgiving manner of her approach. While she never has complete autonomy over her identity, the narrative intimates that her resistance to racial labels allows her a limited control. Transcending "mulatta" stereotypes, Helga serves as the prototype of the black-sentient subjectivity that other "mixed" race characters and figures under investigation in this study embody and appropriate.

Helga's geographic locations connect her attitude to her racial subjectivity. Her physical movements parallel specific changes in her psychology. She is highly conscious of her surroundings and flees when she feels restricted or racially imprisoned. Helga makes some choices as she embraces a new kind of identity in each new place she moves to. While her choices narrow because she is subject to other people's projections and perceptions, they still facilitate her subject formation by allowing her to work against social expectations. In reference to multiracial families, Heather M. Dalmage notes that those who "move in and out of various racial identities [are doing] something that has been called 'traveling'" (23). Key stages in Helga's subject negotiations include her assertions of a black-sentient identity, her resistance to outside readings of her identity and her "traveling." She develops a mixed-race subjectivity when she exercises her prerogative to interpret her family's racial history differently depending on her environment, when she searches for freedom beyond racial classification, and when she projects racial independence. Helga's negotiations resonate with Martiniquan novelist Edouard Glissant's notion of creolization by which we better understand Helga's agency and realize her possibilities as a mixed-race character. Glissant defines creolization as "the transfer (by the slave trade) of a population to another place where they change into something different, into a new set of possibilities" (14). Though not a postcolonial subject or Caribbean Creole, Helga embodies the clash and transformation of differences (read: blackness and whiteness), representing a new set of possibilities shaped by a black diasporic connection. Far from romanticizing her biracial status, this process highlights Helga's potential as a black-sentient subject, a potential unexamined by earlier critics who have either oversimplified Helga's racial dilemma or simply overlooked her racial identity.

Helga's identity choices seem to end when, at the novel's conclusion, Helga dreams about escaping her situation, only to be reminded of reality when "she began to have her fifth child" (135). In some ways, changes to the U.S. census form between 1920 and 1930 parallel Helga's identity choices at the beginning and ending of the novel. The year 1920 was the last time that "Mulatto" was an option on the form; it was no longer available by the time of the 1930 census.[1] If we consider Helga's life as embodying the decade of the 1920s (with its highs and lows, financial irresponsibilities, sexual freedoms, and racial movements), then Helga's bleak situation at the end of the novel corresponds to the disappearance of "Mulatto" from the census. In other words, her final move to Alabama marks the end of her racial autonomy and the end of her mixed-race assertions. If the "Mulatto" option on the census form symbolically represents Helga's biracial aspirations for the bulk of the narrative (which takes place during the 1920s), then the Census Bureau's return to monoracial classifications in 1930 represents Helga's stagnant position in a rural black community into which she doesn't fit. Changes on the census form during this time period thus provide an apt metaphor for Helga's mixed-race identity. In the same way in which the census has historically reflected political interests and ideologies, causing racial classifications to be "internally incoherent, inconsistent across groups, and unstable," Helga's racial identity has been shaped by outsiders' inability to accept her difference and her own political understanding of black oppression, creating a shaky yet definite relationship with blackness (Hochschild and Powell 60).[2]

Larsen's early writings have encouraged some scholars to describe her own personal relationship with blackness as precarious.[3] George Hutchinson suggests that Larsen's early writing did not focus on black characters or themes because "[i]n part, it was a characteristic choice for someone who persistently tested racial boundaries" (196). In *In Search of Nella Larsen: A Biography of the Color Line,* Hutchinson clears up many of these misconceptions, maintaining that such statements lack evidence.[4] Mary Helen Washington also notes that Larsen's correspondence shows that despite Larsen's occasional detachment from blacks, she had "an unmistakable race pride" (48). Larsen was born in 1891 to a black West Indian father and a white Danish mother in Chicago. While some biographers question whether Larsen was completely truthful about her past in her self-descriptions, it seems that, to a great extent, *Quicksand* is autobiographical. Larsen grew up with her mother, who married a white man when Larsen was young. She attended Fisk University, audited classes at the University of Copenhagen, and worked as head nurse at Tuskegee Institute, leaving after one year to work as a nurse in New York. *Quicksand* (1928) and *Passing* (1929) are Larsen's only novels. Despite her literary accomplishments, which include being the first black woman to receive a Guggenheim Fellowship, Larsen died an unrecognized author in her New York apartment in 1964. In her essay "Dear Ms. Larsen, There's a Mirror Looking Back," mixed-race writer Heidi W. Durrow, of Danish and African American descent, describes visiting Larsen's grave in Brooklyn, likening it to Alice Walker's infamous search for Zora Neale Hurston's grave.[5] Durrow views Larsen as "an artistic ancestor and literary role model"; Larsen's "published writing became the permission [she] needed to write the only stories [she] knew how to tell: of being black and Danish, and of being a white woman's child" (101, 105). Throughout the essay Durrow describes herself and Larsen as black women "who are also white" (102). The description is interesting in that it is deceptively complex. Helga, like Durrow and Larsen, cannot be easily classified: to be both a black woman and someone who is white affirms a black identity but also challenges what it means to be black or white in the first place.

Both *Quicksand* and *Passing* explore the role of "race mixing" in complicating personal, familial, and social relations. They reveal the difficulties faced by persons alienated because of race and racial choices. A distinct difference between the protagonists of each narrative has influenced this chapter's focus on *Quicksand.* Though *Passing*'s Clare is multiracial and light enough to pass, her parents are not an interracial couple. Clare's father is mixed race and though her mother's race is never specifically stated, it can be assumed that she is black or perhaps mixed race, but not white (*Passing* 153, 159). There is a difference between being light enough to pass (with presumably a multiracial background like Clare) and being both racially and culturally "mixed" with parents who represent that "mixture." This chapter's analysis of Helga exposes how this difference renders distinct psychological, emotional and social dilemmas.

Quicksand recounts the life of a young mixed-race woman abandoned by her black father and raised by her poor Danish mother. After her mother's death, Helga Crane enrolls in a boarding school and then accepts a teaching position at Naxos, a Negro school. "The South. Naxos. Negro education": Helga comes to hate all three things in part because none of them accepts or permits her difference or "hybridity" (3). Helga's unhappiness and inability to "fit in" or to conform prompt her sudden departure from Naxos to the North, where she finds momentary comfort and contentment. In Harlem, a widowed socialite, Anne Grey, welcomes Helga into her plush home. Helga takes pleasure in the social life enjoyed by New York's black upper class: the theater, lavish dinners and swank parties. Obsessive talk about "the race problem" at teas and get-togethers, however, frustrates Helga, who tires of thinking about race and then tires of America.

A letter and a check from a sympathetic white uncle provide Helga with the opportunity to visit her aunt in Denmark, a woman who, as her uncle writes, "always wanted" her (54). Like Helga's other "homes," Denmark initially strikes Helga as a wonderful "realization of a dream" save for her aunt and uncle's exhibition and exploitation of her "exotic" blackness at every social gathering (67). Helga must temporarily mask her feelings for the sake of her aunt and uncle. She soon grows to resent the flashy costumes she is expected to parade and realizes that she longs for other American Negroes.

A bitter rejection from Dr. Anderson, the man whom, for the bulk of the narrative, Helga has resisted, weakens Helga's spirit upon returning to the States. As depression sets in, she wanders into a church service led by Reverend Pleasant Green, whom she marries the next day because to her he represents the comforts of a settled life. Helga moves to Alabama with her preacher husband and falls into what she finds to be an undesirable role of rural housewife and mother. The novel concludes with Helga's slow emergence out of a deep depression and illness and the unwanted expectancy of her fifth child.

Four strands of criticism have dominated the response to *Quicksand*. While these have value in terms of highlighting different aspects of Helga's character, they have not specifically addressed Helga's journey for a mixed-race acceptance that remains ascribed to a black racial discourse. Early on, critics read *Quicksand* as a tragic novel. In 1948, Hugh M. Gloster characterized

Helga as "a convincing portrait of the tragic mulatto. Sensitive because of her questionable background, Helga cannot integrate herself into either race" (143). Later critics continued to oversimplify Helga's racial dilemma, attributing her instability and unhappiness to her mixedness.[6] Analyzing the narrative in terms of black female sexuality marks a departure from examining Helga's "mulatto" status. Deborah E. McDowell claims that "Helga is divided psychically between a desire for sexual fulfillment and a longing for social respectability" (xvii). Critics like McDowell contend that the main tension of the novel lies between sexual repression and sexual expression.[7] Still other scholars have examined feminist themes in *Quicksand* using psychoanalysis as their theoretical framework. Claudia Tate maintains that Helga's personality is based upon her "vague and insatiable" desires (130). She argues that *Quicksand* is "ultimately controlled by its desire to recover and forget, express and silence a lost primary love at the expense of repudiating another one" (124). These critics treat Helga as a psychological study, which helps readers understand Helga's often bizarre behaviors and impulses.[8]

More recently, George Hutchinson has returned to Helga's biracial identity without simplifying her as a black female or dwelling on her supposedly tragic state. He asserts that "[t]he desire of *Quicksand* is for a world in which races would not exist and women's bodies would not be mortgaged to them. This desire runs up against the harsh confines as the modern institution—the labyrinth—of race" ("Nella Larsen and the Veil of Race" 547). Scholarship that recenters on race is valuable; nevertheless Hutchinson may oversimplify race and biraciality by not recognizing Helga's movements as stages in a kind of racial journey. Hutchinson claims that Helga "accepts a public identity as 'black' while maintaining a private and publicly disallowed mixed-race subjectivity" (544). By contrast, I argue that Helga both privately and publicly claims a black-sentient mixed-race identity, one that is not consistent but informs her decisions, her relationships, and her geographic movements. She asserts what Kerry Ann Rockquemore and David L. Brunsma might call a protean identity: "racial identities [that] are directly tied to [one's] ability to cross boundaries between black, white, and biracial . . . These individuals feel endowed with a degree of cultural savvy in several social worlds and understand their mixed-race status as the way in which they are accepted, however conditionally, in varied interactional settings" (17). At the same time, these individuals can "feel a stronger orientation to" blacks (or whites). In this chapter, I seek to return the focus to how the novel constructs Helga's black-identified mixed-race identity in a way that sheds light on her autonomy.

"She Felt Shut in, Trapped": Defying Racial Scripts

The story begins in the Naxos, a southern institution where students and faculty know their place. In fact, Helga hotly recalls a white preacher declaring that "Naxos Negroes know what was expected of them. They had good sense" (Larsen 3). Upset by the school's accomodationist policy, Helga also feels troubled with the idea of people behaving in a required way either culturally or in terms of specific societal norms. Helga will not follow the social rules that circumscribe her within a singular space. The community shuns her, partly because of her difference, and partly because of her defiance. Instead of trying to hide her difference, Helga flaunts it. Helga's bold and colorful outfits, carefree attitude, high-class tastes, and "mulatto" status often offend her peers at Naxos. While the women at Naxos follow the dean of women's recommendations that "'[d]ark-complected people shouldn't wear yellow, or green or red,'" Helga believes that bright colors complement the various shades of her people (18). The narrator asserts, "[S]omething intuitive, some unanalyzed driving spirit of loyalty to the inherent racial need for gorgeousness told her that bright colors *were* fitting and that dark-complexioned people *should* wear yellow, green, and red" (18). While Helga's celebratory attitude towards dark skin illustrates her rebellious stance toward society's categories and unwritten rules, it also shows a loving relationship to blackness. Meredith Goldsmith writes that "Larsen consistently links the colors green and red to her heroine's sexuality" (101). However, in this instance, Larsen seems to use the colors yellow, green, and red to symbolize black consciousness. In 1920, red, black, and green were adopted by the Marcus Garvey's Universal Negro Improvement Association for their flag to represent the blood, race, and homeland (Africa) of African Americans.[9] Neil J. Savishinsky explains, "Garvey, in his attempts to promote Ethiopia as a model of African strength and independence, chose the colors, red, black, and green as a symbol for his nascent movement because he mistakenly believed them to be the colors of the Ethiopian flag (which actually were, and still are, red, yellow, and green)" (134). If we read Helga's approval of red, yellow, and green as a symbolic embracing of a black consciousness, what do we make of her description of the "queer" colors she wears two paragraphs later? Larsen writes that in Naxos "they felt that the colors were queer; dark purples, royal blues, rich greens, deep reds, in soft luxurious woolens, or heavy, clinging silks. And all the trimmings—when Helga used them at all—seemed to them odd" (18). Jessica G. Rubin notes that Larsen repeatedly uses the word "queer" in *Quicksand,* "appearing no fewer than ten times in this 135-page novel" (144). She asserts, "[N]o one has questioned Helga's heterosexuality, nor do I intend to do so. I will suggest, however, that Larsen purposely invokes transitivity, inversion and blending implicit in any discussion of homosexuality in her creation of Helga Crane" (144). Helga knows that others view her fashion choices as "queer" and "odd," words that also describe how they view her biracial identity or her refusal to assimilate and "fit in," racially and otherwise. Thus the references to and descriptions of colors both point to Helga's affinity with blackness and her desire to blur boundaries.

When Helga thinks that "some unanalyzed driving spirit of loyalty" prompts her to embrace bright colors for blacks, the word "loyalty" is revealing as it speaks to overall feelings of racial loyalty to which Helga often returns. Later, before leaving Denmark, she understands her father's need and expressions of racial loyalty. Helga's love for things others despise is not only a reflection of her aesthetics and rebellion but also an expression of her racial defiance against white oppression. As bell hooks writes, "Loving blackness as political resistance transforms our ways of looking and being, and thus creates the conditions necessary for us to move against the forces of domination and death and reclaim black life" (162).[10] Although Helga's celebration of "[h]armony, radiance, and simplicity, all the essentials of spiritual beauty in the race" doesn't translate into political action, her recognition nonetheless stands as a powerful rejection of racial rules, particularly those created by a legacy of white superiority and internalized by black self-hatred (Larsen 8). Though Helga defiantly assumes a biracial identity, she admits to feeling an unexplainable attachment to blackness. When Helga is in Denmark and tries to explain to her uncle why she can't marry Olsen, she describes her attachment to race as instinctual: "just something—something deep down" (91). Throughout her life experiences, Helga cannot completely separate her biracial identity from a black racial discourse.

Geographically, Helga's various homes in Naxos, Chicago, New York, Denmark, and Alabama represent her evolving self-formation. Helga begins to formulate her own sense of identity out of her various experiences with others and her inability to form connections with the particular racial group that surrounds her in each place. In Harlem, Helga feels akin to whites, while in Denmark, she misses other blacks. Helga's ability to reconstruct her racial affiliation and socialization resonates with mixed-race individuals in a contemporary context (a social practice also criticized by blacks). Indeed mixed-race writers rather consistently bemoan the difficulties of remaining singularly loyal. As biracial writer Malcolm Gladwell explains, "I go back and forth between my two sides. I never feel my whiteness more than when I'm around West Indians, and never feel my West Indianess more than when I'm with whites" (123). Like the character Helga (who, incidentally, is also part West Indian), Gladwell has a choice in terms of identification. Helga frequently meets with scorn and disdain when she tries to "be herself" or act according to how she wants, not how others want her to behave. She typically flees whenever she feels confined or racially imprisoned, further shaping her identity. In Naxos, Helga "could neither conform, nor be happy in her unconformity" (Larsen 7). She thus sets out to find a place for herself, though not without difficulty. Helga soon realizes a "lack somewhere. Always she had considered it a lack of understanding on the part of the community, but in her present and new revolt she realized that the fault had been partly hers. A lack of acquiescence. She hadn't really wanted to be made over" (7). Indeed, Helga resists others' attempts to create an identity for her in favor of negotiating her own. She decides to reject James Vayle's engagement—which would be an identity "makeover" and improvement in terms of social status. Joining the Vayles, a "first family" in Atlanta, would bring Helga material comforts as well as respect from people in high social circles who admire families with prestigious social and historical backgrounds. As Helga learns, "Negro society . . . was as complicated and as rigid in its ramifications as the highest strata of white society" (8). While James's respected familial connections initially attract Helga, her desire to maintain her own individuality dominates. As much as Helga seems to hate her supposedly shameful origins, her past still encourages her to maintain a wavering sense of pride. Even when faced with a new attractive life and change in lifestyle, Helga remains conscious of the importance of her background as a foundation for her identity. Ultimately, assuming a new identity as a Vayle does not mean more than erasing her own background. In a sense, rejecting the Vayles legitimizes Helga's illegitimate past in that she refuses to disregard or ignore her biracial past for a monoracial one.

Helga's unhappiness, both with the people and the environment, prompt her departure from Naxos. She asks herself, "But just what did she want?" (11). This indicates that she doesn't yet consciously comprehend her pursuit of an identity that will please both herself and others, while still allowing her to change her mind without feeling pressured to remain in a boxed subjectivity. For Helga, identity registers as the "something else, some other more ruthless force, a quality within herself, which was frustrating her, had always frustrated her, kept her from getting the things she had wanted. Still wanted" (11). Helga recognizes a lack in her life and despises her uncomfortable emptiness. Her cognizance of what irks her differentiates her from others who seem blindly and unproblematically to accept their social position. Margaret Creighton provides an example of this kind of person, a woman who turns what Helga regards as "probably nice live crinkly hair, perfectly suited to her smooth dark skin and agreeable round features, into a dead straight, greasy, ugly mass" (14). Helga interprets Margaret's hairstyle as a pathetic act of conformity. Margaret represents the majority of the Naxos faculty in that she fears people like Helga when they don't follow rules. She lacks the sense of independence that Helga expresses yet still admires her. Margaret discloses, "'I do wish you'd stay. It's nice having you here, Helga. We all think so. Even the dead ones. We need a few decorations to brighten our sad lives'" (14). Margaret's innocent view of Helga as decoration previews the kind of mentality Helga will contend with later when she becomes an adornment to her relatives' lives in Denmark. The point is that Helga's difference, framed by her racial difference, always draws attention and her attempts to maintain her individuality highlights her difference even more.

When Helga tells Dr. Anderson that she plans to leave Naxos, he convinces her to stay—until he tries to compliment her by saying, "Perhaps I can best explain it by the use of that trite phrase, 'You're a lady.' You have dignity and breeding" (21). Helga becomes enraged. She replies, "If you're speaking of family, Dr. Anderson, why, I haven't any. I was born in a Chicago slum" (21). Dr. Anderson then mistakes Helga's hurt for embarrassment regarding her poor upbringing. In an attempt to clarify his point, he makes another blunder: "That doesn't at all matter, Miss Crane. Financial, economic circumstances can't destroy tendencies inherited from good stock. You yourself prove that!" (21). Offended by his seemingly elitist assumption, Helga proclaims, "The joke is on you, Dr. Anderson. My father was a gambler who deserted my mother, a white immigrant. It is even uncertain that they were married. As I said at first, I don't belong here" (21). This final retort of Helga's shows her contradictory sense of pride, yet also establishes the start of her self-formation process in that she insists upon refusing a prescribed role as "lady" with its connotations of coming from good "stock." Later that evening, Helga regrets the way she responded to Dr. Anderson: "She had outraged her own pride, and she had terribly wronged her mother by her insidious implication" (23). Her oscillation between shame and pride evidence Helga's consciousness regarding her identity formation. Thinking back on her reaction to Dr. Anderson causes her to challenge the validity of his words "good stock" and their symbolic racial implications in a way that rejects racial labels and assumptions.

Although Helga often feels uncomfortable disclosing her family history, external forces sometimes push her to assert them. Her dialogue with Dr. Anderson shows that outsiders can subtly influence Helga's racial allegiance, at least enough to affect her identity choices. Others seem less cognizant of their identity in that they play out whatever role society gives them. Helga has a certain degree of agency in that she chooses how she wants to be identified. Clare Kendry's actions in *Passing* represent a similar kind of restricted yet conscious decision. Though Clare maintains her front as a white woman, her unexpected meeting with Irene alters Clare's understanding of her identity. In a letter to Irene, Clare admits, "It may be, 'Rene dear, it may just be, that, after all, your way may be the wiser and infinitely happier one. I'm not sure just now. At least not so sure as I have been" (Larsen, *Passing* 178). Clare must rethink her options in terms of her racial identity after seeing her black friend from childhood. The point here is that actions of and reactions from individuals and communities frequently inform race and identity choices, just as Helga's heated discussion with Dr. Anderson informs her biracial subjectivity. Mixed-race writer James McBride captures this sense of fluidity in identity choices in his memoir when he reveals how, as a college student, his interactions with others triggered his racial subjectivity: "During the rare, inopportune social moments when I found myself squeezed between black and white, I fled to the black side, just as my [white] mother had done" (*Color of Water* 261–62). It is worth noting that McBride does not flee to his white side since whites have not historically and often do not accept mixed-race people as "their own" or as white (while blacks often accept mixed-race people as "their own"). The same theory applies to Helga who, though accepted by white Danes in a limited sense, gets shunned by American whites such as her uncle and his wife, who reminds Helga that "my husband is not your uncle. No indeed!" (Larsen 29). This incident informs all of Helga's decisions, each of which is abruptly and hastily marked.

Helga's move from Naxos to Chicago marks the initial shift in her subject negotiation. In Chicago, she feels at home: "She, Helga Crane, who had no home" (30). Yet, Helga's "shameful" background haunts her even as she attempts to start this new life. When she tries to get a job at the YWCA, the woman at the employment agency "regarded her with an appraising look and asked for her history, past and present, not forgetting the 'references'" (33). In this sense, references act as a metaphor for family or "good stock," something that Helga does not have. Even Mrs. Hayes-Rore recoils at Helga's "unfortunate" past: "The woman felt that the story, dealing as it did with race intermingling and possibly adultery, was beyond definite discussion. For among black people, as among white people, it is tacitly understood that these things are not mentioned—and therefore they do not exist" (39). Dalmage calls this kind of disapproval "*border patrolling,* discrimination that comes from both sides," aimed at those who cross racial boundaries (42). For both racial groups, miscegenation brings shame—for whites because it exposes their immoral wrongdoing and for blacks because it painfully reminds them of their suffering. Blacks become highly class-conscious, and in an attempt to ignore race mixing, they evaluate each other based upon family name, history, and class. Paradoxically, though, each of these categories interconnects: black and white histories always merge together at some point. Moreover, black standards of beauty were increasingly determined by one's closeness to whites in terms of facial features and skin color. This contradictory social order places Helga in a precarious plight since she is a mixed-race woman who was raised in a lower-middle-class environment. Helga's mixed-race identity is multifaceted, making her relationship to blackness equally complex. Her childhood experience at a Negro boarding school acts as a metaphor for her racial subjectivity. At school, Helga learns that her darkness is not "loathsome" and that she "for the first time could breathe freely" (Larsen 23). Yet, at the same time "[t]here had been always a feeling strangeness, of outsideness" at the school because of her racial difference (23). Similarly, Helga rests on the periphery of a black identity, maintaining a distant but real connection to blackness. Her black-sentient mixed-race identity thus allows her to "breathe" more comfortably. Helga's early school experiences speak back to her celebratory attitude toward dark skin and "crinkly" hair, given that at her Negro school she learned one could "consider oneself without repulsion" (23). This translates into her learning to be proud of her black self later in life, a pride and understanding that does not usurp but instead provides a framework for her mixed-race identity.

While Helga's biological background and low class status are a social disadvantage, she receives certain benefits from her biraciality, including the ability to move about more easily than other blacks (to Europe, for example) and recognition and approval of her beauty. Thus, Helga gets trapped in the dilemma of choosing shame or pride about her past. Social systems at work in both black and white communities pressure her to choose. Helga must consider the backgrounds of her friends and associates to maintain a favorable social position. For example, she determines that hiding her biraciality will procure advantages in New York. When Mrs. Hayes-Rore tells her she won't mention her family background, Helga's gratitude was "so great . . . that she reached out and took her new friend's slightly soiled hand in one of her own fastidious ones" (41). Helga's decision to feel neither self-respect nor disgrace about her past suggests the start of her conscious negotiations regarding her identity. While history may have mandated scandal about such origins, Helga decides, at least partially, not to feel shame. Throughout her stay in Harlem, she keeps her past a secret: "Sinister folk [whites], she considered them, who had stolen her birthright. Their past contributions to her life, which had been but shame and grief, she had hidden away from brown folk in a locked closet" (45). Hutchinson argues, "[In] exchange for her new sense of belonging, Helga has locked her mother away" (231). The metaphor of a locked closet is interesting, given Helga's desire for "a profusion of lovely clothes" throughout the novel (11).[11] If a closet is where one puts clothing, what does it mean that Helga locks feelings of "shame and grief" (and "whiteness") in this space? Drawing on Judith Butler's *Bodies That Matter*, Goldstein asserts that "[t]he metaphor of the closet, with its abundance of garments representing a plethora of identities from which the subject can choose freely, is telling" (98). I argue that Helga's description of the "locked closet" reveals that she recognizes the performativity of race, another thing that can be worn, at the same time she understands how racial connections (and disconnections) shape belonging, informing her black-sentient mixed-race identity. Since Anne and Helga's associates uphold ideals of bourgeois uplift, Helga realizes the necessity of omitting her background and "performing" a black bourgeois identity. Yet, Helga does not always hide her background. Later, in Denmark, Helga often announces her difference. This seeming indecisiveness along with her recognition of how one's family history and racial background can hinder or help one's social position, underscores her attempted authority over how she will be perceived.

Helga soon begins to feel restless and unhappy in Harlem: "Not only did the crowds of nameless folk on the street annoy her, she began also actually to dislike her friends" (Larsen 48). In particular, Anne's obsession with "the race problem" begins to irritate Helga, who tires of the topic. Harlem will not allow her to look past or switch her racial affiliations. Anne's constant race talk "stirred memories, probed hidden wounds, whose poignant ache bred in her surprising oppression and corroded the fabric of her quietism" (49). Even Dr. Anderson notices Helga's anxiety: "You're still seeking for something, I think" (50). Helga begins to resist the black subjectivity she once welcomed in Harlem in favor of choosing her own identity. In this instance, choice serves as only a partly useful term because Helga does not have true freedom of choice: her social circle also influences her decisions. Anne makes her views on miscegenation and race mingling clear. She tells Helga that Audrey Denney, who socializes with whites, is "outrageous, treacherous, in fact. That's what's the matter with the Negro race. They won't stick together. She certainly ought to be ostracized. I've nothing but contempt for her, as has every other self-respecting Negro" (61). Helga decides to leave Harlem because she feels unhappy and cannot be herself, especially around people like Anne, who hold such narrow views. In this sense, Helga has only limited control over her decision to leave since her failing relationship with Anne and with Harlem, as well as a force within herself, push her: "Somewhere, within her, in a deep recess, crouched discontent. She began to lose confidence in the fullness of her life, the glow began to fade from her conception of it. . . . She became a little frightened, and then shocked to discover that, for some unknown reason, it was of herself she was afraid" (47). Helga seems to fear the part of herself that is complacent with her racial status. Until this point, Helga seems satisfied with her social and political position in Harlem. Though she is "established, secure, comfortable" (45), she becomes exasperated by the contradictory and backward social politics of Harlemites like Anne who work to uplift the race, yet "turned up her finely carved nose at their lusty churches, their picturesque parades, their naïve clowning on the streets" (48). This inconsistent racial ideology parallels the thinking of blacks such as Mrs. Hayes-Rore, who advises Helga to keep her racial background a secret. Helga seeks a community more progressive and accepting in terms of race, more specifically a community that will not deny her black mixed-race identity, which also challenges racial scripts. Anne's insistence on a black solidarity that frowns upon interaction with whites is as damaging to Helga as any other racial proscription as she refuses to be limited in her racial expressions.

Still, Helga's black-sentient identity does not always resonate. For example, Helga soon begins to resent other blacks in Harlem: "It was as if she were shut up, boxed up, with hundreds of her race, closed up with that something in the racial character which had always been, to her, inexplicable, alien. Why, she demanded in fierce rebellion, should she be yoked to these despised black folks?" (54–55). Helga rejects the assumption that because she may physically resemble black people, she must necessarily be "boxed up" with them. She rationalizes that "in spite of her racial markings," she did not "belong to these dark segregated people. She was different. She felt it. It wasn't merely a matter of color. It was something broader, deeper, that made folk kin" (55). Helga's sentiment anticipates contemporary discussions of what defines communal or familial ties. Rebecca Walker writes, "My blood is made from water and so it is bloodwater that I am made of, and so it is a constant empathic link with others which claims me, not only carefully drawn lines of relation" (*Black, White, and Jewish* 320). Helga insists that race does not dictate bonds in the same way that Walker insists upon a more encompassing criterion for community. Yet Helga contradicts her own beliefs, often affirming a kinship with blacks that affects her mixed-race identity. For example, Helga does not always feel disassociated from other black people. Later, at Anne's dinner party, she marvels "at the gradations within this oppressed race of *hers*" (Larsen 59, my italics). Helga's wavering identification with black people indicates her discomfort with societal definitions of racial belonging.

Today, the question "What is black?" remains thorny and exhausting, particularly for biracial subjects whose identity depends on variables such as biology, family, upbringing, community, skin color, and race consciousness. In "To Be Real," Danzy Senna explains that she "no longer believe[s] in a single 'authentic Negro experience.' I have come to understand that my multiplicity is inherent in my blackness, not opposed to it, and that none of my 'identities' are distinct from one another" (18). Senna's belief in the "wholeness" of her racial self echoes sentiments expressed by a growing number of mixed-race writers and activists who see an unbreakable connection between mixed-race identity and black identity. Helga's literary characterization presciently underscores these avowals.

Helga's feelings of isolation provoke her visit to Denmark so that she, like Audrey Denney, can easily have "the courage, so placidly to ignore racial barriers" (Larsen 62). Helga admires Audrey's freedoms. As a mixed-race woman, Audrey "goes about with white people" and seems to socialize in interracial crowds without reservation (60). Audrey's characterization anticipates Clare Kendry's in *Passing.* Although Clare gives up her former life to pass as a white woman, she still yearns for the company of other blacks and will do anything to attend her black friends' social functions. Clare and Audrey both represent women who want to live free from racial classifications despite outside disapproval or disdain. Helga hopes that living in Copenhagen will allow her the same type of freedom she imagines Audrey has, and this move marks a new stage in her sense of herself as a social subject.

During the trip to Denmark, Helga stands on the ship's deck, "reveling like a released bird in her returned feeling of happiness and freedom, that blessed sense of belonging to herself alone and not to a race" (64). Jeanne Scheper argues that "Helga Crane is like a migratory bird ready to fly: flying and then caught, caught and then escaping, escaping and then staying, staying and then fleeing" (683). I want to suggest that the bird imagery (Helga twice refers to herself as a peacock, a bird that can only fly short distances) intimates Helga's connection to her black identity and a black sociohistoric consciousness. Before Helga describes herself as a "released bird," she enjoys the "lovely" weather "with the serene calm of the lingering September summer, under whose sky the sea was smooth, like a length of watered silk, ruffled by the stir of any wind" (Larsen 64). The nature imagery recalls the first lines of Paul Laurence Dunbar's infamous caged-bird poem, "Sympathy" (1899), wherein the summer imagery is equally tranquil and the water is serene:

> I KNOW what the caged bird feels, alas!
> When the sun is bright on the upland slopes;
> When the wind stirs soft through the springing grass,
> And the river flows like a stream of glass (15)

Though Helga's description of herself as a "released bird" highlights her freedom from "the great superfluity of human beings, yellow, brown and black, which . . . had so oppressed her," she soon realizes she is nothing more than a "curio. A peacock," a hireling of sorts who is subject to a racist European gaze (Larsen 63, 73). Later, when Helga hears black performers sing "an old ragtime song" (82) at a vaudeville house, her disquietude recalls Dunbar's last line: "I know why the caged bird sings!" (16). In short, though she feels like a free bird, her blackness makes it difficult for her to escape completely. Her eventual feelings of being caged in Denmark prompt her "urgent longings" for black America (Larsen 83).

Still, Helga's "blessed sense of belonging . . . not to a race" encourages her awareness of herself and is a common characteristic in the mixed-race subjectivity of many other mixed-race literary characters who appear after *Quicksand* (64). Though Helga wants *not* to belong to a race, she wants to continue to reap the benefits of racial affiliation when it serves her interests. She finds it easy and convenient to disassociate from blacks when Harlem begins to bore her and when hidden feelings for Dr. Anderson frustrate her. Yet, as the epigraph from *Passing* that begins this chapter suggests, racial bonds are difficult to let go of completely. In *Passing*, Brian, Irene's husband, says he does not know why this is so, a sentiment that supports Helga's later contention that her black racial ties are real but inexplicable.

Receiving Blackness Abroad

Helga's move to Denmark simply exchanges old feelings of unhappiness and entrapment for new feelings of unhappiness and discomfort. Helga's aunt and uncle treat her like a prized show dog, displaying her at every social function and fawning over her exotic and foreign look. In response to her aunt's comment that she is "different," Helga thinks, "Did it mean that the difference was to be stressed, accented? Helga wasn't so sure that she liked that. Hitherto all her efforts had been toward similarity to those about her" (72). The exception, perhaps, is Helga's stay in Naxos, where she both attempts to assimilate and asserts her individualism in a place that "tolerated no innovations, no individualism" (4). In Denmark, Helga's showcasing of her difference invokes Frantz Fanon's theory of racial fetishization: "I was responsible . . . for my body, for my race, my ancestors. I subjected myself to an objective examination, I discovered my blackness, my ethnic characteristics; and I was battered down by tom-toms, cannibalism, intellectual deficiency, fetishism" (112). When Helga's aunt drapes her in exotic clothing and jewelry, she, too, is battered down by the tom-toms. However, Helga's efforts to conform and to announce her difference are not always consistent.

Helga's contradictory identification with blackness surfaces during the aforementioned vaudeville scene when Helga and Olsen visit a circus where two black men sing minstrel songs. When Helga sees the minstrel act for the first time, she sits "silent, motionless," while the audience cheers (Larsen 82). Helga feels ashamed of the exaggerated act and regards the audience's enjoyment of such foolish behavior with disgust. Yet, the singers attract and intrigue Helga. She returns to the circus by herself again and again, "gazing intently and solemnly at the gesticulating black figures, an ironical and silently speculative spectator. For she knew that into her plan for her life had thrust itself a suspensive conflict in which were fused doubts, rebellion, expediency, and urgent longings" (83). Initially, Helga plans to find a place where people will accept her "racelessness" without question. While discontent with Denmark already brews in Helga, watching the circus act makes her realize the futility of that plan. The applause and excited shouts from the white audience spark her desire to leave Denmark immediately and bring her to the realization that not even in Europe can she escape racial stereotypes. Moreover, Helga feels an "urgent longing" for home and black Americans. Soon after these visits to the circus, Helga decides to identify more strongly with her blackness because she no longer sees an advantage in trying to claim a kind of "racelessness" in Denmark. Helga leaves because the Danes regard her as Other (black, foreign, exotic) and exploit her difference. In Denmark, Helga discerns that not just black Americans have trouble recognizing her biraciality; even whites in a foreign country cannot appreciate her racial expressions. She reasons that if Danish people can take pleasure in grossly stereotyped black figures, then they will never see past her own blackness.

Even though Helga wants outsiders to understand her as a mixed-race subject, she still understands and feels the ties of race. Though she does not abide by society's unwritten rules about race, she experiences racial bonds and connections. When she declines Axel Olsen's marriage proposal, she tries to explain that "[i]t isn't just you, not just personal, you understand. It's deeper, broader than that. It's racial" (88). This statement reveals Helga's own insecurities regarding her racial position. Although she accepts her mixedness in Denmark, she refuses to pass on racial struggles to the children born from such a union: "She had no words which could adequately, and without laceration to her pride, convey to him [Olsen] the pitfalls into which very easily they might step" (88). The rejection leads Olsen to assert that his portrait of Helga reflects "the true Helga Crane. Therefore—a tragedy. For someone" (88). Helga, too, sees the distorted painting as tragic, representing Olsen's failed attempt to see beyond the limits of the tragic mulatto archetype. In other words, what may signify a possible tragedy in the text is not Helga's psyche but other people's inability to see her as "untragic," demonstrated in Olsen's failure to paint the real multidimensional Helga.

"Homesick . . . for Negroes": Rac(e)ing Home

Helga resolves to return to America after hearing a rendering of "Swing Low, Sweet Chariot." Sitting in the concert hall, she thinks, "I'm homesick, not for America, but for Negroes. That's the trouble" (92). This marks the first time Helga feels a truly deep racial connection to others:

> For the first time Helga Crane felt sympathy rather than contempt and hatred for that father, who so often and so angrily she had blamed for his desertion of her mother. She understood, now, his rejection, his repudiation, of the formal calm her mother had represented. She understood his yearning, his intolerable need for the inexhaustible humor and the incessant hope of his own kind, his need for those things, not material, indigenous to all Negro environments. She understood and could sympathize with his facile surrender to the irresistible ties of race, now that they dragged at her own heart. (92)

Yet, Helga still craves the freedom to live her life unscripted by race. Though she wants to return home to socialize among other blacks, the prospect of leaving Denmark saddens her: "Why couldn't she have two lives, or why couldn't she be satisfied in one place?" (93). Helga's desire to have two lives intimates her aspiration to relate with whomever she wants on a personal and social level and suggests her friends' and family's inability to let her do so. Here the narrative reminds us of an essential challenge mixed-race people face: trying to live in accordance with social expectations. Malcolm Gladwell explains, "If you mix black and white, you don't obliterate these categories; you merely create a third category, a category that demands for its very existence, an even greater commitment to nuances of racial taxonomy" (124). While this problem does not affect just mixed-race people, the social expectations they face can be more difficult to reconcile. Helga's question also reveals her complex understanding of herself as black and biracial or mixed race, a description she does not see as conflicted or contradictory. Outsiders would perhaps interpret these identities as disparate, but Helga chooses to express this dual identity because she does feel black racial ties. It is important to note that Helga does not feel racial ties in terms of her whiteness. Although there are times when she wants to disassociate from blacks, and other times when she dreams of a white Copenhagen "where there were no Negroes, no problems, no prejudice," she never articulates a yearning or longing for her mother's race (Larsen 55). This is no doubt in part shaped by her childhood and her experiences as a student and teacher in all-black environments. At the same time, Helga's blackness informs her black-sentient mixed-race identity because her black identity has shaped her sociopolitical consciousness, albeit inconsistently, evidenced when she is forced to stand up for blackness against racism, oftentimes to her own surprise.

After returning to the United States, Helga continues to shock, upset, and excite others with her appearance. In Denmark, Helga learned "to expect and accept admiration as her due. This attitude, she found, was as effective in New York as across the sea. It was, in fact, even more so. And it was amusing too" (98). Her friends in New York still notice Helga's difference from them and her desire to project that difference. At her friend's party, Helga expresses her desire to meet Audrey Denney, a black woman who boldly socializes in interracial circles. Helen Travenor tells her, "Audrey's an awfully interesting person and Anne's said some pretty awful things about her. *You'll* like her, Helga" (100). This enthusiastic recommendation from a friend suggests Helga's continuous, outward wishes to identify with whomever she wants, blacks and whites. Later, during a conversation with James Vayle, Helga affirms her blackness. When James admits he would find it difficult to live overseas, away from black people, Helga reminds him, "I'm a Negro too, you know" (102). Helga's racial proclamation contradicts some of her previous feelings. Still, her insistence that she is "Negro" seems to generally underscore her recognition of others' attempts to place her on the "inside" or "outside." Indeed, James's reply, "Well, Helga, you were always a little different, a little dissatisfied, though I don't pretend to understand you at all," indicates that outsiders refuse to see Helga as "one race" at the same time that they paradoxically disavow her racial mixedness (102). The dissatisfaction James recognizes, along with Dr. Anderson's rejection, leads Helga to "run away" again, though this time she does not know where to go. She finds that Harlem has not changed in terms of racial boundaries, and she therefore seeks an "out" from the city.

Helga's drifting into a black church demonstrates her awareness of her identity formation. Suffering from shame and humiliation, Helga "felt alone, isolated from all other beings, separated even from her own anterior existence by the disaster of yesterday" (109). Disconnected from her previous identity, Helga is not living as she has planned, despite her shifting geographic, racial, and identity positions. Her frequent movements indicate her unsuccessful attempts to feel free and secure. Helga's aimless wandering into the church suggests her hopelessness, yet it also reveals her agency. In other words, Helga commits herself to being swept into the religious moment at the church. Instead of walking away from the intensity and religious fervor in the room, "Helga too began to weep, at first silently, softly; then with great sucking sobs.

Her nerves were so torn, so aching, her body so wet, so cold! It was a relief to cry unrestrainedly, and she gave herself freely to soothing tears" (112). Unlike earlier mulatta characters who uncontrollably fall into catastrophic binds, Helga does not lack power in terms of the direction her life will take. However, remembering Dr. Anderson's rejection of her also facilitates Helga's walking into the church. When Anderson reveals that his kissing Helga was a drunken mistake, she feels "belittled and ridiculed" (107). To Helga, Anderson's rejection is in essence also a rejection of Helga's racial choices in that he has chosen Anne (a woman who disapproved of race mingling and projected an uncompromising black identity) over Helga, a woman whose actions and worldview represent the opposite of hers. Anderson's romantic brush-off (including his symbolic inability to accept her) provides Helga with the fortitude to let the church's powerful direction sway her. Ironically, although Anderson and Anne are racial uplifters, Anderson's gray eyes (often a signifier of mixedness) and Anne's last name (Grey) figuratively symbolize racial mixture, the literal blending of black and white that Helga aspires to balance with a recognition of her blackness. The marital union between Anderson and Anne highlights Helga's loneliness, both romantically and in terms of her associations with others whose views on race are narrow-minded. Helga wishes to be "gray" and "black," yet Anderson and Anne refuse to see or accept her biraciality despite their superficial and symbolic connections to mixednesss. Anderson's gray eyes do not connote a deeper understand of mixed race, and Anne's name is meaningless given her narrow views on race.

The hysteria that surrounds Helga in the church both entertains and repulses her. After the preacher mistakes her for a prostitute, Helga remains "amused, angry, disdainful, . . . listening to the preacher praying for her soul. But though she was contemptuous, she was being too well entertained to leave" (113). Instead of correcting the preacher, Helga simply takes in her surroundings. The mysteriousness of the rituals attracts her: "[T]here crept upon her an indistinct horror of an unknown world" (113). The enigmatic quality of this "world" captivates Helga. Hitherto, Helga has had little success "fitting into" the world. She therefore sees potential in this simultaneously horrific yet enchanting religious community. This "show" mesmerizes Helga because it offers a new option for her in terms of living as a black-sentient mixed-race subject. While she watches the congregation, "a curious influence penetrated her; she felt an echo of the weird orgy resound in her own heart; she felt herself possessed by the same madness; she too felt a brutal desire to shout and to sling herself about" (113). After this bizarre moment, Helga becomes sick, a result of the previous night's drinking, her confused emotions, and the chaos of the evening. She then participates in the religious ceremony by uncontrollably chanting in a strange tongue, asking for God's mercy. The congregation celebrates Helga for her "conversion" as a "miraculous calm came upon her. Life seemed to expand, and to become very easy. Helga Crane felt within her a supreme aspiration toward the regaining of simple happiness, a happiness unburdened by the complexities of the lives she had known" (114).

While it may seem that Helga gives into fate's whims, she exerts a surprising degree of control regarding this change in her life. I read Helga's desire for "simple happiness . . . unburdened by the complexities" of life as a deeper conscious desire and aspiration for a life free from racial burdens and classification. The all-black church and its promise of security and acceptance entice Helga, who has attempted to live in four different places yet felt rejected in each. She will not have to face the challenges of racial classification in a homogeneous black environment whose community members share the same economic, racial, and religious background. The black communities of Naxos and Harlem were fraught with jealousy, contradictions, and divisions along race, color, and class lines. Denmark's all-white environment exploits Helga's difference instead of simply accepting it. Thus, Helga hopes that the black rural Alabama setting will be more accepting and less divided by class than the other places in which she has lived.

The ending of the novel indicates Helga's attempt to write her own story. Dissatisfied with her prospects in New York City or Denmark, Helga determines she will welcome "a chance at stability, at permanent happiness" (117). Thus, Helga trades in her life as Helga Crane for a new life as the wife of the Reverend Pleasant Green in a small Alabama town. This town initially appears simple to Helga, so simple that identity issues do not disturb her. Instead, "the novelty of the thing, the change, fascinated her. There was a recurrence of the feeling that now, at last, she had found a place for herself, that she was really living" (118). Helga holds a relatively high social position in the black church and does not have to think about racial affiliations. Freed of worrying about her position as a racial subject, Helga finds momentary "truth" in religion: "She believed in it. Because in its coming it had brought this other thing, this anaesthetic satisfaction for her senses. . . . This one time in her life, she was convinced, she had not clutched a shadow and missed the actuality" (118). Helga convinces herself that her former yearning for acceptance and understanding of her racial mixedness has subsided. Living in the small town makes Helga feel "compensated for all previous humiliations and disappointments. . . . If she remembered that she had had something like this feeling before, she put the unwelcome memory from her with the thought: 'This time I know I'm right. This time it will last'" (118). Though she does not hold romantic or affectionate feelings for her husband, Helga convinces herself to feel "at peace, and secure" (121).

Helga soon begins to feel the pressure, stress, and monotony of being mother and wife. After giving birth to her fourth child, emotional distress turns into physical sickness and hopelessness regarding her predicament returns. Helga hangs on to the security and comfort of an illness that allows her to avoid facing certain truths. However, not only has depression set in, but she has also failed to find a satisfactory sociocultural space to inhabit. After Helga awakens from her depression she remains

> silent and still, wanting to linger forever in that serene haven, that effortless calm where nothing was expected of her. There she could watch the figures of the past drift by. There was her mother, whom she had loved from a distance and finally so scornfully blamed. . . . Audrey Denney, placid, taking quietly and without fuss the things which she wanted. (129)

As Helga reflects on the past, she remembers people who have entered her life and directly or indirectly helped shape her identity: her mother, Robert Anderson, Anne Grey, Axel Olsen, Audrey Denney, her aunt and uncle. She thinks, "It was refreshingly delicious, this immersion in the past. But it was finished now. It was over" (129). Part of what makes this reflection so "delicious" is that it allows Helga to trace the racial negotiations she has made throughout her life. Each person on whom she reflects marks a different stage in Helga's evolution of self-identity. Although social pressures often affect Helga's decisions, her awareness of how others perceive and accept her identity precipitates her geographic moves and projections of identity. Helga's consciousness regarding these choices shows that her plight informs her choices and that they are not just random or casual reactions.

Quicksand ends ironically, with Helga losing the strong sense of agency she grasped through the rest of the narrative. Her pessimism about life, particularly black life, resonates as she ponders God's existence:

> Into that yawning gap of unspeakable brutality had gone, too, her belief in the miracle and wonder of life. Only scorn, resentment, and hate remained—and ridicule. Life wasn't a miracle, a wonder. It was, for Negroes at least, only a great disappointment. Something to be got through with as best one could. No one was interested in them or helped them. (130)

At times like this, Helga affiliates with her blackness, feeling powerless and recognizing the effects of racism on black life. Yet, accepting society's definitions regarding race and power is not characteristic of Helga. During her "long process of getting well," she briefly returns to her "old self": "[A]t first she had felt only an astonished anger at the quagmire in which she had engulfed herself. She had ruined her life. Made it impossible ever again to do the things that she wanted, have the things that she loved, mingle with the people she liked" (133). This vexation embodies what Helga has hitherto represented in the novel: a woman who consciously goes after what she wants and associates with whomever she desires to associate, regardless of race and boundaries.

Helga momentarily awakens out of her emotionally and physically disabling coma. Dismissing religion as an illusion, she decides that she needs to garner real strength: "For she had to admit that it wasn't new, this feeling of dissatisfaction, of asphyxiation. Something like it she had experienced before. In Naxos. In New York. In Copenhagen. This differed only in degree" (134). She therefore ponders the possibility of leaving her husband and attempts to find ways to reconcile her role of mother. She decides that after she grows stronger and better able to reason, she will plan an escape out of her dreary rural life. In the meantime, she finds it "so pleasant to think about freedom and cities, about clothes and books. . . . It was so hard to think out a feasible way of retrieving all these agreeable, desired things. Just then. Later. When she got up. By and by. She must rest. Get strong. Sleep. Then, afterward, she could work out some arrangement" (135). Yet, the confines of motherhood shatter Helga's optimism about her future plans. The novel ends by notifying us that hardly had Helga left her "bed and become able to walk again without pain, hardly had the children returned from the homes of the neighbors, when she began to have her fifth child" (135). This bleak ending marks a surprising turn for Helga, considering that she usually has the ability to get out of uncomfortable or disagreeable binds easily. Much has been written about what this ending suggests about Larsen's view of the patriarchal institution of marriage and the confining aspects of motherhood.[12] Yet, the conclusion of the novel also suggests the futility of Helga's dream of ultimate happiness and freedom as a "raceless" subject.

The fact that the novel does not have an optimistic ending for Helga does not render Helga a tragic mulatta. Werner Sollors writes,

> [T]he use of the term "Tragic Mulatto" in critical literature seems to carry the sense of violent action, sentimentality, and denouement in an unhappy ending. . . . It is evidence of "heavy" emotions, tough confrontations between the recognizable forces of good

> and evil, innocence beleaguered by perfidious villainy, disastrous turns of the plot, the power of coincidence, and tears at the end. (242–43)

Historically, the tragic endings of mulatto characters have intimated the disastrous effects of miscegenation. In other words, mixed-race characters (and people) were thought to be doomed to unfortunate or miserable lives because of their biraciality. This also suggests a lack of control these characters have in their lives. While *Quicksand*'s ending implies an unfortunate turn of plot for the novel and its readers, Helga's lack of control at the end does not negate her agency through the rest of the novel. Far from tragic, Helga enacts agency and self-awareness. While numerous articles have focused on Helga's repression and lack of freedom, she actually has choice and power in terms of her identity. Though other characters continue to see her either as they see themselves or as they want her to be, Helga maintains the privilege of changing her mind by asserting new identities. It is not so much Helga's racial mixture that shapes the narrative but the way in which she contends with alienation, exploitation, and misunderstanding from others.

Chapter Three

Homeward Bound: Negotiating Borders in Lucinda Roy's *Lady Moses* and Danzy Senna's *Caucasia*

> I prefer to think of a-world-in-which-race-does-not-matter as something other than a theme park or a failed and always-failing dream, or as the father's house of many rooms. I am thinking of it as home.
>
> —Toni Morrison, "Home" (3)

> However dissimilar individual bodies are, the compelling idea of common, racially indicative bodily characteristics offers a welcome short-cut into the favored forms of solidarity and connection, even if they are effectively denied divergent patterns in life chances and everyday experiences.
>
> —Paul Gilroy, *Against Race* (25)

Even when *Quicksand*'s Helga thinks she has found a home, she is profoundly aware of the fact that "[s]he, Helga Crane, . . . had no home" (Larsen 30). Helga's feelings of non-belonging and unsettlement, largely because of her racial background, are also markers of the black experience in America. In *Burnin' Down the House: Home in African American Literature,* Valerie Sweeney Prince asserts that "the century of African American literature shows that home is ubiquitous and nowhere at the same time" (2). Torn from their ancestral origins, African Americans have sought to find "home," both literal places and psychic spaces. A review of fiction featuring mixed-race characters also reveals that the concept of home is fraught with uncertainty, tension, and ambiguity for those who border the black/white divide.[1] As Danzy Senna explains, "It's as if by being mixed race you are a perpetual immigrant. . . . You don't really have a homeland, so you're sort of perpetually homeless" ("Race and Other Flammable Topics"). This chapter concerns itself with two novels published in 1998, Lucinda Roy's *Lady Moses* and Danzy Senna's *Caucasia,* both of which feature mixed-race protagonists who feel like foreigners in their bodies and/or communities. In his empirical study of British mixed-race families, Suki Aki proposes:

> Homes are constructed within a matrix of psychic and geographic spaces—they are conceived as both real and imagined, and are lived through domestic and (inter)national locations. It is these complex ties between home, nationality and family that help inform the central area of inquiry, the negotiation of mixed-race identity. (123)

Jacinta Moses in *Lady Moses* and Birdie Lee in *Caucasia* initially locate home in blackness: Jacinta views Africa as her homeland, while Birdie understands black culture as "home." Yet Jacinta's white British mother and geographic displacement and Birdie's white body agitate against their visions of and connections to home. They experience what Homi Bhaba describes as "unhomeliness": "Although the unhomely is a paradigmatic postcolonial experience, it has a resonance that can be heard distinctly, if erratically, in fictions that negotiate the powers of cultural difference in a range of historical conditions and social contradictions" ("The World and the Home" 142). Culturally displaced and trapped between two cultures, Jacinta and Birdie seek racial homes via their black fathers, whose cultures, assertions of citizenship, and racial pride offer a promising sanctuary. Ultimately, each embraces a black-sentient mixed-race "home" even while questioning the limits and challenging the foundation of that "home."

Both novels emphasize the importance of community and geographic place in the formation of racial identities. Jacinta grows up in London but later lives in the United States and Africa. The three sections of the novel—"London," "The New World," and "Lunama"—reflect her travels. In part II of *Caucasia,* Birdie passes for white while she lives with her mother; this section is appropriately titled "from caucasia, with love," suggesting that passing is a specific physical locale. Birdie also lives in several different places, including Boston, upstate New York, New Hampshire, and California. The point is that, like Helga Crane, each character searches for home (literal and symbolic), moving from city to city, region to region. In fact, each novel ends with the protagonist living far from her childhood home: Boston-raised Birdie ends up in California, while London-raised Jacinta ultimately chooses the United States.

Despite their different nationalities, both girls share a hyperawareness about racial prejudice and discrimination in their countries and communities. When she moves to the United States, Jacinta is "fascinated" by African Americans "because they took this land as their own. Black Britons didn't do that in the same way. We were always aliens; in the corners of our eyes was the fear of repatriation" (Roy, *Lady Moses* 206).[2] Jacinta and Birdie come of age during the late 1960s and mid-1970s respectively; racism and disapproval of interracial relationships shape each girl's childhood. Jacinta is repeatedly called a "wog," first by a little boy who tells her he cannot play with her and later by the Beadycap children who "used words like 'wog' and 'half-caste' all the time" (32). Before she is sent to an all-black school, Birdie's mother homeschools Birdie and her sister while Birdie's father schools her in other ways: "Study them [white people], Birdie. And take note. Always take notes" (Senna, *Caucasia* 52). Both girls are aware that they live in black-and-white worlds; as Deck, Birdie's father, says, "In a country as racist as this, you're either black or you're white" (23). Jacinta seems to register a similar conclusion in a diary entry: "I am a colored girl living in a white country. If I have a child by a white man, he'll be a quadroon" (*Lady Moses* 36). Jacinta's words suggest that despite her British upbringing, she subscribes to a one-drop rule more typically associated with the United States. As Jayne O. Ifekwunigwe argues, "[T]he Black essentialism of the one drop rule is integral to our understandings of both colonial and contemporary Black/White social stratification in the former British Empire and the future United Kingdom, respectively" (5).[3] England and the United States have different racial histories, but the experiences of Jacinta and Birdie suggest that each character views herself as both black and mixed race. By the end of each novel, the protagonist seems to question racial categories while at the same time claiming a black consciousness.

Simon Says Africa: Finding Father, Finding Self

Lady Moses is narrated by Jacinta Louise Buttercup Moses, a British mixed-race woman whose African father dies when she is young, leaving her depressed and emotionally distant mother to take care of her. Before he dies, Jacinta's father, Simon, charms her with powerful stories about "good and evil, glory and despair," stories that take Jacinta to her father's welcoming homeland.

When her father gets a collection of his writings published, the family "danced around our kitchen in the sky, told each other we were famous, and planned our trips to visit the queen and her butler at Buckingham Palace, and to go back home to West Africa" (14). It is telling that the family fantasizes about visiting the palace and then settling in West Africa. These two dream trips symbolize Jacinta's various cultural and social influences. From her mother Jacinta "learned to be a social and intellectual snob"; from her father she learns that "without our story [of the Moses family] there is a big hole in the world, and people will not know how to talk to each other. And people will not remember to cherish what is different" (30, 13). Both worldviews shape Jacinta's sense of self when she travels abroad, seeking "beauty and adventure" and home (155). As an adult, she learns to appreciate her difference.

Before Jacinta visits Africa, she mostly identifies as "coloured." When she plays with her black childhood friend, Alison, she seems to feel closer to Africa, her imagined home. After questioning Alison whether she ever wanted to be white, Jacinta realizes "for the first time that our homes were places where our skins belonged" (90). As a thirteen-year-old, Jacinta equates home with black acceptance, not taking into account the complexities of skin and belonging. After all, when she visits her father's country as an adult, her friend Esther says she is "too white," and Murunghi villagers call her "Poro," or white (282). She later learns, as Tracy Fisher writes, that "[t]he politics of belonging is a contested space. It is full of contradictions and struggles, it is imbued with power, and is often rooted in homogeneous assumptions about gender, race, and nation" (176). While her brown skin connects her to blackness in England, it estranges her in Africa. After Jacinta and Alison celebrate their racial difference ("Who wants to be freckly and pointy-nosed anyway? Who wants to have greasy wads of hair and fat babies that look like loaves of white bread?"), she is confronted with racism and challenged and ridiculed about her imagined "home," Africa, and her home country, Britain (*Lady Moses* 91). Her neighbor/renter, Mary Beadycap, slings racial epithets at them and yells, "This is *our* country . . . not yours. Go home and swing on trees, why don't 'cha?" (92). Socially, Jacinta is excluded from any complete sense of English belonging; yet, born in Britain, she cannot technically claim Africa as her birthright. As Ifekwunigwe writes, "The outcome of the prescribed specificity of white Englishness is that Black sons and daughters of the English-African Diaspora are denied full citizenship. . . . [M]estis(se) children with White English mothers or fathers are also denied access to an English identity that they can rightfully claim on the basis of parentage" (42). Strangers, acquaintances, and family deny Jacinta an English identity. Such rejection (most strikingly portrayed when her mother calls her "coloured" following a difficult visit to the hospital before Simon's death) encourages Jacinta to begin to embrace a black identity.

However, despite Jacinta's embracing a black identity, she does want to be like everybody else. When she is twelve, she becomes obsessed with remodeling her house on Lavender Street because "[t]he house was a dump. Lavender Sweep was a dump" (*Lady Moses* 35). Jacinta's discomfort in her living space symbolizes her overall estrangement: her desire to renovate, improve, and clean is intimately connected with her desire to fit in and rightfully occupy a space/place. Feeling even less grounded as her mother becomes increasingly detached, Jacinta intensifies her home-improvement plans. She purchases home-improvement books, paints and wallpapers, and designs elaborate remodeling plans. Jacinta is often forced to confront her racial identity in or around her home, a literal place and metaphoric space that brings her unrest. When Mary Beadycap sees the results of Jacinta's "decorating weekend," she makes fun of the colorful home makeover: "It's bloomin' awful. . . . You wogs is all color blind, me dad says. Look at that Alison Bean's house. Pink and blue and yellow all over! Yuk!" (75). Mary's brother Maurice also registers Jacinta as abnormal and racially Other when he sneers at her and Alison and calls them "[b]irds of a feather" as they sit at the front door of the house. His statement unveils Jacinta's resentment over being recognized as black like her friend: "Part of me wanted to deny the association. My mother was white, after all. But Alison was my friend. Why did I feel ashamed?" (40). Shame returns when Jacinta reflects on the "shabbiness" of her home (68). She repeatedly mentions her desire to show off a dream house to "snobby Josephine Marsh and the other girls at school" so that they can "coo with delight at our tasteful stair carpet and expensive-looking draperies" (75). However, Jacinta knows that first and foremost she must clean: "There was dirt everywhere. I could never bring Josephine Marsh to a place like this" (76). It is important to note that Jacinta considers Josephine her "other best friend" (aside from family friend Alfred) and that her desire to escape her socioeconomic status is linked to her racial identity. After all, she associates whiteness with "slave owners and racists and wealthy bastards living in Chelsea with . . . caviar and champagne" (91). In a diary entry, she describes Josephine as follows:

> A white girl with long fair hair. She wears it in a ponytail. It reminds me of the Tressy doll I used to have whose hair grew. I still remember the ads with the American woman's voice telling me about the doll's secret. . . . If I found the secret I could wind out her hair from the hole in the top of her head. I could make it grow the way white people's hair grew. I'd have power. (36)

The connection Jacinta makes between whiteness and power returns every time other people remind her of her racial difference. Twice a white hospital environment makes her feel alienated. When she visits her father before his death, the nurses stare at her and her mother "with disdain" (18). When she becomes a hospital patient herself (having intentionally burned her hand following an incident with Maurice), visitors stare, making Jacinta hyperaware of her difference: "They expected my mother to look more like me. But she was white, with a straight little nose and small lips . . . and I was a colored girl, and that was that. . . . I tried to pretend they were dead" (54). When Jacinta's cleaning intensifies months later, it reflects her identity struggles.

Owen E. Brady and Derek C. Maus assert that "the relationship between home and self is reciprocal: home defines the individual, yet the individual defines home through choices about values, human relationships, and self-expression. Individuals are both made by and makers of the ideological and emotional complex called home" (x). As she tries to be a home "maker" or renovator, Jacinta's efforts to remodel are futile, an indication of her crisis of identity. When she is unable to remove "the brown tea stain that had been a permanent mark" on the sink, Jacinta's frustration builds, and she experiences shame, recalling the shame she felt when Maurice likened her and Alison Bean. She explains, "[T]he more I scrubbed, the worse the stain seemed to become. Gradually, as the scouring pad from the Brillo factory that had killed my father left its metal threads in the small cuts on my hands, I felt a hatred swell in me until I found myself trembling with shame" (*Lady Moses* 76–77). In both instances of shame, Jacinta's insecurities and flaws are exposed: while she often embraces blackness, she also resists its "stain."[4] Gloria Anzaldua's discussion of the "deep sense of racial shame" that envelops the Chicano mestizo around Anglos, Gringos, and Native Americans provides a helpful comparison. Just as Jacinta is embarrassed over being linked with black friend, "the Chicano [in the Gringo world] suffers from excessive humility and self-effacement, shame of self and self-deprecation" (105). Linda Alcott explains, "For Anzaldua, developing an alternative positive articulation of mestizo consciousness and identity is essential to provide some degree of coherence and to avoid the incessant cultural collisions or violent compensations that result from the shame and frustration of self-negation" (280–81). For Jacinta, developing a black-sentient mixed-race identity provides a positive concept of home while avoiding the determinist boundaries of home. When Jacinta cries out, "It [the sink] will never, ever be clean! I hate this house! . . . I need more space," she articulates her desire to move beyond the traditional boundaries of home that can repress and limit (*Lady Moses* 77).

Jacinta's cleaning only angers her already emotionally unstable mother, who attacks her when Jacinta rants about the house. Not long after the attack, a neighbor calls social services, and Jacinta must go to a children's home. There, she creates a second self, "Simone Madagascar because, although she wasn't me, she had enough of Simon in her name and enough of Africa to be different" (102). Jacinta's split into two selves evinces her yearning for a black identity symbolically free from a (white) British identity that excludes her. Unlike her real name, Jacinta Louise Buttercup Moses, which pays homage to her mother (Louise Buttercup) and her African aunt (Jacinta Moses), Simone Madagascar only speaks only to the black (African) identity that Jacinta idealizes.[5]

Like *Caucasia*'s Birdie, who becomes Jesse Goldman when she and her mother go on the run, Jacinta temporarily "passes" as Simone, who then passes for Jacinta: "Playing the role of Jacinta again, I climbed into Ruskin's car" (104). Birdie also splits into two selves, referring to her passing self, Jesse, in the third person at school: "I saw myself from above that first day, saw the rush of embarrassment what a strange creative I really was: a pitiful creature called Jesse for lack of a better name. . . . She looked old-fashioned to me. Like someone who has been kept in a box, missed a century, collected dust" (*Caucasia* 187). Jacinta similarly sees herself from above during her conversation with her godfather, Ruskin Garland: "Simone was looking down at us both. She would see the bald spot of Ruskin's head. It didn't interest her in the least" (*Lady Moses* 103). Like Birdie's Jesse, Simone is both a part of her and separate. In "Therapeutic Perspectives on Biracial Identity Formation and Internalized Oppression," Helena Jia Hershel argues, "Living in an invalidating situation causes an internal split between one's ideal self-representation . . . and one's socially constructed self. . . . This split is a psychological defense to protect from painful encounters and invalidation" (173). Indeed, when Jacinta learns she will be going to a children's home, she thinks, "They could send Jacinta Louise Buttercup Moses wherever they wanted. The only person they could never touch was me" (95). On the one hand Jacinta's Jacinta/Simone split comes from her need to "sever [her] connections" to bad memories of her recent past. Yet, on another level, her creation of Simone speaks to her self-alienation. When Ruskin calls Jacinta a "half-caste" and "mulatto," she rejects those terms; and when Ruskin asks, "What do you want me to call you?" she replies, "Don't call me anything" (108). Jacinta's attitude is partly a response to Ruskin's inappropriate sexual advances: she is disgusted with Ruskin's behavior and angry that he has worked things so that Jacinta will be sent to Mrs. Butcher's. However, her response—"Don't call me anything"—also represents Jacinta's early inclination to reject labels that confine her identity, an instinct she does not embrace until later.

In both *Lady Moses* and *Caucasia,* protagonists Jacinta and Birdie witness those who intentionally cross, or at least blur, socially accepted sexual and gender boundaries. Birdie spends time with her mother in Aurora, a woman's commune where her mother "found 'Sapphic bliss' . . . with an Australian woman named Bernadette who rode a Harley" (*Caucasia* 115). Later she writes a story about a teenage boy and his girlfriend, but "it wasn't clear to [her] which one of them [she] was supposed to be identifying with—the burly, macho Richie, who lay on top, or his soft, ultrafeminine girlfriend . . . who lay on the bottom" (147). Her adolescent innocence suggests she has not yet been pressured to fit into a certain mold when it comes to her burgeoning sexuality. Same-sex desire is also not new to Jacinta. Her surrogate parent, Alfred, who lives in the basement of the house, is gay and talks openly with Jacinta about his identity, eventually urging her to see beyond boundaries that limit or restrict. When Jacinta marries a white American, Manny, Alfred concludes his wedding card with, "May people see in you that racial differences can be reconciled into beauty, and that black and white are not opposite but complementary shades of the same spirit," an indication of his progressive views on racial divisions (173). In his examination of Englishness, hybridity, and colonial discourse, Robert J. C. Young maintains, "[A]t one point, hybridity and homosexuality did coincide to become identified with each other, namely as forms of degeneration. The norm/deviation model of race as of sexuality meant that 'perversions' such as homosexuality became associated with the degenerate products of miscegenation" (24). Jacinta recognizes her connection to Alfred, whom the Beadycap siblings call "queer" and "queen." When he sneaks into her hospital room dressed as a woman, she thinks, "He was different, like me. We'd scaled the Wall of Cruelty and escaped from Ugly for a while" (66). Understanding the pain of the outsider status through Alfred's story and her own, Jacinta is compelled to question the rigidity of all kinds of societal boundaries—social, cultural, and racial. In fact, after moving to Africa with her husband and daughter, Jacinta is open to falling in love with a woman after hearing Esther Cole, a singer her nanny and friend Assatu once called her lover, perform. She describes her experience in the audience by using a metaphor of home: "I can't remember what Esther sang about that night, but I thought it had something to do with peace. In the West we call it inner peace, but for me in Africa it was stillness. It is standing in the heart of the bush and feeling its pulse and calling it home" (257). Though Jacinta never develops a romantic or sexual relationship with Esther, they share an intimate moment that leads Jacinta to realize, "If I could have fallen in love then, I would have" (277).

In a review of the novel, Abby Frucht describes the first half as "an account of a quest for identity that is complicated by Jacinta's biracial heritage and Alfred's ambiguous sexuality" (35). From Alfred, Jacinta does learn to value fluidity. However, unlike Frucht who argues that "the spirit of the novel is tested by Jacinta's sentimentalized Africa—and by the white-black, male-female polarization that replaces her earlier far more fluid considerations of identity," I read Jacinta as developing a black-sentient mixed-race identity when she goes to Africa. As a young person, she vacillates but is less concerned with blurring boundaries. Alfred influences Jacinta, but this manifests once Jacinta has distance from her childhood and has matured. After Louise is released from a mental institution, Alfred offers advice that will later shape her identity formation:

> I just think you should remember that we're all more intertwined than the culture lets us be. . . . [Y]ou think you're a coloured girl with a beginning and a middle and an end to your story. Well, perhaps it's not like that at all. Perhaps we're all each other's stories. Perhaps we're like rivers—we all run into each other and our identities are not as separate as they try to tell you they are. (134)

Jacinta's response suggests that her teenage feelings of abandonment and alienation resist such fluidity: "I know *exactly* who I am. . . . I am a coloured girl . . . and I know *exactly* where the tip of me begins and where the end of me ends" (134). While she accepts Alfred's sexuality, she is not completely ready to embrace fluid borders.

In part III, "The New World," Jacinta moves with her new husband to the United States, where she seems content to stay. Though Manny wants to go to Africa, Jacinta comes gradually "to see Africa as a place we'd visit and America as our home" (210). In the United States, she trades in not belonging for admiration; her fellow MFA classmates and professors are charmed by her racial difference. However, once Jacinta graduates and lives in Africa with Manny and Lady, their daughter, she reconnects with her father and herself. She describes it as "entering one of Simon's stories" and reveals, "It made me believe in God" (249). Jacinta's new environment destroys binary thinking. As a child, there were times when it was easier to think in terms of black and white. During one fight with her mother, Jacinta tells her that "white is a damn ugly color" and affirms a racial difference between herself and her mother: "I'm black, not like you" (56). Patricia Hill Collins writes that in binary thinking, "difference is defined in oppositional terms. One part is not simply different from its counterpart; it is inherently opposed to its 'other.' Whites and Blacks, males and females, thought and feeling are not complementary counterparts—they are fundamentally different entities related only through their definitions as opposites" (70). For Jacinta this binary thinking contributes to her negative self image. When her mother calls her coloured, Jacinta recalls, "It made me shrivel up and remember how white she was. It made me want straight hair and a nose as thin as a knife" (21). During this moment, she renounces a black or coloured identity: "I wasn't a coloured child. I was Jacinta Louise Buttercup Moses. I was Jacinta-in-the-Story" (21). Here Jacinta's distinction between "coloured" and "Jacinta-in-the-Story" stands out, given that the Story-Jacinta in her father's stories is an African girl. In other words, Jacinta resists the label "coloured" because in Britain it represents the racial Other. Jacinta can escape that as Story-Jacinta.

When Jacinta first arrives in Lunama to be the Story-Jacinta, she observes, "Objects in shadow became voids, they lost the essence of what they were in sunlight and turned inside out into their opposites. There were trees and not-trees, men and not-men, snakes and not-snakes, things were lost altogether in the intensity of light and dark" (249). While binaries do not dissolve in Africa, Jacinta's reconnection with her father and her increasing self-acceptance prompts her to see beyond binaries. Even after her mother dies, Jacinta sees beyond the limits of experience. She recalls Hubert's belief in "*becoming* the day rather than just experiencing it" and notes that it is "[a]s if there's no separating the experience from who you are. I have to look at Lady to remember I haven't become death too" (144). This suggests an Africana worldview in which there is a blurring between life and death. Scientist Thomas Odhiambo explains, "In the African religious traditions we say that intuitional revelation is a source of memory from the living dead. The living individuals maintain a constant, enduring relationship with the living dead. This belief explains our strong awareness of immortality and continuity and connectedness" (119). It is not a coincidence that Jacinta comes to this revelation about life and death following her trip to her father's country. At her mother's funeral, she says:

> I hadn't thought enough about my mother's race and my own. I was mixed race. Louise Buttercup was white, my father was African. Yet I wasn't simply a bringing together of opposites. I was me. Distinct. A race apart. I didn't just want to know Esther; I wanted to know other people like myself. It would be a luxury to talk with someone who understood what blackness meant from a white perspective and what whiteness meant inside the dark. (285)

It is important to remember that when Jacinta narrates in the present (at the age of thirty-six), she identifies herself as a "woman of color," suggesting that while she has come to terms with her mixedness, she still identifies as "coloured" or "of color" (4). In an interview, Lucinda Roy confirms, "Jacinta has a terrible time in the beginning not understanding really which world she belongs to. Only when she gets to Africa does she begin to understand who she is" ("Searching for Belonging").

Toward the end of the novel, Jacinta is both confused and more settled. She becomes more aware of her husband's deception and instability, has an affair with John Turay, an African man she meets, and is reunited with her childhood neighbor, Maurice Beadycap, who terrorizes her. Yet, Jacinta also comes to terms with her father's death, embraces her mixed-race identity, and finally becomes "Story-Jacinta" when she, Peace Corps volunteer Lionel, John, and a twelve-year-old named Isatu come upon an elephant that Lionel and Isatu were convinced was a dinosaur or beast. Recalling the moment she saw the elephant, Jacinta tells John, "It was as if we were entering his [Simon's] story, as if we had become the characters he wrote about. And the girl, Jacinta, the one who rides the elephant, she was me and she was Isatu as well. . . . The elephant was Simon—just for a second" (334). Jacinta's reading of the Story-Jacinta as both herself and Isatu intimates her black-sentient mixed-race identity; she is both "mixed race," something she affirms after visiting Murunghi, and African, an identity she has long associated with black consciousness. Simon again appears before Jacinta's eyes later, after she, Manny, and Lady get into a car accident and Jacinta drifts in and out of consciousness. She dreams that she is back in the Jeep with Manny; however, instead of the car crashing, they almost run into an animal, "[b]igger than a small elephant, frozen by the headlights" (373). When her father materializes, he leads drummers dancing. Jacinta exclaims, "We were in the dance! Lady and me. In the dance with my father, Africa!" (373). Here Africa is simultaneously her homeland and her father. However, Jacinta still has not found home in her father's country despite telling John, "I'm here to stay. I've come home" (356). Following her husband's sudden death, she doesn't return to England but goes back to Virginia with her daughter. When her mother dies, Jacinta gives the house to Alfred as it had been "a warren, not a home" (46). It is not surprising that she returns to the United States, a place she associates with limitless possibilities when she and Manny first arrive: "I couldn't believe how much space there was to roam around in: houses had dozens, sometimes hundreds of feet between them" (189). If her childhood home is like a walled-in prison, Virginia is like an open field. Her astonishment with the spatial freedom she experiences in the United States connects to her assertions of a black mixed-race identity; in Britain, she did not feel she had the metaphoric space to claim an identity. "The African Americans in this country fascinated me because they took this land as their own." Jacinta muses. "Black Britons didn't do that in the same way. We were always aliens; in the corners of our eyes was the fear of repatriation. I wanted to find a home like the Africa of Simon's stories—a place where no one would question my right to put down roots" (206).

Homesick and Passing in *Caucasia*

Ironically, in *Caucasia,* despite Birdie Lee's African American patrilineal "roots," she is often prevented from claiming black citizenship, suggesting that home is more than acceptance or familiarity or approval. In *Caucasia,* Birdie's search for home is much more abstract because it is an imagined space, a racial locale where she will be recognized and accepted as black and mixed. Her physically white body misrepresents her identity that remains ascribed to, yet not confined by, "blackness." Despite others' attempts to bleach her past, present, and future, Birdie wants to be seen as a person of color and maintain a mixed-race identity. When she overhears a man insult her father with, "You're the one with the white daughter," she is silenced: "[T]he words caught in [her] throat" (14, 15). Unlike her fictional predecessor, *Quicksand*'s Helga Crane, Birdie is not frustrated by flawed choices; rather, her frustration comes from other people's expectations, which always derive from the whiteness of her body. In short, Birdie struggles to strike a balance between being "black and proud" and representing her white mother's heritage. Yet, she cannot map out her racial and psychological identity without investing in the corporeal—the site of the cultural and racial assumptions she resists.

Birdie embarks on her journey after her activist parents decide to split up the family to evade the Federal Bureau of Investigation. The mother, Sandy, and the father, Deck, pair each of their daughters, Birdie and Cole, with the parent she most physically resembles. While Cole flees to Brazil with her black father and his black girlfriend, Birdie must pass as the fictional persona her white mother creates—Jesse Goldman, a white, half-Jewish girl with a deceased Jewish father. Birdie and her mother jump from state to state, fabricating lies and watching out for police who never come to arrest her mother. They finally settle in a small New Hampshire town where Birdie's unhappy immersion in working-class white culture and her desire to return to her former life prompt her to run away and find her father and sister.

Before Birdie moves to "Caucasia," she finds solace in the attic of her two-level brownstone. Unlike Jacinta's brick house, Birdie's brownstone offers comfort. Her world is her sister: "I had some vague understanding that beyond our window outside the attic, lay danger—the world, Boston, and all the [racial] problems that came with the city. When Cole and I were alone in our attic, speaking Elemeno and making cities out of stuffed animals, it seemed that the outside world was as far away as Timbuktu—some place that could never touch me" (4). Birdie's discomfort and confusion about race cause her to desire a kind of invisibility. Although Cole does not suffer from the same kind of public scrutiny, she also yearns for a space or a place where race does not exist. To escape the hegemony of racial typology, Cole creates the imaginary land of Elemeno.[6] Though the word "Elemeno" sounds like a child's rushed pronunciation of the letters L, M, N, and O, it also sounds like a variation on the word "eliminate," suggesting the elimination of racial categories. Cole tells Birdie that the Elemenos "could turn not just from black to white, but from brown to yellow to purple to green, and back again. She said they were a shifting people, constantly changing their form, color, pattern, in a quest for invisibility" (7). Cole creates an imaginary people who attempt invisibility as "less a game of make-believe than a fight for the survival of their species" (7). Cole and Birdie's awareness of the volatile nature of race relations in their city makes the idea of disappearing particularly appealing to them. Similar to Jacinta's description of Britain as "a racist island filled with Beadycaps and squalor," Birdie describes Boston in 1975 as "a battleground. . . . Forced integration. Roxbury. South Boston. Separate but not quite equal. God made the Irish number one. A fight, a fight, a nigga and a white" (6). Racial divisions and related tensions surround them in their neighborhood and within their immediate family, especially when their parents' arguments turn racial. The power of the Elemenos "lay precisely in their ability to disappear into any surrounding" (7). Though playing make-believe captivates Birdie at seven years old, she still wonders, "What was the point of surviving if you had to disappear?" (7). In questioning why people cannot be accepted for themselves, Birdie evinces an awakening to her mixed-race subjectivity. Her question challenges the idea that people have to disappear, pass, or somehow change in order to survive or live happily.

In the prologue of Ralph Ellison's *Invisible Man,* the protagonist lives "in a border area" outside of Harlem, similar to the figurative border Birdie straddles when she passes as white (5). Like the Invisible Man, Birdie is both distant from and a part of the communities in which she lives. The Invisible Man steals electricity from the Monopolated Light & Power "in a section of the basement that was shut off and forgotten during the nineteenth century" (6). Though he makes clear that he has "found a home" in this basement, by the epilogue he makes a decision to leave: "I'm shaking off the old skin and I'll leave it here in the hole. I'm coming out, no less invisible without it, but coming out nevertheless" (6, 581). The Invisible Man's decision to leave his hole parallels Birdie's search for home, not necessarily a tangible place but rather a psychic place where she feels comfortable and secure. Birdie is hyperaware of how others inhabit their homes as she is in pursuit of a welcome and acceptance. When Birdie's mother and father separate, achieving a home-like atmosphere is elusive: "Ever since he [her father] had left us that bright July morning, he acted as if the house were contaminated" (46). When she visits her friend Maria's house, she is awestruck, referring to it as "the most exquisite home I had ever laid eyes on" (58). While Birdie is mostly impressed by the elaborate décor, her reaction reveals that, like Jacinta, she envies others' spaces, particularly those she categorizes as "normal." When Birdie and her mother go on the run, she lays her head to rest in several different spaces and environments that frequently change (including a van, motels, and a commune), a reflection of the various masks Birdie wears. When she and her mother go to appraise the Marshes' rental guesthouse, Birdie notes that it looked "like a ginger-bread cottage, promising sweets and familial comfort" (124). Indeed, when they rent from the Marshes, she thinks, "A part of me believed New Hampshire was as temporary as any of those motel rooms. . . . But another part of me yearned, like my mother, to stay still, to land on this broad country earth and make a home, for once" (133).

The first few lines of *Caucasia* also suggest a strong thematic connection to *Invisible Man*. Though the Invisible Man feels erased because he is black and therefore unimportant in the eyes of U.S. whites, both he and Birdie suffer erasure. "A long time ago I disappeared," Birdie asserts, "One day I was here, the next I was gone. It happened as quickly as that" (1). Birdie's disappearance figures both literally and symbolically. Symbolically, Birdie's blackness disappears when she and her mother escape from Boston. Literally, Birdie physically vanishes from her school, her neighborhood, and her life as Birdie Lee. Birdie's disappearance parallels the figurative invisibility of the protagonist in *Invisible Man*. Both protagonists move from place to place, kept on the run because of other people's attempts to define them. The Invisible Man explains, "I am invisible, understand, simply because people refuse to see me" (Ellison 3). Racism and white employers keep the Invisible Man on the run while paranoia keeps Birdie and her mother running. "I was a nobody," Birdie recalls, "just a body without a name or a history, sitting beside my mother in the front seat of our car, moving forward on the highway, not stopping" (1). Both Birdie and the Invisible Man feel as if they are losing their identities. Birdie's perception of herself as "a body without a name or a history" recalls Frantz Fanon's sense of his corporeal self in a colonized condition. Under the white male gaze, Fanon feels erased: "In the white world the man of color encounters difficulties in the development of his bodily schema" (110). Similarly, Birdie's body becomes erased under the white gaze when she passes for white. As Fanon explains, "Consciousness of the body is solely a negating activity. It is a third-person consciousness. The body is surrounded by an atmosphere of certain uncertainty" (110–11). The paradox of "certain uncertainty" speaks to Birdie's understanding of her surroundings. She knows that her body sits beside her mother in a moving car, yet she remains uncertain regarding the details of her own body ("without a name or a history"). Passing prohibits Birdie from self-identifying. Like Fanon, Birdie exists "triply": she "occupie[s] space" and moves toward "the evanescent other, hostile but not opaque, transparent, not there" (*Caucasia* 112). She disappears. Birdie's disappearance is marked by her awareness of how her body has been manipulated in order to pass: "[W]hen I stopped being nobody, I would become white—white as my skin, hair, bones, allowed. My body would fill in the blanks, tell me who I should become, and I would let it speak for me" (1). Again, like Fanon, Birdie's body represents her, even before she has a chance to tell her story. In describing a child's voice crying, "Look at the nigger! . . . Mama, a Negro," Fanon explains that his "body was given back to me sprawled out, distorted, recolored, clad in mourning in that white winter day" (113). In the same vein, Birdie's body is "given back" to her white and unrecognizable.

While she is on the run, Birdie's desire for a more stable literal home signifies her need for a racial home. While she occasionally welcomes invisibility when she wants to avoid alienation, more often she wishes she had the stronger presence of her sister. Throughout her wavering, Birdie always searches for "self." Recalling her childhood, Birdie remembers, "Before I ever saw myself, I saw my sister. When I was still too small for mirrors, I saw her as the reflection that proved my own existence" (*Caucasia* 5). Yet Cole's tan skin and curly hair do not show up in Birdie's reflection: she phenotypically looks white. Before seeing a mirror, Birdie regards Cole's face as "me and I was that face and that was how the story went" (5). Birdie soon learns about their difference, however, when she overhears her mother refer to her as "a little Sicilian" (23). Hearing these comments marks the beginning of Birdie's "body betrayal"—her feeling that her body decodes her, makes her invisible. In a moment of realization in front of the bathroom mirror, Birdie reflects:

> I tried to think what Sicilian meant by reading my own face. I glanced at my sister's reflection behind me. . . . Her hair was curly and mine was straight, and I figured that this fact must have something to do with the fighting [between her parents] and the way the eyes of strangers flickered surprise, sometimes amusement, sometimes disbelief, when my mother introduced us as sisters. (24)

Outsiders' ready acceptance of Cole as a person of color makes it more difficult for Birdie to accept her body. It also leaves Birdie overshadowed by her older sister. Birdie's body, both her features and color, acts as an enemy informant, announcing to the world an identity she resists. When Birdie's mother registers the two girls in a "black power school," the secretary reacts coldly to Birdie. Later, Birdie's classmates challenge her presence at Nkrumah Academy and her blackness: "Who's that? . . . She a Rican or something? . . . I thought this was supposed to be a black school" (36). Without Cole right by her side, Birdie cannot explain her connection to blackness; her body exposes a different story. Her white skin pushes her out of community acceptance. Rebecca Walker affirms a similar sense of alienation in "Higher Yellow" (2000), referring to her light skin as "the colonizing tinge that taints and marks me as an outsider and pushes me to the periphery of brown and black worlds I have longed to call my own" (247). Birdie feels pushed into a different (white) space without Cole's presence.

Birdie seems to vanish symbolically because she is a mixed-race person who looks white. As Walker reminds us, "[T]he body is a sign, a text to be read and interpreted. For each body part there is at least one widely accepted script already written, a bit of subtext that fleshes out, so to speak, the extremity in question" ("Higher Yellow" 245). People see Birdie's white skin instead of her individuality. Deck Lee cannot see his daughter's blackness. After Birdie's parents separate, Deck seems to look through her rather than at her. "He never had much to say to me," Birdie attests. "In fact, he never seemed to see me at all. Cole was my father's special one. . . . She was his prodigy—his young, gifted, and black. At the time, I wasn't sure why it was Cole and not me, but I knew that when they came together I disappeared" (*Caucasia* 47). Even Cole's name connotes black (coal, colored), and thus Cole represents the blackness Deck tries to hold onto despite anxieties that he "sold out" by marrying a white woman. Birdie tries to impress her father during their visits by doing silly things to make him laugh or by showing off her knowledge of black history. Occasionally this foolery grabs her father's attention. Birdie momentarily becomes visible. One time after she tells her father, "Stay black, stay strong, brotherman," Birdie's father sees her, as if for the first time: "My father flashed me a fierce look of bewilderment, then burst into laughter as he ruffled my hair, as if he had just discovered I could talk when he pulled the string on the back of my neck" (63). Yet, these moments do not last long, and Birdie never stops feeling fatherless. This lonely feeling persists when Birdie's father leaves the country with his girlfriend and Cole, and it continues when Birdie reunites with him seven years later.

When the teenaged Birdie reconnects with her father, he still ignores her. Birdie finds her father living in California and feels a familiar sense of disappointment and betrayal when she learns that he has been in the United States for over five years and has not contacted her. When her father unexpectedly finds Birdie in his kitchen, he tells her, "So, welcome home," even though Birdie has never been to his apartment (330). She notes of the place: "There were no photographs, no sign of anyone's personal taste," and nothing in the rooms to suggest the familiarity of a home (329). While she has sought out a racial home via her father, Deck ironically attempted to make Brazil, his idealized "Xanadu" and "grand Mulatto Nation," his "racial paradise" and home (303).[7] When she confronts him about his absence, he answers her with his usual detached, theoretical, academic jargon. Birdie divulges, "Papa, do you even know where I've been? Do you even care? I've been living as a white girl, a Jewish girl. I've waited and waited, and I kept the box of crap you gave me. But you never came" (334). Deck's response suggests that he still cannot *see* his daughter. He proposes that "there's no such thing as passing. We're all just pretending. Race is a complete illusion, make-believe. It's a costume. We all wear one. You just switched yours at some point. That's just the absurdity of the whole race game" (334). Deck's academic analysis of passing again evokes Birdie's invisibility: he ignores the pain she associates with passing for white. By dismissing and trivializing Birdie's passing as not really passing, as just "switching" costumes, Deck invalidates her feelings of invisibility. His articulation of the social construction of race denies racial essence, thereby neglecting mixed-race issues such as his daughter's real angst. Though Birdie also recognizes the fallacy of race, her understanding of its "real" implications mirrors how she thinks of her own body. Though she rejects the idea of the "bodily" as real or true, she also invests in its ability to mark her closer to blackness.

When Birdie passes for white, she vanishes from her old life. She and her mother suddenly trade in their lives as a multicultural family for one easier for whites to accept. Birdie remembers, "[A]t the Wellington Diner in Maine, surrounded by the thick smoky scent of pine trees and the broad flesh of country women, I was knighted a half-Jewish girl named Jesse Goldman, with a white mama named Sheila—and the world was our pearl" (111). Birdie's momentary enthusiasm seems to speak back to Zora Neale Hurston's famous line from "How It Feels To Be Colored Me": "No, I do not weep at the world—I am too busy sharpening my oyster knife" (153). Given Hurston's proclamation, "BUT I AM NOT tragically colored," three sentences before, Birdie's description of "the world" as "our pearl" seems to suggest her desire not to be tragically colored, even if it means passing. From the beginning, however, Birdie's life on the run lacks substance. She recalls, "In those years, I felt myself to be incomplete—a gray blur, a body motion, forever galloping toward completion—half a girl, half-caste, half-mast, and half-baked, not quite ready for consumption" (116). Immersed in lies and deceit, Birdie begins to feel her black self fade away. While her mother leads her "from motel to motel in a mournful hush, seeming for the first time in her life without any desires—for words, food, or home," Birdie yearns for a literal place and a symbolic racial site to call home (107). In this sense, *Caucasia* recalls Gayle Wald's description of racial passing narratives that

> are concerned with elucidating concepts of "home" in relation to social categories of race, class, gender, sexuality, and nationality. In particular, they represent the struggles of subjects to imagine a "home" that would not demand their subjection to, or confinement within, the various defining discourses alternatively imposed and wielded by the dominant culture. (51)

Birdie's lies slowly become more and more like reality, particularly when she and her mother settle in New Hampshire. At times, Birdie's mother acts as if Birdie is never black or mixed race in the first place. When she tells Birdie about her illegal activist activities, she explains, "Having a black child made me see things differently. Made it all the more personal. It hurts to see your baby [referring to Cole] come into the world like this, so you want to change it" (233). When Birdie's mother refers to Cole as her only black child, she erases Birdie from blackness, causing Birdie to feel racially invisible. This contrasts with Jacinta's mother who calls Jacinta "coloured," making her "want straight hair and a nose as thin as a knife" (Roy, *Lady Moses* 21). Still, both girls feel alienated from their mothers. Birdie thinks, "My mother did that sometimes, spoke of Cole as if she had been her only black child. It was as if my mother believed that Cole and I were so different. As if she believed I was white, believed I was Jesse" (Senna, *Caucasia* 233). Her mother's comments are particularly hard for Birdie given her own self-definition as both black and mixed. Regardless of her physical body that often passes, inadvertently or purposely, Birdie sees herself as connected to a black past and history. This is evident when Birdie mentally "sides" with black teenagers with whom Jim gets into a confrontation on their return from a trip to New York. After that incident, Birdie considers herself "a spy in enemy territory," a statement that recalls real-life racial spies such as Walter White who used their "white" bodies for political purposes (228).[8]

When Birdie assumes the identity of Jesse, she begins to think of herself in the third person, invoking Fanon's description of third-person consciousness. Birdie is displaced, no longer within her own body. "I experienced a sense of watching myself from above," Birdie explains. "It happened only occasionally. I would, quite literally, feel myself rising above a scene, looking down at myself, hearing myself speak. I would gaze down at the thin girl, drawing patterns in the dirt, and watch this girl with the detachment of a stranger" (162). Here Birdie appears indistinguishable among whites. Her invisibility mirrors the Invisible Man's effacement when others either fail to see him at all or see him as indistinguishable from any other black man. Birdie continues, "I would look at my own body the way that I looked at another's. I would think, 'You,' not 'I,' in those moments, and as long as the girl was 'you,' I didn't feel that I lived those scenes, only that I witnessed them" (162). Though Birdie does not literally vanish in the eyes of other people, she fades before her own eyes, rendering herself invisible to her own mind. The fact that Birdie considers herself black, or at least more black than white, makes her passing feel like a vanishing. Writer and artist Adrian Piper's elucidation of her black identification confirms Birdie's identity choices:

> [I]t is not entirely surprising that many white-looking individuals of African ancestry are able to jettison this doubly alienated and alienating social identity entirely, as irrelevant to the fully mature and complex individuals they know themselves to be. I take the fervent affirmation and embrace of black identity to be a countermeasure to, and thus, evidence of, this alienation, rather than as incompatible with it. (246)

The fact that Birdie identifies more as black speaks to her alienation and explains her third-person consciousness. Though others identify her body as white, she recognizes herself as "other," creating that "certain uncertainty" Fanon describes. Birdie strives to think beyond race. She struggles to reject imprisoning labels of color while knowing she wants to "be black like somebody else," different from biracial girls such as Samantha, who seems sad and trapped in her "cinnamon skin" with her "confused, half-nappy hair" (274).

The possibility of being racially outed complicates Birdie's black-sentient mixed-race identity. Since she frequently feels invisible, she wants people to see her. However, on the run, Birdie must deny these desires in order to pass. Birdie slips when she looks through Nicholas's racist *Tintin* comic book: "They've made *us* look like animals" (173, my emphasis). Nicholas catches

Birdie's mistake and then looks at her differently, "sideways through his slittish red eyes" (173). When Nicholas begins calling her Pocahontas because of her ability to tan quickly, Birdie must act cautiously so as not to show her anxiety. Thus, while Birdie knows that "Cole was the girl I wanted to look like, Dot was the woman I wanted to look like," she must hide her secret preferences (174). Birdie's textuality—via body—becomes a site (and sight) of confusion, contradiction, and mythology.

Passing entangles and doubles since Birdie passes not just for white but also for Jewish. Initially, Birdie describes her Jewishness as "a performance we [Birdie and her mother] put on together for the public" (119). At times, they stress this identification and at other times they do not. Birdie's mother justifies this false identity by trying to differentiate between passing for white and passing for Jewish: "[S]he . . . liked to remind me that I wasn't really passing because Jews weren't really white, more like an off-white. She said they were the closest I was going to get to black and still stay white. 'Tragic history, kinky hair, good politics'" (119). In a cruel twist, Birdie's attempt to pass for something other than black nevertheless subjects her to prejudice and discrimination. Ironically, Birdie and her mother pass in order to disappear, yet Birdie's "Jewishness" makes her stand out. One day, when some teenage boys harass Birdie and her friends, one boy throws pennies specifically at Birdie. He shouts, "Fuckin' kike. I'm talkin' to you. Do you want another penny?" (209). An identity intended to protect Birdie and her mother from the "feds" makes her vulnerable to her peers. After Birdie remembers the Star of David necklace around her neck, she "realized then that they were throwing pennies at me because I was Jesse Goldman, daughter of David Goldman. I felt a pang of loyalty toward this imaginary father, and touched the necklace" (209). Birdie's momentary loyalty parallels the alliance Jacinta feels with Jewish people: "Jews and black people had a lot in common, I believed. I planned revolutions where we would help each other escape persecution" (Roy 33). In both cases, the girls unconsciously connect their allegiance to blackness to their sense of kinship with Jews. In effect, when passing for Jewish, the advantages associated with visibility and invisibility reverse. As a mixed-race subject, Birdie dreams of complete acceptance. She does not want invisibility or racial denial. In response to Mona's question regarding her religion, Birdie says, "Well, not *really* Jewish," absolving her from social location within yet another ethnic or religious minority (210). Announcing a Jewish identity proves too socially debilitating for Birdie.

While Birdie "passes" for something she both is and is not (white), she also passes for something she is and is not (black). To "camouflage" her whiteness in the black world, Birdie must find ways to look more black. She depends on her "white" body to make a "black" statement. When she goes over to Maria's house, Birdie pretends she has a life like Maria's:

> . . . just a girl who lived and had always lived in this splendid pink-and-purple palace where all the furniture matched, a girl whose mother worked late nights as a nurse and whose big brother was in the Army. I imagined my name was not Birdie or Jesse or even Patrice, but Yolonda, and that Maria was one of my many cousins. I imagined myself Cape Verdean. (59)

Birdie's fantasy of being like Maria, a Cape Verdean–American, is similar to her passing for Jewish in that she temporarily "becomes" another ethnicity that embodies diversity. In "Passing for White, Passing for Jewish: Mixed Race Identity in Danzy Senna and Rebecca Walker," Lori Harrison-Kahan argues that in *Caucasia* (and *Black, White, and Jewish: Autobiography of a Shifting Self*), "Jewishness operates as a figure for multiplicity by illuminating other ethnic, racial, sexual, gender, and class identifications that compose sub-narratives of these texts" (24). A Cape Verdean identity also represents a blurring of racial and ethnic boundaries: "The Cape Verdean-American ethnic experience . . . combines both immigrant origin *and* color within the dichotomous 'Black-White calculus' and thus brings together issues of ethnicity, race, and national origin" (Pires-Hester 486). Thus, even when Birdie embraces "blackness," she represents racial plurality. Birdie's fantasy becomes momentarily real to her when Maria does her hair. Using a curling iron and hairspray, Maria transforms Birdie's straight hair into a head of curls. As the girls lie atop Maria's mother's bed, Birdie relishes her new look, which would allow her to "pass" for black: "The tint of the ceiling mirror darkened me, and with my newfound curls, I found that if I pouted my lips and squinted to blur my vision in just the right way, my face transformed into something resembling Cole's" (*Caucasia* 60). Birdie wants others to acknowledge her blackness, but she knows that her curls will not last and that physical blackness will remain a fantasy. Despite her efforts to say "nigger the ways kids in school did, dropping the 'er' so that it became not a slur, but a term of endearment," Birdie cannot appropriate blackness as easily as Cole, whose blackness is always visible (54). When Birdie turns twelve, she realizes the futility of her dreams: "There had been a time when I thought I was just going through a phase. That if I was patient and good enough, I would transform into a black swan" (154). By depicting Birdie's painful awareness of the absurdity of her dream, Senna critiques the impossible standards by which others define blackness. As a mixed-race subject, Birdie becomes entrapped in this restrictive criterion.

During a drive back from a weekend vacation in New York City, Birdie feels torn between her passing body and black consciousness. Yet after Mona calls the black youths who throw rocks at Jim's car "niggas," Birdie thinks: "I didn't want the teenagers to think I belonged with these white people in the car. It struck me how little I felt toward Mona and Jim. It scared me a little, how easily they could become strangers to me. How easily they could become cowering white folks, nothing more, nothing less" (224). Before this incident, Birdie ignores any racial insensitivity she hears while she passes as Jesse, even befriending people who would reject her if they knew her racial background. Part passing necessity, part adolescent peer pressure to fit in, Birdie joins Mona's clique. Yet caution always underscores Birdie's comfort: "And when I hear those inevitable words come out of Mona's mouth, Mona's mother's mouth, Dennis's mouth—nigga, spic, fuckin' darkie—I only look away into the distance, my features tensing slightly, sometimes a little laugh escaping" (198). The fact that Birdie so quickly turns against Mona and Jim suggests her affinity toward blackness and rejection of what whiteness represents.

Both Birdie's and Jacinta's voyages to find their fathers mark their journey toward racial freedom. In part three of *Caucasia,* Birdie's black-sentient identity emerges with vigor. On one level, Birdie's decision to find Cole and her father signals her desire to end her mother's real-life game of pretend. On another level, her search for Cole suggests her desire to connect with her sister racially, familially, and emotionally. Ironically, Birdie relies on her body, whose white attributes cause her great anxiety and pain when she grows up in Boston, to help fulfill her mission. Birdie reflects on living in Boston: "My body remembered the city. And, outside, déjà vu hurt my eyes, made me squint as if to block out brightness, though the sky was gray" (251). Birdie does not simply say that she remembered the city: Senna underscores that Birdie's *body* remembers the city. It seems that when Birdie feels nervous about her actions or ideas, she relies on the corporeal. For example, though Birdie knows she must find her aunt, she does not know how her plan will work. Later, she describes her walk from the donut shop to the subway station as an unconscious movement: "My body had led me to the T station" (251). The language here implies how Birdie grants her physical body authority to follow through with psychological decisions that nearly overwhelm her. Writer/poet Akilah Oliver, author of *the she said dialogues: flesh memory,* explains that "flesh memory," a concept she uses in her performance piece *Sacred Naked Nature Girls,* "holds actual experiences, it holds imaginary experiences, it holds memory that may or may not be a direct result of what we've lived." Her elucidation of flesh memory helpfully explains Birdie's corporeal "memory":

> There is a text, a language, a mythology, a truth, a reality, an invented reality as well as a literal translation of everything that we've ever experienced and known, whether we know it directly or know it through some type of genetic memory, whether through osmosis or our environment. Our body holds its own truth and its own reality that may or may not correspond directly with what actually transpired in any given situation. . . . Flesh memory is more than just memory, it's the way we re-invent scenarios and worlds and languages and images to transcribe what we see, what we feel, what we think. It's a language that's activated in our bodies. (qtd. in Fusco)

Déjà vu hits Birdie, suggesting that though she may be experiencing this particular adventure for the first time, her body already understands her journey.

Finding her paternal aunt Dot helps Birdie reconnect with her blackness and with her various identities. Dot's philosophical theories make more sense to Birdie than her father's, "which had been based on bodies and where they fit in the world" (*Caucasia* 273). On the one hand, Deck's theories hurt because they render Birdie invisible and, in effect, homeless. Dot's theories, on the other hand, privilege the spiritual over the corporeal. These theories intrigue Birdie, especially her conclusions on color: "There's skin color, eye color, hair color, and then there's invisible color—that color rising above you. It's the color of your soul, and it rests just beyond the skin" (273). The idea of an invisible color attracts Birdie, particularly because her mixed-race identity often makes her feel erased. An invisible color (which Dot later describes as dark red for Birdie) gives Birdie a place in the world that does not reduce her racial "color." Birdie ponders, "I wondered if I'd ever transcend the skin, the body. If I would ever believe in something I couldn't see" (273). Later, when Birdie reflects on her passing for white, she muses about whether "such a thing were possible," suggesting her deconstruction of the visible (346).

Ironically, finding her father yields Birdie no insight about her body or racial transcendence. Instead, her initial meeting with Deck leaves her empty because he lacks tenderness. In an attempt to explain how he has spent the last seven years, he points to his book, *The Petrified Monkey: Race, Blood, and the Origins of Hypocrisy,* in which he argues that "the mulatto in America functions as a canary in the coal mine. The canaries . . . were used by coal miners to gauge how poisonous the air underground was. . . . [M]ulattos had historically been the gauge of how poisonous American race relations were" (335).[9] Deck surmises that the fact "mulattos" had become less tragic over the years proved a gradual improvement of race relations. His chart of mulattos and their tragic deaths illustrate that the "fate of the mulatto in history and literature . . . will manifest the symptoms that will eventually infect the rest of the nation" (335). Birdie's possibilities reflect the aims of the larger multiracial movement to "dismantle dominant racial ideologies and group boundaries and to create connections across communities into a community of humanity" (Nakashima 81). Still, progressive multiracial literature does not equal more progressive thinking just as Deck's theories do not minimize Birdie's racial struggles.

Through talking with Cole, Birdie comes to a solid sense of herself as a mixed-race subject. Literary critic Michele Hunter argues that the "identification that occurs between the two sisters introduces a 'third space' of experience" that offers non-oppositional ways to think about difference (303). Yet, their mutual connection to blackness also suggests their black-sentient possibilities. Cole tells Birdie that in Brazil she "yearned for America, for Black America, whose pathology she at least could call her own" (346). Ironically, though she resents the impositions both black and white America fix on her body and identity, Birdie yearns for black America without leaving the country. After their emotional reunion, the sisters discuss their father's new race theories. Cole reminds Birdie, "He's right, you know. About it all being constructed. But . . . that doesn't mean it doesn't exist" (348). Cole's statement rings true for Birdie, who feels the strains of racial identification more profoundly than does her sister. Birdie reflects on the difficulties of racial categories:

> I thought of Samantha, in that thick forest, with her cheap white shoes and blue eye shadow. I thought of Stuart at the party, laughing along to all those jokes spoken to him in fake slang. That was how they had learned to survive. Everybody had their own way of surviving. . . . And then I thought of me, the silent me that was Jesse Goldman, the one who hadn't uttered a word. . . . I had become somebody I didn't like. Somebody who had no voice or color or conviction. I wasn't sure that was survival at all. (349)

Birdie's reflection on her own racial passing and Samantha's and Stuart's social passing reconcile her with her mixed-race identity. She tells Cole, "They say you don't have to choose. But the thing is, you do. Because there are consequences if you don't" (349). "Yeah," Cole adds, "and there are consequences if you do" (349). Birdie advocates disregarding the consequences of "not choosing." Her adolescence validates this philosophy because she attempts to blur or ignore all kinds of societal boundaries, believing that freedom comes in abiding by one's own self-image, not color laws.

When Birdie notices a light-skinned girl on a school bus near Cole's house, she identifies her as "black like me, a mixed girl" (353). Some critics read this as evidence of Birdie's "post-ethnicity."[10] Kathryn Rummell writes, "By choosing to affiliate with 'mixed'ness, rather than blackness, Birdie rejects the racial binary that limited earlier passers in favor of a postethnic affiliation" (12). However, such critics overlook the fact that Birdie describes the girl on the bus as "black like me," affirming that she sees herself as both "black" and "mixed" since she shares not the girl's cinnamon skin color but seemingly her racial identity. There are times when both Birdie and Jacinta find race harmful and restrictive; however, they still recognize a profound relationship to blackness. In a letter Jacinta writes to Alfred, she shares, "You taught me about the accident of gender and Simon taught me about the profundity of race," demonstrating that she accepts the fluidity of identity while also understanding its consequences and ramifications (295). Itabari Njeri suggests that a black identity and a mixed-race identity need not diverge: "[E]very Black person with White ancestry should, no matter how they came by it, own it. That is not a rejection of African American identity, but an affirmation of the complex ancestry that defines us as an ethnic group" ("Sushi and Grits" 38). Is it equally valuable for black/white mixed-race individuals to own "blackness" even if they reject race as "real"? For Birdie, the expectation that she is "white" (or must pretend to be) both encourages her desire to live without racial scripts *and* urges her toward blackness. Sarah Willie, a self-described "multicultural" writer with "Black African ancestry," contends, "A defense of a multiracial identity is complicated because it entails simultaneously embracing community and individuality in a society where people tend to see that goal as two discrete goals, oppositional and conflictual" (278). Similarly, Birdie embraces the black community that she is both a part of and separate from, while wondering if she will "ever transcend the skin, the body" (273). Her desire seems inconsistent yet manifests the artifice of race; it is both real and not real, palpable and elusive.

Jacinta's and Birdie's respective, evolving, black-sentient mixed-race identities reflect and go beyond current trends with regard to multiracial identification. In *Race Mixing: Black-White Marriage in Postwar America,* Renee C. Romano contends that the majority of mixed-race children before the 1970s were raised by their parents to identify as black. However, she writes that since the 1970s, "an increasing number of black-white couples have decided to raise their children as biracial . . . rather than telling their children they are black" (279). While this move in part reflects changing social and racial dynamics over time, it also points to a slow shift away from blackness. Many critics of a separate multiracial racial category, for example, have noted that white parents of biracial children are leading the multicultural movement and deliberately leading their children away from blackness because of its stigma (Romano 284). Tangible and abstract obstacles such as Jacinta's and Birdie's bodies, families, and social constructions of race frustrate Jacinta and Birdie from identifying as "just black" or "all white." The black-sentient position of these literary characters thus offers possibilities for identity that remain historically grounded in blackness without being imprisoning.

Chapter Four

"This Is How Memory Works": Boundary Crossing, Belonging, and Blackness in Mixed-Race Autobiographies

> [I]f mixed-race theory has a narrative, it is embodied in the tension, conflicts and deliberations that inhere in discursive genres like the personal essay or memoir, which remain the voiced alternatives to official histories or systematic philosophies.
>
> —Raquel Scherr Salgado, "Misceg-narrations" (53)

"I am at once no one of the races and I am all of them. I belong to no one of them and I belong to all" ("The Crock of Problems" 58).[1] Jean Toomer's declaration intimates the difficulties of racial classification and allegiance for most Americans whose racial heritage is undeniably complicated and mixed. Toomer, who claimed many "racial and national strains," including "Spanish, Dutch, Welsh, Jewish, Negro, Indian [Native American], German and French," later attempted to construct an American identity that would eliminate the need to cling to racial categories (58). Explaining this to a black friend, he said, *"I am not talking about whites or blacks, I am talking about Americans. I am an American. You are an American. Everyone is an American"* ("The Cane Years" 121). In his resistance to racial pigeonholing, Toomer chooses a category that may be vulnerable but is certainly more encompassing and less restrictive than the mutually exclusive black or white. The desire to live beyond race that Toomer advocated has strongly resurfaced in the past two decades, particularly with the establishment of multiracial organizations dedicated to changing how America constructs and recognizes racial identity. These groups fall roughly into three categories of political movements based on their objectives and philosophies. In the first is the Association of MultiEthnic Americans, which purports to "educate/advocate on behalf of multiethnic people" (*AMEA*). This organization has challenged legislation to allow individuals to claim multiple racial categories, particularly on the U.S. census form.[2] A different and more extreme example of the multiracial movement, exhibited in the online writings of *The Multiracial Activist,* calls for the dismantling of racial categories altogether—presumably including multiracial categorization on official forms—claiming that "'racial' categories breed 'racism' instead of fighting 'racism.'" [3] Finally, a third category consists of organizations calling for a separate "mulatto" community. *The Mulatto People* claims that their organization differs from other multiracial organizations, which, they think, "seem to focus on 'freedom to identify as whatever they chose.'" They "strongly discourage any racially mixed person, be they mulatto, hapa, mestizo, meti, or haole from choosing a monoracial race to identify as." Although these organizations are small and lack widespread recognition or support, numerous websites are dedicated to this disturbing separatist philosophy.[4]

This chapter explores the issues of identity that preoccupied Toomer by examining writers whose racial subjectivities often contrast with the sociopolitical ideologies of multiracial organizations. James McBride and Rebecca Walker express a Toomer-like vision in resisting classification in their autobiographies, *The Color of Water: A Black Man's Tribute to His White Mother* (1996) and *Black, White, and Jewish: Autobiography of a Shifting Self* (2001). In acknowledging that they have been shaped by more than one racial identity, both writers recognize their biraciality. However, both also remain politically invested concerning issues affecting the black community. This chapter argues that this emerging "fourth group," not of organizations but of what I call "writer-activists," asserts black-sentient mixed-race identities through their desire to dismantle the conception of race, challenging what it means to be black without ignoring its value in terms of social policy and solidarity. Important to their identity formation, each writer grew up (at least partly) in a black community. The point is not that a black-sentient identity depends upon having a "black" upbringing but rather that both writers witness and feel connections to blackness. While such connections may be forged via personal relationships, experiences, and communal ties, they are also formed by a consciousness shaped by an understanding of one's history and ancestral ties. Barack Obama describes how his white mother shaped his black consciousness as a child: she taught him to "embrace black people generally," and thus he learned "[t]o be black was to be the beneficiary of a great inheritance, a special destiny, glorious burdens that only we were strong enough to bear" (*Dreams from My Father* 50, 51). This chapter therefore also briefly addresses Obama's memoir, *Dreams from My Father: A Story of Race and Inheritance*

(1995), originally published before *The Color of Water* and *Black, White, and Jewish*. While the focus of Obama's memoir is not the development of a mixed-race identity, some of its episodes point to the tensions that may arise when a mixed-race individual predominantly assumes a black identity. And while I would not classify Obama as a member of this fourth "writer-activist" group, his autobiography details his activism in the traditional sense—his organizing work on the South Side of Chicago. Like McBride's and Walker's "writer-activism," Obama's community organizing relates to his cross-cultural and cross-racial connections.[5]

Although mixed-race people obviously have several racial and/or ethnic ties, many black-sentient mixed-race subjects recognize how, in the United States, blackness informs one's additional subject positions and urges one to question racial hierarchies, racial "rules," and race itself. Thus Danzy Senna contends that she identifies as black but is "less interested in giving this answer, than I am in examining the question itself." She continues, "What do we mean when we talk about 'identity'? I think it's important to interrogate the questioner. Why do we need to safely identify people? And what do each of my potential answers (black, white, mixed, just human) mean to you?" (qtd. in Bowman 26). Like Senna, McBride and Walker reserve the right to identify differently than others expect. Moreover, they express indignation with the presupposition that their bodies speak for them. When McBride and Walker were children, their social environments, along with their urgency of assimilation and the insecurity of not fitting in, shaped their self-identification. As adults, they seem to accept black-sentient mixed-race identity as an affirmation of their proximity to a black legacy despite personal memories of traversing the neither/nor racial divide.

Warring Colors: Growing Up Black and White

James McBride's memoir is part biography of his mother and part autobiography. Ruth McBride was born the daughter of an Orthodox Jewish rabbi who disowned her and mourned her as dead when she married a black man. Her father's hatred and her mother's imposed rejection made Ruth's young adult life painful and alienated: she ran away from her "whiteness" (and Jewish identity) but could never "become" black. McBride's coming of age during the 1960s and 1970s was consumed by complicated identity formation as one of twelve mixed-race siblings. His black father died before his birth and his black stepfather died when he was fourteen. McBride always searches for his racial identity, yet never seems to be able come to terms with it. His mother's avoidance of racial topics only furthers his puzzlement. He recollects that the issue of race "was like the power of the moon in my house. It's what made the river flow, the ocean swell, and the tide rise, but it was a silent power, intractable, indomitable, indisputable, and thus completely ignorable" (*Color of Water* 94). McBride's water analogy is fitting, given the fluidity of racial identity in his life. Still, McBride's preoccupation with his and his mother's racial "place" begins when he is just a kindergartner. McBride slowly notices that his mother does not resemble his classmates' mothers. When he mentions this fact to his mother, she reminds him, "I'm not them." After McBride asks who she is, his mother unhelpfully responds, "I'm your mother" (12). McBride then appeals, "Why don't you look like Rodney's mother, or Pete's mother? How come you don't look like me?" (12). The realization of his mother's physical difference from him marks McBride's first memories of race. He does not seem to think about his mother's apparent whiteness before this point; he is only aware of "the stares of the black women" when she picks him up from the bus stop (12). McBride's question recalls that of James Weldon Johnson's ex-colored man who, after looking himself in the mirror, asks his mother, "[A]m I white? Are you white?" His mother's response, "No I am not white, but you—your father is one of the greatest men in the county" (Johnson 12), suggests, as Valerie Smith contends, that she "will neither lie nor speak the truth" (61). McBride's mother similarly evades racial "truths," prompting her son to seek racial "facts," questioning his mother and investigating her past.

McBride's consciousness of racial difference also recalls the fictional Birdie Lee's first awareness of herself as other than black. Though Birdie knows her mother is white, she gradually notes herself as different, even when compared to her biracial sister. Remembering her mother's reference to her as a "little Sicilian," Birdie "tried to think what Sicilian meant by reading [her] own face" in the mirror (Senna, *Caucasia* 24). After she "glanced at my sister's reflection behind me," she understands why the "eyes of strangers flickered surprise" when they find out she and Cole are sisters (24). Comparing herself to her sister allows Birdie to understand how outsiders classify her differently from her sister based on their physical differences. Her observations contrast with the childhood remembrances of McBride, who initially notices his mother's difference from him without giving much attention to outsiders' assumptions. McBride recalls, "I had what black folks called 'good' hair, because it was curly as opposed to nappy. I was light-skinned or brown-skinned. . . . Yet I myself had no idea who I was" (*Color of Water* 91). McBride continues, "I loved my mother yet looked nothing like her. Neither did I look like the role models in my life—my stepfather, my godparents, other relatives—all of whom were black" (91). Although Birdie's situation differs, she also looks nothing like the people she admires, especially her sister, and she yearns to look other than how she looks.

For McBride, on the other hand, this physical difference prompts a desire to pinpoint his racial identity. Yet McBride's mother offers him little solace in this racial labyrinth. Her responses avoid the issue and instead read like a list of clichéd immigrant advice on education as the road to success in America: "I do look like you. I'm your mother. You ask too many questions. Educate your mind. School is important. Forget Rodney and Pete. Forget their mothers. You remember school. Forget everything else" (13). While Ruth needs her secrecy to forget painful childhood memories of her mother's abuse by her father and her own sexual abuse, her children know only that their mother prefers them to keep to themselves. This rejection of the outside world does not work for McBride, who needs answers to figure out his place.

Stephen Butterfield suggests that black autobiographies differ from white autobiographies particularly in offering a "different perception of history and revealing divergent, often completely opposite meanings to human action" (2). He conceives the black self as a "conscious political identity, drawing sustenance from the past experience of a group" (3). This reliance on the past reflects the process by which black-sentient mixed-race subjects understand themselves. McBride's and Walker's mixed-race autobiographies counterpoise "group" experience with outsider alienation, establishing a vulnerable relationship with blackness. McBride asserts that during times when he felt "squeezed between black and white," he embraced "the black side, just as my mother had done, and did not emerge unless driven out by smoke and fire" (*Color of Water* 261–62). As a child, McBride's embarrassment over his mother's whiteness prompts him to escape into blackness. He describes his mother as oblivious to her surroundings unless she or her family faced danger. When Ruth rides her outdated bike through her black neighborhood, unaware of any animosity, McBride dreads the thought of his friends seeing her and her whiteness: "She was already white, that was bad enough" (8). Though McBride's humiliation echoes the embarrassment most children feel about their parents' public behavior, he knows that his mother threatens his racial allegiance. McBride perceives a public alliance with his mother as social death in his black neighborhood. At the age of ten, he feels "ashamed of her" and doesn't want the neighborhood kids to associate them together: "I grew secretive, cautious, passive, angry, and fearful, always afraid that the baddest cat on the block would call her a 'honky,'" and thus disrespect his mother and also insinuate McBride's proclivity to whiteness (100–101). McBride tries to control his racial representation by hiding his mother, choosing to go out alone rather than attract undesired attention. Stuart Hall's understanding of black representation speaks to McBride's identity. Hall suggests, "we tend to privilege experience itself, as if black life is lived experience outside of representation." He continues, "Instead it is only through the way in which we represent and imagine ourselves that we come to know how we are constituted and who we are" (30). McBride primarily imagines himself as black, although his mother's whiteness unsettles that identification. He describes his desire to discover his mother's racial identity as "something inside me," recalling Helga Crane's explanation of her racial instincts as "something deep down inside of me" (Larsen 91). McBride compares his inner turmoil and need to know his mother's origins to "a constant itch that got bigger and bigger as I grew . . . It was in my blood" (*Color of Water* 23). McBride's language is intriguing here because it recalls dangerous nineteenth- and twentieth-century racist discourse with regard to blood quantification and also points to the importance of one's consciousness and self-awareness in terms of racial identification. The affirmation of knowing that he represents more than black suggests that McBride's steadfast mixed-race identification is something that symbolically stays with him, even while he affirms a black identity. "It was in my blood" suggests an undeniable presence of something; for McBride "it" is a gut feeling that his mother is in fact different despite her assertions to the contrary. However, it more generally speaks to black-sentient mixed-race identity in that the statement symbolically suggests an embrace of all aspects of one's identity.

As an adult, McBride identifies as both a "black white man" and a "black man," pointing to both his acceptance of a multiracial identity and his comfort with blackness ("What Color Is Jesus?" 184). His constant questioning about how he should identify reveals that even as a child, McBride balanced his mixed-race identity with his blackness. For example, one day he asks his mother the meaning of the term "tragic mulatto." After she learns that he read it in a book, McBride's mother evades her son's questions:

> "Don't read that book anymore." She sucked her teeth. "Tragic mulatto. What a stupid thing to call somebody! Somebody call you that?"
>
> "No."
>
> "Don't ever use that term."
>
> "Am I black or white?"
>
> "You're a human being," she snapped. "Educate yourself or you'll be a nobody!"
>
> "Will I be a black nobody or just a nobody?"
>
> "If you're a nobody," she said dryly, "it doesn't matter what color you are."
>
> "That doesn't make sense," I said. (*Color of Water* 92)

Their dialogue illustrates McBride's perplexity about his racial belonging. His questions always invoke a black/white binary in that he never asks whether he is biracial (as opposed to black or white). But his inquisitive searching seems a result of the time period, the 1960s, and not necessarily his distance from biraciality. McBride is perhaps right to point out that his mother's final statement does not make sense, given the fact that race matters, particularly with regard to whether or not a person is viewed as a nobody in society. At his young age, McBride is aware of the power of race in determining how he sees himself and how others view him. Interestingly, immediately after he asks whether he is black or white, he does not ask whether he will be a *white* nobody or a black nobody. On the one hand, the exclusion of "white" may intimate McBride's early awareness that lacking a racial descriptor often means white. On the other hand, his question—"Will I be a black nobody?"—symbolizes that despite his confusions, the 1960s did not allow for many other possibilities, such as "biracial."

The flourishing black pride of the 1960s urges McBride to embrace blackness while at least partially jettisoning whiteness and his white mother. As he asserts, "Mommy was the wrong color for black pride and black power, which nearly rent my house in two" (96). Though McBride remembers thinking "it would be easier if we were all just one color, black or white," he "didn't want to be white" (103). McBride's older siblings strongly influence his black identification and remain seemingly free from his particular identity struggles. Yet his young mind "feared black power very deeply," thinking it "could be the end of [his] mother" (26). He surmises that his young age during the black power movement accounts for this difference between him and his brothers and sisters. McBride contends, "Although each [sibling] had drawn from the same bowl of crazy logic Mommy served up, none seemed to share my own confusion" (93).

The majority of McBride's siblings, older and more settled, seemed fairly comfortable with their blackness. When McBride asks whether he and his siblings are black or white, his brother David replies, "*I'm* black," then adds, "But *you* may be a Negro. You better check with Billy upstairs" (93). David's response, albeit sarcastic, shows the diversity of racial identification even within families. That siblings may identify differently resists the notion of a singular racial experience and asserts that racial identification, including black consciousness, is ultimately a choice. The idea reverberates in *Quicksand* when Helga Crane often chooses, even switches her racial identity. The right of the individual to choose stands as one of the main tenets of a sect of multiracial activists. Maria P. P. Root embraces the usefulness of choice in her essay "A

Bill of Rights for Racially Mixed People." She maintains, "*I have the right* / to identify myself differently than strangers expect me to identify / to identify myself differently from how my parents identify me / to identify myself differently from my brothers and sisters" (7). Root's proclamation works to dispel the blood myth which proposes that blood lineage determines race. Rejecting such archaic ideologies as the "one-drop" rule simultaneously throws out the idea of race as necessarily biological. Still, considering that all McBride's siblings had "some sort of color confusion at one time or another" (*Color of Water* 52), David's racial assertion suggests his recognition of a black politics inherent in claiming "black" over "Negro" (or "mixed"). Similarly, a black-sentient mixed-race identity privileges a black politics. For the characters in this study, a black politic is often shaped by an understanding of how blackness is condemned, despised, or oppressed in American society: Helga Crane encounters racial oppression and prejudice in the United States and abroad; Jacinta Moses confronts race inequalities in Britain and the United States; and Birdie Lee claims affinity with blackness during the turbulent 1970s. In addition, McBride's and Walker's various experiences teach them that while black connotes "cool" in some circumstances, it is also vilified. The point is that having personal insight into racial inequalities contributes to developing a black consciousness and mixed-race subjectivity.

Even though Ruth ignores her son's race questions, McBride learns that his bond with other black people transcends skin color. In his essay "What Color Is Jesus?" he remembers his mother's response to his inquiries about blackness: "Forget about black. You are a human being" (194). Yet, McBride's experiences prove more powerful than naïve humanist proclamations. As the "token Negro" in otherwise all-white schools, McBride discovers that even though his mother will not recognize race, his classmates do. During a short lesson on "Negro history," McBride hears that "James is a nigger! followed by a ripple of tittering and giggling across the room" (*Color of Water* 89). McBride becomes enraged yet does nothing. This pivotal moment harkens to Fanon's elucidation of how he came to understand what it meant to be called a "dirty nigger":

> I came into the world imbued with the will to find a meaning in things, my spirit filled with the desire to attain to the source of the world, and then I found that I was an object in the midst of other objects. (109)

Fanon's understanding encapsulates McBride's perception of himself in the eyes of his white classmates as "other." Moreover, Fanon intimates the connection blackness necessitates between one's personal identity and communal identity. After a girl points him out as a Negro, Fanon realizes his simultaneous responsibilities for "my body, my race, for my ancestors" (*Color of Water* 112). No longer can he independently "find meanings in things." Instead, the experience of racism makes him "black in relation to the white man" and therefore he begins to think of himself that way. Similarly, when a classmate calls McBride a nigger, he is no longer a human being like others but a stereotype and caricature of blackness who represents, to his classmates, his "race" and "ancestors." This identification connects him to blackness through shared experience. The incident serves as a catalyst for his future rage over racism: "[O]nly later did the anger come bursting out of me, roaring out of me with such blast-furnace force that I would wonder who that person was and where it all came from" (90). The connection Fanon makes between his subjectivity and his responsibility for his ancestry speaks to McBride's racial responsibility. In an interview, McBride suggests that "in order to accept yourself, [you] have to accept the totality of your past . . . but have to disregard what needs to be discarded so you can face the future with an open heart" (interview with Bill Zimmerman). He continues, "I'm not pure anything. There are no pure Asians, Africans, white in this world . . . what have you done to make the world a better place right now?" His question implies a primary concern with progressive action as opposed to belaboring which words best describe his or other people's racial identity. McBride assures people that he remains "proud of my Jewish heritage, my Jewish blood . . . my African American blood." Still, he continues, "there's a certain point where that pride ends and the reality of where we live today begins. . . . It's good to have pride about your identity but what you do in the world as a grown person is what really counts." Here, McBride joins a cluster of contemporary mixed-race writers such as Lisa Jones, Danzy Senna, and Rebecca Walker who seem more interested in "doing" rather than "being" and satisfying other people's need for racial identification. This approach suggests a new way of positioning oneself in terms of racial identification. Concerning the damage caused by racial and other internal "splits," Walker claims that she "stopped choosing sides and accepted and embraced all of my complex and complicated self" and "became a real human being" (interview, *PBS Online*). This variation of a black-sentient mixed-race identity does not focus on the ethics or pressures of racial allegiance but on pertinent racial issues such as discrimination, racism, and prejudice.

Wearing Masks of Racial Belonging

In her autobiography, Rebecca Walker refers to memory and legacy, two terms that underscore the foundations of a black-sentient mixed-race identity.

Walker's "bad" memory, which, she claims, forgets to "remind me at all times of who I definitively am," acts as a metaphor for her feelings about her mixed racial identity: without a solid memory, she feels "amorphous, missing the unbroken black outline around my body that everyone else seems to have" (2). Walker's legacy as an African American, on the other hand, impels her to stand by blackness, as when a drunken Jewish student challenges her ethnicity and Walker must tell him to leave "in a voice I want him to be sure is black" (25). For many mixed-race people, their experiences and social positioning as alienated or "in-between" prompts them to resent racial scripts and classification. At the same time, a solely "biracial" identity can tend to devalue blackness, particularly given how blackness is disparaged in American culture. Acknowledging her personal memory and cultural legacy allows Walker and mixed-race subjects to remain loyal to both their personal and political identities. At the same time, Walker has recently explained that she claims "biracial" or "multiracial" "only because there has yet to be a way of breaking through the need to racially identify and be identified by the culture at large" (Washington, "Obama's True Colors").

Rebecca Walker's childhood is one of displacement and non-belonging. She never feels completely comfortable in any of her "homes," yet her parents do not seem to notice. Instead, in her eyes, they "did not hold me tight, but encouraged me to go. They did not buffer, protect, watch out for, or look after me" (*Black, White, and Jewish* 4–5). Walker remembers being "left alone to discover the world and my place in it" (5). She always feels like an outsider or a foreigner in a different land, and this estrangement makes her crave (racial) boundaries and borders, relying on her surroundings to define her.[6] Walker asserts that

> most of my life I have been defined by others, primarily reactive, going along with the prevailing view. . . . Having to remember my own life means that I have to feel it, too. I have to pay attention to the thoughts that float, uninvited, to mind. . . . Remembering my own life means knowing that everything can look one way from the outside but there is always another story to be told. (74)

In other words, though Walker may appear to "fit," inside she feels self-conscious and awkward. For this reason, she sometimes wants "to be told what to do." She describes freedom as "overwhelming": "I want to know constraints, boundaries. I want to know the limits of who I am. Tell me what I cannot do. Let me master myself within articulated limitations" (4). Walker's desire to be told who she is parallels McBride's obsessive questioning of his siblings about their racial identity. Implicit in McBride's questioning is a desire for racial belonging. Walker longs to be welcomed in a group because without this acceptance she feels lost. Her desire for boundaries reveals a contradiction in oversimplified versions of progressive identity politics. Although not conforming to a specific "identity" is attractive, the disadvantages include a potential loss of community based on that identity. While opponents of racial classification generally embrace open, fluid spaces, Walker suggests that limitless boundaries can blight rather than embolden identity formation. She contradictorily "sides" with those invested in racial labels in her yearning for limitations. Inherent in Walker's contradiction is the need to belong versus the desire for personal freedom.

Walker vacillates between feeling uncertain and feeling confident about her racial background. A self-described "border crosser," she bluntly defies "mulatto" stereotypes when she asserts, "I am not a bastard, the product of rape, the child of some devil. I am a Movement Child. My parents tell me I can do anything I put my mind to, that I can be anything I want. . . . I am not tragic" (24). Yet when Walker's parents begin to grow apart and their idealism fades, Walker "no longer make[s] sense." She painfully concedes, "I am a remnant, a throwaway, a painful reminder of a happier and more optimistic but ultimately unsustainable time. Who am I if I am not a Movement Child?" (60). Walker does not know *who* she is, particularly after her parents separate. This unknowing makes one of her first encounters with racial prejudice at school especially difficult. When a boy she likes informs her that he "doesn't like black girls," Walker cannot process her rejection (69). This disavowal unsettles her perception of herself: "[I]s this what I am, a black girl?" (69). At this point the pressure to conform overwhelms her. "[S]uddenly I don't know what I am and I don't know how to be not what he thinks I am. I don't know how to be a not black girl," she says, never acknowledging that "not black" really means "white" (69). Walker's third-grade rejection by the boy she likes is reminiscent of W. E. B. Du Bois's description, in *The Souls of Black Folk* (1903), of having his visiting card rejected by a white girl. After this moment, Du Bois realizes that he is "shut out from their [white] world by a vast veil," and this informs his sense of double consciousness: "[T]he Negro is a sort of seventh son, born with a veil, and gifted with second-sight in this American world—a world which yields him no true self-consciousness, but only lets him see himself through the revelation of the other world" (2). Whereas Du Bois suggests double consciousness does not lead one to "bleach his Negro soul in a flood of white Americanism" (2), Walker's fears of being confirmed as black lead to a distorted double consciousness: she rejects blackness in an effort to appear as a "not black girl" (*Black, White, and Jewish* 69). Worried about her mother "outing" her, she thinks, "How else can I explain that Bryan Katon doesn't like black girls and if she comes he will definitely know that I am, in fact, a black girl, and all of my other efforts to be a not black girl will be washed away?" (71). The childhood pressures on Walker to fit in prompt her insistence years later not to conform. As an adult, Walker does not "choose labels that society tosses." While she once gladly accepted these labels, a mature Walker upholds her decision to identify in multiple ways. She discloses, "When pressed I say that my ancestry is African American, Russian Jew and Cherokee with some Irish thrown in." She continues, "To the question, 'What are you?' I might say those four and add student of Buddhism, or I might simply say 'I am being'" (qtd. in Bowman 25). Walker's various descriptions open up the possibilities of self-identification and displace race as the key identifier. Yet, as a result of her personal "color complex," Walker also admits to privileging blackness, locating beauty in darkness. To her, darkness includes "words *community, belonging, stability, justice, righteousness* and *moral superiority.*" She reveals that in her "weaker moments" she believes, "To be black is to be a part of the solution" ("Higher Yellow" 245). These seeming contradictions reveal a desire to uphold and "belong" to blackness while remaining racially "free-standing."

Contradiction and conflict become a part of Walker's young life when her parents divorce. In the third grade Walker's uneasiness with her identity increases. According to her parents' divorce agreement, she switches home every two years:

> Now as I move from place to place, from Jewish to black, from D.C. to San Francisco, from status quo middle class to radical artist bohemia, it is less like jumping from station to station on the same radio dial and more like moving from planet to planet between universes that never overlap. (*Black, White, and Jewish* 115)

Walker must alternately switch subjectivities according to whose daughter she is and where she lives. During the summer between junior high and high school, she leaves San Francisco and attends a Jewish camp her father and stepmother choose. There, Walker tries to "pass" as another white Jewish camper: "I wear Capezios and Guess jeans and Lacoste shirts, and I assume the appropriate air of petulant entitlement" (177). In addition to appropriating new ways to dress and talk at camp, Walker hides mannerisms that might give her "otherness" away. She remembers, "When I get there I do what I do everywhere else, I heighten the characteristics I share with the people around me and minimize, as best I can, the ones that don't belong. At Fire Lake I am a Jap, but not one" (182–83). Homi Bhabha's notion of colonial mimicry is useful in understanding Walker's attempt to socially convert into a white Jewish girl. Bhabha writes, "[C]olonial mimicry is the desire for a reformed, recognizable other, as a subject of a difference that is almost the same but not quite. . . . [I]n order to be effective, mimicry must continually produce its slippage, its excess, its difference" (*Location of Culture* 86). In this vein, Walker's attempt to pass for white is inherently futile. She asserts, "I am a Jap, but not one," or as Bhabha might conclude, almost a "Jap" but not quite white. Walker always resists her conversion into a white upper-class camper even as she desperately tries to conform. Her passing is always undermined by her otherness:

> When I ask Jody or Pam why people are sometimes quiet or reserved around me, they say that I am intimidating, which doesn't really answer my question, but gives me a general idea of how I am perceived. It doesn't occur to me that intimidating might be another word for black. (*Black, White, and Jewish* 178)

Though Walker tries to disclaim her connection to blackness at camp, even she acknowledges that masking does not always work: "I move my body like I belong but I also hold it back" (183). Walker's struggle against her racial passing recalls Bhabha's notion of mimicry as a means of resistance. "I never get it quite right," Walker further admits, "never get the voice to match up with the clothes, never can completely shake free of my blackness: my respect for elders, my impatience with white-girl snottiness, the no-shit attitude I couldn't quite perfect back with Lisa in San Francisco but which comes to me natural as rain at Fire Lake, where it makes other girls defer to me, look up to me, fear me" (177–78). In Walker's case, taking mimicry out of the colonial context but still in a white/other context allows us to see the impossibility of Walker's passing and also intimates the resistance inherent in her attempt. As Bhabha explains, "[M]imicry rearticulates presence in terms of its 'otherness,' that which it disavows" (*Location of Culture* 91). Walker never completely disassociates from her blackness. She writes that she cannot disrespect her elders or suppress her defiant attitude, which seem like superficial markers of an essentialized black identity but speak to survival mechanisms necessary when one's life is framed by a history of oppression and inequality. Walker also indicates that her ties to blackness shape her interactions with others and her positioning in the world. In other words, Walker's blackness prepares her to fight or resist constantly, and she carries these tools wherever she goes: "My parents raised me to believe I am entitled to whatever is available. . . . This, to counteract the idea that being black or being a woman, or being Jewish, means having to settle for less. . . . This, the legacy of two parents who spent a great deal of their energy fighting for it" (*Black, White, and Jewish* 185). Walker's appreciation of her legacy, particularly one rooted in the civil rights movement and handed down from her parents, both civil rights activists, solidifies her understanding of herself as part of a larger black struggle.

After summer camp, Rebecca lives with her father and stepmother in the Bronx. Here, belonging means being authenticated as Latino, which she is not. Her ethnic passing parallels Birdie Lee's passing for Jewish. Since Walker's friends are mostly Puerto Rican and Dominican, she transforms into a Nuyorican like her friend Melissa: "After being around her so much I talk like her, shaking my head and pushing my whole mouth forward, pursing my lips for all that attitude she picked up somewhere between San Juan, which she's never seen, and the Bronx, where she grew up" (191). Walker temporarily accepts this new identity and feels as if she belongs. Though her new friends never come over to her house (and her father never gets out of the car when he drops her off), hanging out in the Bronx provides her inclusion. Living in the Bronx "means walking around with my friends Sam and Jesus and Theresa and Melissa and being seen as I feel I truly am: a Puertor-riquena, a mulatta, breathed out with all that Spanish flavor. A girl of color with attitude" (198). Walker's move from vaguely Jewish to ambiguous "girl of color" allows her to run away from her father's "lily-white" life. In Larchmont, she performs Jewishness in the same way she performs "Latina-ness" in the Bronx. When she passes, her quest for authenticity boils down to adapting or adopting physical, racial, and cultural signifiers that still invite scrutiny and remind her of her racial vulnerability. When a biracial person of some black heritage passes for a "person of color," the very fact that s/he must pass highlights the preposterous and fallible notion of racial authenticity. As James Davis asks in his book title, "*Who Is Black?*" How do we define "blackness," "person of color," "Latino"? Danzy Senna reflects on her own passing for Latino: "In a 1980s twist on the classic tragic mulatto, I was determined to pass as black. And if that wasn't possible, at least with my hair-sprayed 'crunchy curls' I could pass as Puerto Rican" ("To Be Real" 9). Such racial masquerade, what I call "transverse passing," describes a black mixed-race person passing for another ethnicity of color, often black Latino.[7] Ironically, light-skinned people of color who pass for other minorities must still authenticate themselves as people of color. I refer to this kind of passing as "transverse passing" to highlight the intersection of multiple racial systems represented by the black Latino or other racial and ethnic identities. This reversal of "light-skin" privilege seems an indirect reaction to the difficult ironies found in the color politics in black and Latino communities where the worship of "light" skin contradicts the challenging of those who do not seem "black enough." Walker knows how her light-skin privilege works to her advantage: "I carried on my skin the same power to hurt by being the one chosen over another, the one better regarded" ("Pale as I Am" 168). Though advantaged by her light skin, it is also a liability to her sense of blackness, as at school when she surmises she is "not black enough" for the "tough black girls" to like her (*Black, White, and Jewish* 99). Walker's security in belonging with her Latina clique (a third "category" to which she does not belong) subsumes all of these politics: her "passing" illustrates how belonging and legitimacy war with each other.

As Walker moves from city to suburb, she feels as much a weary go-between as *Caucasia*'s Birdie Lee, who negotiates her position as a white Jewish girl in New England. Walker's role as racial and cultural translator recalls that of mixed-race leaders such as Booker T. Washington and literary characters who were often expected to act as negotiators between black and white.[8] Late-nineteenth- and early-twentieth-century mulatto archetypes were used as empathetic go-betweens between white readers and black people via black characters; so, too, Walker is expected to transition and translate seamlessly from black to white, all the while acting as a bridge between black and white worlds. In early American literature, mulatto characters were intended to gain white sympathy, yet they created new destructive stereotypes of blackness.[9] For Walker, the responsibility of translator also proves too heavy to bear. She wears "a mask of unfazable calm. With it firmly in place, my features express serene indifference. My cheeks, eyes, lips, all are placid, welcoming, nonthreatening" (184). Here, nonthreatening can also refer to Walker's racially "ambiguous" facial features, instrumental to her role as a border crosser. Yet Walker feels uneasy and awkward in her mask, pretending to fit in whenever she moves between black and white. "Beneath the mask, behind the cool, unperturbed exterior there is rage," she continues. "There is pure liquid fire threatening to annihilate. And I am afraid" (187). The point here is that heavy expectations placed on "biracialness" to always decode and translate often create anxiety, not possibilities. Walker envisions a less racially scripted world. "What do we become," she asks, "when we put down the scripts written by history and memory, when each person before us can be seen free of the cultural or personal narrative we've inherited or devised? When we, ourselves, can taste that freedom?" (305). Walker's conception of freedom encapsulates the overall vision of each of the characters in this work who want to be free from the binds of race rules. It should be noted, however, that usually only light-skinned, often upper-class subjects have the luxury of crossing borders or thinking about race in abstract terms.

Walker's friendship with Jesse, "a white boy who talks and acts black," highlights her precarious position as "a border crosser, a human bridge" (229, 242).[10] Like Walker, Jesse is constantly made fun of for projecting an identity people do not expect: "Downstairs in his two rooms he's surrounded by black people who jokingly make fun of him for being the blackest white boy on the planet, and upstairs he's surrounded by his white family, who love him to death even when they can't quite figure out what he's doing with his life and why he talks the way he does" (242). Similarly, Walker's family and friends tease her, making her envious of Jesse's ability to "do all of this moving up and down and in and out so seamlessly" (242). Walker feels defensive about her border crossing, particularly when her boyfriend Michael exposes her racial "otherness." She laments that "he starts to call me half breed now that I got to Urban [High School], half breed because he says my white comes out when I'm at Urban. . . . He tells me I sound like a white girl. He tells me that he forgets sometimes that I'm not a real sister" (266). This comment places Walker in a racial black hole she cannot easily escape: she does not "fit in" with her white peers and is challenged for not being black enough. Poet/writer Toi Derricotte captures the pain of such moments—of being told, "She think she white." Derricotte reveals this snide comment as a hateful attack "said with a bitterness, irony, disgust, and even a humor that only one raised with generations of historical pain can understand. It was not only a judgment, it was a punishment as well, for it embodied the consequence of exile, of exclusion" (162). When Michael tells Rebecca she sounds white, he immediately becomes her enemy. Walker cannot ignore the jokes in the same way Jesse does. She contends, "He says this like he's joking, with a big bright white smile, but I don't hear it as a joke. I hear it as territory I'm supposed to defend" (*Black, White, and Jewish* 266). Derricotte explains that being racially challenged moves one "outside of love, community" and places "that territory in another person's head that made her the thing hated" (162). Michael's comment also places Walker in another cultural and racial realm, and she realizes that to Michael she is "other." As a result, she begins keeping her thoughts and feelings to herself, particularly during her internship in New York: "I don't tell Michael about all the things that might mark me more in his eyes as the half-breed race traitor I feel I am becoming" (*Black, White, and Jewish* 269). Michael's joking accusations highlight the ambiguous qualifications for racial authenticity. When Walker grows older, her black cousins also make fun of her when she does "things they think are strange or weird, things they think are not black" (85). In general, these affronts make blackness narrow and limiting, not allowing for diversity of black experiences.

Only after their adolescence do Walker and McBride find a comfortable racial space to call home. For Walker, anonymity works better than conformity at high school: "It's easier to be quiet, aloof, removed than it is to slip and be made fun of for liking the wrong thing, talking the wrong way, being the wrong person, the half-breed oreo freak" (269). Both Walker and McBride simply want to make their classmates and friends happy and at ease, a natural adolescent reaction to feeling different and excluded. Though Walker trains herself not to break "the code, not saying something too white around black people, or too black around white," her inability to use the code inevitably breaks down, forcing her out of the "quiet, aloof, and removed" space she inhabits (269). Yet when her white boyfriend's friend "casually says something about some dumb nigger," Walker suddenly takes sides: "This image of white boys out of control, drunk and hurling the word nigger around, frightens me, reminds me of lynching photographs," and it no doubt also reminds her of her black relatives in the South and her "legacy of slavery and discrimination" (285–86, 304). Being called "nigger," or just overhearing the epithet, is something of a rite of passage for black people, a social initiation into racism. When Walker hears the term, she feels further away from her boyfriend and his (and her) whiteness: "Looking into Andrew's smiling brown eyes I feel deep uneasiness, like suddenly I'm separate from him" (286). As we have seen, Birdie Lee experiences a similar moment when her friend Mona calls some black teenagers niggers. In that moment, Mona and Jim turn into "strangers" and "cowering white folks" to Birdie (Senna, *Caucasia* 224). In these instances, a cultural memory becomes personal. When Andrew's friend Zack racially maligns Walker, she tells Andrew he must "beat him into this century," consciously calling up the history of black pain (286).

Memory and legacy symbolize Walker's simultaneous racial identities. Claiming that "memory is stronger than legacies," she writes,

> Memory works like this: I am always standing outside the gate, wanting to be let in. I am always terrified that this is where I will have to live: forever wanting, never fulfilled, always outside. . . . This is how memory works: I wear a mask of belonging because this is what I am supposed to do, because belonging is my birthright. But behind the mask lurks a far more mutilating truth: I am not fit, there is something wrong with me, I am not correct. (185–86)

Though she acknowledges the role of legacy in informing her subject formation, her everyday experiences in the world equally affect her. Still, as Suki

Ali asserts, "Memory is a process that constantly invokes and reinvents past events through the lens of the present and the imagined future. The social and the self are linked in the continuous co-productive venture" (36). Walker understands that her sense of social displacement results in her feeling the most comfortable in airports, indeterminate spaces that seem to encompass the past, present, and future in that travelers are either returning from and remembering a trip, anticipating a trip, or en route. "I do not have to define this body [in airports]," Walker writes. "I do not have to belong to one camp, school, or race, one fixed set of qualifiers, adjectives based on someone else's experience" (*Black, White, and Jewish* 4). Though Walker wishes to break free from racial constraints, she nevertheless recognizes the value of legacy and racial responsibility. When her mother shows her an old picture of a great ancestor who was a slave, Walker thinks, "I would not have been born had Grandmother Poole not done her walking, had she not fought off whatever demons wanted to keep her from moving, from being free" (149). When Walker wonders "if I would have been as brave," her sadness and empathy connects her to black family history. At the same time, however, she questions whether Grandmother Poole would "see the lightness of my skin as a sign of danger, the evidence of brutality" were she to have anonymously approached her in the past. Moreover, when Walker looks at the picture for the "thread that makes the life of this ancestor intersect with my own," she feels "lost" (148). She stands at a crossroads defined by her simultaneous rejection and recognition of racial boundaries. She admits:

> I stand with those who stand with me. I am tired of claiming for claiming's sake, hiding behind masks of culture, creed, religion. My blood is made from water and so it is bloodwater that I am made of, and so it is a constant empathic link with others which claims me, not only carefully drawn lines of relation. I exist somewhere between black and white, family and friend. I am flesh and blood, yes, but I am also ether. This, too, is how memory works. (319–20)

This powerful ending to Walker's autobiography acknowledges racial familial connections but ultimately recognizes how she is more than black and white. Her use of the word "ether" establishes her embracing open spaces, metaphorically filling all physical and nonphysical spaces without regard to racial categories. I see Walker's black-sentient mixed-race identity as reconciliation between her black identity and her desire to remain racially neutral.

Neither Tragic Mulatto Nor Racial Translator, Yet Both

In the introduction to his memoir, *Dreams from My Father: A Story of Race and Inheritance,* Barack Obama discloses, "[W]hen people who don't know me well, black or white, discover my background . . . I see the split-second adjustments they have to make. . . . They no longer know who I am." He continues, "[T]hey guess at my troubled heart, I suppose—the mixed blood, the divided soul, the ghostly image of the tragic mulatto strapped between two worlds" (xv). Responding to assumptions about his identity, Obama explains that "the tragedy is not mine," but rather a tragedy owned by all Americans who confront or deny American's racial problems. In other words, the racial issues of an individual are the issues of the nation. Obama's memoir reveals his efforts to avoid "identity tragedy." Barbara Foley asserts that *Dreams from My Father* is "a story about stories, and about the construction of identities—personal, familial, community, and national—through the stories that people tell about themselves or others" (4). In this sense Obama's stories provide context for two writers who are in or close to his generation, McBride and Walker, who demonstrate black-sentient mixed-race identity in its variations.[11] When Obama recounts his college experiences, he describes a conversation he has with Joyce, another mixed-race student. After asking her whether she is going to the Black Students' Association meeting, Joyce responds, "I'm not black. I'm multiracial. . . . Why should I have to choose between them [her Italian father and African/French/Native American mother]?" (99). Initially, Obama scoffs at Joyce's claims of multiraciality, repeating a common critique of the multiracial movement: "They ['people like Joyce'] talked about the richness of their multicultural heritage and it sounded real good, until you noticed that they avoided black people" (99). Here, Obama echoes Danzy Senna's question, "[W]hy is it so important for many mixed people not to be defined as black?" ("Passing and the Problematic of Multiracial Pride" 86). However, despite Obama's critique of Joyce, a paragraph later he admits to "being too hard on poor Joyce" and sympathizes with her. "I understood her, her and all the other black kids who felt the way she did," he continues, "In their mannerisms, their speech, their mixed-up hearts, I kept recognizing pieces of myself" (*Dreams from My Father* 100). Bertram Ashe importantly points out that Obama conflates the struggles of biraciality with the struggles of black suburban students who embraced individualism over assertions of blackness. He argues that Obama's identity search is "less about being biracial and more about being bicultural," maintaining that Obama's "examination of Joyce . . . emerges as a key blaxploration moment in his text" or what Ashe reads as a "post-soul" exploration of blackness (Ashe 104, 110). Indeed, Obama's memoir largely focuses on his efforts to be accepted as black despite the cross-cultural, transnational experiences that set him apart. Still, I think it is important to note that Obama also states, "Their confusion made me question my own racial credentials all over again, Ray's trump card still lurking in the back of my mind" (Obama 100). The trump card refers to the previous chapter when Obama tells his friend Ray to "give the bad-assed nigger pose a rest," to which Ray replies, "Speak for your own self." Following Ray's comment, Obama thinks, "And I would know Ray had flashed his trump card, one that, to his credit, he rarely played. I was different, after all, potentially suspect; I had no idea who my own self was" (82). Ray's trump card stops Obama, who recognizes his biraciality, particularly given his earlier discussion of the term "white folks":

> Sometimes I would find myself talking to Ray about *white folks* this or *white folks* that, and I would suddenly remember my mother's smile, and the words that I spoke would seem awkward and false. Or I would be helping Gramps dry the dishes after dinner and Toot would come in to say she was going to sleep, and those same words—*white folks*—would flash in my head like a bright neon sign, and I would suddenly grow quiet, as if I had secrets to keep. (81)

Obama's admission of confusion, along with his unwillingness to dismiss his whiteness, suggests that he is working through what it means to be both black and white. McBride similarly participates in what he feels is betrayal when, "standing on the street with a group of black [college] students . . . one of them said, 'Forget these whiteys. They're all rich. They got no problems.'" McBride concurs, although he immediately thinks, "[I]nside my pocket was the folded letter holding the heartbroken words of an old white lady who had always gone out of her way to help me—and many others like me [during high school and college]. It hurt me a little bit to stand there and lie" (McBride, *Color of Water* 187). The point is that both men feel a sense of responsibility to both sides of their ancestry that makes it difficult for them to disavow connections. Obama's assertion that "identity might begin with the fact of my race, but it didn't, couldn't, end there. At least that's what I would chose to believe" intimates both his challenging of racial scripts *and* his awareness of the power of race (*Dreams from My Father* 111).

Obama attempts to understand the complexities of black manhood by reading a list of African American male literati greats: James Baldwin, Ralph

Ellison, Langston Hughes, Richard Wright, W. E. B. Du Bois, and Malcolm X. Malcolm X's autobiography particularly influences Obama; as Tara Green states, "Malcolm X resonates more clearly to him than the others since his mother was biracial" (121). While Obama notes Malcolm X's "wish he'd once had . . . that the white blood that ran through him . . . might somehow be expunged," he also asserts, "I knew as well that traveling down the road to self-respect my own white blood would never recede into mere abstraction. I was left to wonder what else I would be severing if and when I left my mother and my grandparents at some uncharted border" (*Dreams from My Father* 86). Obama's language here speaks to how he simultaneously circumvents racial dichotomies and racial indeterminacy. Growing up, Obama avoids abstractions. He describes himself as "living out a caricature of black male adolescence" in pursuit of a specific kind of racial authenticity (79). Still, valuing his multiraciality, he doesn't want any part of his racial background to be abstract. Like McBride and Walker, he also describes himself as a border crosser as a young adult: "As it was, I learned to slip back and forth between my black and white worlds, understanding that each possessed its own language and customs and structures of meaning, convinced that with a bit of translation on my part the two worlds would eventually cohere" (82). Here, Obama sounds a bit like Joyce, who resents the idea that she should live in separate black and white worlds. Obama's reference to leaving his white family "at some uncharted border" is interesting, as one might expect the phrase "uncharted territory" to denote a description of his white family's hypothetical, uncertain "destination." Obama's use of "uncharted border" perhaps reveals how Obama would feel if severed from his white family—subject to borders and confines.

Obama largely identifies as black throughout his memoir. Still, his reflections and exploration of what constitutes racial ties, familial connections, and communal bonds resembles the writings of McBride and Walker. His book's subtitle, *A Story of Race and Inheritance,* speaks to the complicated relationship between identity and heritage. Rebecca Walker views racial inheritance as a disruption in the United States, "where I always seem to be waiting for a bomb to drop and where I feel I am always being reminded of the significance for better or worse, of my racial inheritance" (302). For Obama, the notion of inheritance and family is elusive:

> What is a family? Is it just a genetic chain, parents and offspring, people like me? Or is it a social construct. . . . Or is it something else entirely: a store of shared memories, say? An ambit of love? A reach across the world? (327)

His questions sound similar to questions one might ask about race: Is it a real or superficial indication of kinship? Is it a social construction? How does racial memory shape identity? His answer is to create "a series of circles around myself with borders that shifted as time passed and faces changed but that nevertheless offered the illusion of control" (327–28). He includes in these circles close friends and family "where love was constant and claims unquestioned," colleagues and people he knows who constitute "a realm of negotiated love, commitments freely chosen," and a much larger circle "widened to embrace a nation or a race, or a particular moral course, and the commitments were no longer tied to a face or a name but were actually commitments I'd made to myself" (328). Thus he moves from a smaller group of people to a much larger community—not unlike Walker who refuses to place limits on racial and familial ties.

Walker challenges the notion that her specific race or ethnicity limits her ability to relate with all people. "Do you think of black people as your people?" her lover asks her. Walker's response shows her sense of connectedness with all oppressed groups:

> What I do feel is an instant affinity with beings who suffer, whether they are my own, whatever that means, or not. Do I identify with the legacy of slavery and discrimination in this country? Yes. Do I identify with the legacy of anti-Jewish sentiment and exclusion? Yes. Do I identify with the internment of Japanese-Americans during World War Two? Yes. . . . Do I feel I have to choose one of these allegiances in order to know who I am or in order to pay proper respect to my ancestors? No. (*Black, White, and Jewish* 305)

Her questions broaden the criteria for allegiance, belonging, and family, ultimately looking to fundamental links of human empathy and understanding in lieu of racial or ethnic ties.

Still, Walker feels a responsibility toward her blackness, which she describes as "an affinity with blackness, with an experience of living in the world with non-white skin" (311). McBride also recognizes his closeness to blackness: "My view of the world is not merely that of a black man but that of a black man with something of a Jewish soul" (*Color of Water* 103). For Walker, her ties to blackness shade, yet do not obscure, her ties to her Jewishness. Her name change from "Rebecca Levanthal" to "Rebecca Levanthal Walker" represents her ties to blackness. She justifies this change by claiming: "I do not feel an affinity with whiteness, with what Jewishness has become" (*Black, White, and Jewish* 311). Walker privileges her black identity implicit in her mother's maiden name while still acknowledging her connection to her white Jewish identity. Walker's name change corresponds to McBride's sense of himself as black and Jewish: "I don't consider myself Jewish, but when I look at Holocaust photographs of Jewish women whose children have been wrenched from them by Nazi soldiers, the women look like my own mother and I think to myself, *There but for the grace of God goes my mother—and by extension, myself*" (*Color of Water* 103). McBride's perception of himself as black with a "Jewish soul" speaks to the peculiar yet connected relationship between blacks and Jews, two historically oppressed groups. It is not surprising, for example, that *Caucasia*'s Sandy Lee fabricates a Jewish identity for her daughter Birdie or that *Lady Moses*'s Jacinta links black slavery to the extermination of the Jews.[12] Though neither character is Jewish, both feel a connection or special loyalty, Jacinta toward persecuted Jews and Birdie toward her imaginary Jewish father when she is called a "fuckin' kike" (Senna, *Caucasia* 209). The shared experience of suffering explains much of this cross-ethnic bond. After writing out the words of the hymn "O Come, O Come Emmanuel," Jacinta connects black and Jewish suffering: "As 'captive Israel mourned in lonely exile' I thought about all the coloured children across the world who were mourning too. Jews and black people had a lot in common" (Roy, *Lady Moses* 33). This compassion matches McBride's blood ties and empathetic connections with the Jews of Nazi Germany.

In *Black, Jewish, and Interracial: It's Not the Color of Your Skin, but the Race of Your Kin, and Other Myths of Identity*, Katya Gibel Azoulay claims, "To be Jewish and Black and interracial—is to occupy a three-tier standpoint position that is inherently political but neither an essentialist idea nor a constuctionalist social category; it is a standpoint position from which to challenge racialist nationalism and misguided prejudice" (187). Such a position also aptly describes the political slant of a black-sentient politic. Walker's stance is political in that she rejects a segregationist outlook, not just in a physical sense but also in terms of personal allegiance. In challenging the presupposition that what connects people is skin color and race, Walker suggests there is more to one's identity than belonging to a certain group. Her lover's question "[W]hen someone black starts talking about 'my people' have been oppressed for so long, do you identify with those people?" prompts Walker to object to what "my people" implies, namely rigid categories and exclusion (304). Both McBride and Walker refuse to engage in the politics of exclusion, as McBride's humanist, albeit somewhat trite, proclamation demonstrates: "I belong to the world of one God, one people" (104).

McBride and Walker resent other people's assumptions regarding what people presume to be their identity. Walker's annoyance with people who criticize her for not being black enough or for not knowing enough about Judaism dissipates only after she stops "shifting between houses and communities, keeping [her] father and [her] mother and their respective worlds separate" ("Black, White and Jewish," *Glamour* 184). McBride registers a similar frustration with outside expectations: "Being mixed is like the tingling feeling you have in your nose just before you sneeze—you're waiting for it to happen but it never does. Given my black face and upbringing it was easy for me to flee into the anonymity of blackness, yet I felt frustrated to live in a world that considers the color of your face an immediate political statement whether you like it or not" (*Color of Water* 262). Biracial people repeat this sentiment over and over in personal essays collected in anthologies such as *What Are You? Voices of Mixed-Race Young People* and *Miscegenation Blues: Voices of Mixed Race Women.* Mark Durrow, interviewed in *Black, White, Other: Biracial Americans Talk about Race and Identity,* underscores McBride's irritation with outsiders' presumptions: "The comment I kept getting from kids was, 'You're not white you're black,' or 'You're not black you're white.' People saw me the way they wanted to" (qtd. in Funderburg 151). Although people do not have control over how they are perceived, they can still assert agency over how they define their personal and political identities. However, the indignation of McBride and others about racial assumptions does not make room for the sentiments of many in the mixed-race movement who fight against what they view as unfair or unnecessary racial presumptions. What is the difference between resenting how one is perceived racially and resenting one's blackness? What is the connection between refusing to choose "sides" in one's personal life (as McBride does) and refusing to choose "sides" on school forms? Race must be viewed within a larger historical and social context. Politically claiming a multiracial category on official forms such as that used in the census can ignore the legacy of the civil rights movement despite the multiracial movement's reliance on the rhetoric and philosophies of the civil rights movement. In short, there seems to be a difference between politicizing one's identity and asserting a specific social identity. Nobles writes that "[m]ultiracial activists have argued that if the government asks a race question, it is obliged to use categories that approximate self-identifications" (137). Though writer-activists such as Walker and McBride may assert a biracial subjectivity, their political stance remains rooted in the struggle for racial equality. The complexities of such political identities suggest that self-identifications are complex and not always reliable or stable markers of how people identify in different settings.

Choosing Anything But Black: Moving from "Multiracial" to "White"?

Advocates for creating a multiracial category on the census form claim they want people to acknowledge all their ethnicities. Project RACE maintains, "Biracial and multiracial people do not have a box to check on forms. Being forced to choose only one race forces us to deny one of our parents. . . . Multiracial people should have the option of recognizing all of their heritage" (*Project RACE*). On the surface, the intent behind this objective seems ideologically in line with the views of McBride and Walker and many other writer-activists. For example, AMEA's mission states, "Every child, every person, who is multiethnic/multiracial has the same right as anyone else to assert a personal identity that embraces the fullness and integrity of their actual ancestry" (*AMEA*).[13] No doubt this declaration rings true for writers such as Walker who embraces her black, Jewish, Native American, and Irish ancestry. Yet AMEA's seeming "elitist" insistence on multiracial people as a "community" shows how they diverge from other political activists. "Our community," AMEA asserts, "has the potential of becoming a stable core around which the ethnic pluralism of this country is unified" (*AMEA*). The goal of a flourishing multiracial community can be potentially polarizing, particularly given the ways in which other mixed-race communities have functioned outside the United States, most notably in Brazil. A 1995 *Ebony* magazine article gives voice to a fear of such polarizing on the first page of the article "Am I Black, White or In Between?" with the question "Is There A Plot to Create A 'Colored' Buffer Race in America?" (Normant 108). There is a fine line between a racial community that buffers other racial communities and one that encourages diversity and non-racialist thinking. On another note, AMEA's focus on one's "actual ancestry" reverts attention and importance back on bloodlines, a dangerous practice which implies that race is in fact biological and not a construction. Walker describes blood ties as "critical, the thread which forces us to stay connected," but maintains that these same ties are "less important, that all blood is basically the same" (318–19). She thus values other bonds as much as she respects ancestry. Viewing one's identity in a multilayered way is crucial to a black-sentient mixed-race identity that relies on more than biology.

The 2000 census form was the first to allow people to check more than one box to reflect their ancestry. Three main arguments against the inclusion of multiple racial options dominated public and private thought. First and foremost, census racial data has been used for racially discriminatory purposes in the workplace and other areas where racial classification is important. Some argue that marking multiple racial categories confuses and conceals this crucial data.[14] Many black organizations feared that a possible decrease in population could affect resources allocated to black social programs. For example, there was worry that affirmative action programs would be affected negatively.[15] A common fear was that a separate grouping would create a discriminatory system similar to that in South Africa, where many people see "coloureds" as superior to blacks. Census results report that less than 3 percent of the population reported more than one race (with only 11 percent of that segment specifically claiming white and black).[16] Regardless of what actual changes the 2000 census results will produce in the future, many people seem encouraged by the promise multiple categories offers. Author Mat Johnson declares, "Call us what we are, biracial." He continues, "I used to feel that everybody should just shut up and be black. With the Census stuff, I was like, 'Oh, come on!' I thought they [the people lobbying the government] were mixed people who really didn't want to be black. That turned me off. But now I see value in it. You can say 'biracial' and people don't look at you like you're speaking French. This is really a change" (qtd. in Bowman 25). The idea that the presence or acknowledgment of multiracial people and their backgrounds will increase public awareness about the slippery lines of race has its promise, yet the census may not provide the appropriate forum for these attempts.[17] The question is how much consciousness is raised with the right to choose among multiple boxes on the census form or the right to check more than one. Melissa Nobles's *Shades of Citizenship: Race and the Census in Modern Politics* argues that censuses *can* shape racial discourses and that, historically, they have contributed to how Americans think about race. Still, those like McBride maintain, "[Y]ou can't change someone's opinion about you no matter how many boxes you check" ("What Color Is Jesus?" 196). Although it remains to be seen, allowing a person the selection of multiple boxes may increase awareness about mixed-race identity, but paper and pencil choices will not prevent intrusive "what are you" questions, stop racial discrimination and bigotry, or erase long-standing racial divisions. Embracing a mixed-race subjectivity seems to stand opposite to preoccupation with boxes on forms. If one rejects conventional notions of race, then he or she is theoretically also rejecting the idea that checking more than one box adequately suffices for an identity description. The dilemma is how to balance ideological goals with current racial inequalities.

The Orthodox Jewish practice of mourning the dead acts as a metaphor for the way in which blackness is conceived by some multiracial organizations. In sum, many multiracial activists privilege personal anxieties over pressing needs affecting people of color. Rebecca Walker, James McBride, and Lisa

Jones all share the same experience of their Jewish families punishing their white parent after she or he married their black parent. As McBride's mother reveals, *"My family mourned me when I married your father. They said kaddish and sat shiva. That's how Orthodox Jews mourn their dead. They say prayers, turn their mirrors down, sit on boxes for seven days, and cover their heads"* (*Color of Water* 2). The particular practice of forgetting someone's existence mirrors those mixed-race organizations whose embracing of a multiracial political identity often denies blackness. While such denial is perhaps not their avowed objective, some multiracial organizations, as a few critics have noted, have disaffiliated themselves from blackness. In other words, is "multiracial" another step closer to "whiteness"? What seems justified is questioning the motivation and goal in the use of biraciality in fiction, politics, and the media. As biracial people move from "tragic mulattos" to multiracials in literature and popular culture, they embody the disruption of racial classification, reminding us of the construction of race while prompting political mobilization around racial issues.

Chapter Five

B(l)ack to Last Drop? Mariah Carey, Halle Berry, and the Complexities of Racial Identity in Popular Culture

> Current media offers biracial girls few positive examples of biracial people. Many successful models, actresses, and sports figures are biracial, but their multicultural heritage is not often highlighted. . . . Biracial children need to be taught about both/all their ethnic heritages and be exposed to multiracial heroines like Joan Baez, Halle Berry, Mariah Carey, and Frida Kahlo.
>
> —Wanda M. L. Lee, "Therapeutic Considerations in Work with Biracial Girls" (212)

> Celebrities such as Cameron Diaz, Keanu Reeves, and Benjamin Bratt are all multiracial but are read as white and have access to white privilege, while other figures and high-profile multiracials, such as Halle Berry, Paula Abdul, Mariah Carey, and Barack Obama, are continually read as black. The difference is physical.
>
> —Meredith McCarroll, "'Claiming': White Ambition, Multiracial Identity, and the New American Racial Passing" (219)

In December 2009, comedian and talk-show host George Lopez posed the question "What color are you?" to Mariah Carey when she appeared on *Lopez Tonight*.[1] Her response—"In this country, black"—connects Carey to another mixed-race star, Halle Berry, who has also identified herself by evoking the historical one-drop system of racial classification in United States. After explaining, "No, for real. It's the law since slavery . . . any amount of black in you, you are black," Carey went on to clarify that her mother is of Irish descent and that her father, an African American, had a Venezuelan paternal grandmother. Lopez joked that he was pleased with her Latino ancestry, saying, "We gotta have a little piece for us!"—a statement that speaks to America's desire to racially "claim" public figures and celebrities (*Lopez Tonight*).[2] Comedian Dave Chappelle exposes this tendency in his skit "The Racial Draft" (2004). He begins, "You know what's cool about being an American? We all mixed up. I'm talking about genetically. . . . My wife is Asian and I'm black and we argue about which half of Tiger Woods is hitting the ball so good. Derek Jeter is another guy like that. Halle Berry is somebody else. We've all got to start arguing about who is what" ("The Racial Draft").[3] Chappelle's reference to Halle Berry demonstrates the extent to which people are invested in her race, despite her self-described identity. In the March 2011 issue of *Ebony* magazine, Berry revealed that she sees herself and her mixed-race daughter (with white model Gabriel Aubry) as black:[4]

> I had to decide for myself and that's what she's going to have to decide—how she identifies in the world. And I think, largely, that will be based on how the world identifies her. That's how I identify myself. But I feel like she's Black. I'm Black and I'm her mother, and I believe in the one-drop theory. (Barnett, "On the Very Solid")

Berry's comment created a small media buzz, prompting reactions and commentary on various websites, from celebrity gossip site *TMZ* to *Psychology Today*. Rebecca Walker responded to Berry's comment two issues later, writing, "[N]one of my feelings of admiration and respect kept me from thinking she had . . . lost her mind when I read her pledge of allegiance to the one-drop rule when discussing her daughter's race" (Walker, "Ebony Debate: One-Drop Rule"). That Carey and Berry have made reference to the one-drop ideology after the 2000 census and the election of a mixed-race president suggests that the racial past of the United States continues to shape mixed-race identity in the twenty-first century: even our most well-known mixed-race celebrities are not "post-race."

This chapter examines the public personas of Mariah Carey and Halle Berry, two celebrities who have directly and indirectly, consistently (Berry) or sometimes (Carey), identified as black while always, as Berry says, embracing "the white side of who I am, too" (qtd. in Barnett). Drawing from Richard

Dyer's *Stars,* I read these celebrities by analyzing autobiographical representations, celebrity statuses, public reception, and the publicity surrounding their representations. Dyer writes, "Stars are, like characters in stories, representations of people. Thus they relate to ideas about what people are (or are supposed to be) like" (*Stars* 22). Recognizing that we can never know how much agency stars have in their image, I acknowledge that biographies or interviews are not necessarily "truths." However, the interviews, career moves (in, for example, choice of movie roles or music), public reception, and publicity that I examine all play a part in creating Carey's and Berry's images.

The epigraphs that begin this chapter reveal that, on the one hand, Carey and Berry are viewed as "multiracial heroines," potential role models for mixed-race adolescents who want to see reflections of themselves in Hollywood or the music industry. On the other hand, these celebrities are categorized as black despite subtle or directed assertions that they are multiracial. Interestingly, both stars have also made career moves that clash with or contribute to their public images as mixed-race celebrities, often recalling the tragic mulatta stereotype. In fact, *Egotrip's Big Book or Racism!* cites both women in their "Top 10 Tragic Mulattos," a comic list of celebrities whose private lives have, in some way, been marked by tragedy. Further, both women's love lives are cited as reasons for their label as "tragic." While Carey and Berry have been linked with numerous romantic partners throughout their careers, both have had recent public fights with white men with whom they were (or were rumored to be) romantically involved. In 2002 and again in 2009, Eminiem's ugly exchange with Carey, whom he claimed he dated, went public via his rap lyrics; and Berry's custody battle with her daughter's father hit the Web in early 2011. The disputes, fighting, and public reaction to and aftermath of both interracial relationships or disputes contradictorily signal both racial fluidity and racial fixedness, prompting the question: can one be both black and biracial in popular culture? The various identities Carey and Berry encode mirror the desires of the American public and media, manifested in a simultaneous disavowal and celebration of mixed race. At once, we are both uncomfortable with and fascinated by mixed-race people and their bodies in particular.

In previous chapters, I have argued that an individual embracing a black-sentient mixed-race identity suggests a strong connection with a black consciousness despite much personal frustration with (or even rejection of) race or racial identification. While Carey and Berry do not per se represent black-sentient mixed-race identities, as "characters" their images are inextricably connected to blackness. At the same time, both stars are often associated with multiraciality because of their "mulatta" performances and, perhaps just as important, the media's frequent focus on their racial identities and repeated discussions of their mixed-race backgrounds. This chapter explores the evolution of the representation of these stars' racial identities in popular culture. I argue that discourse in the media about feuds within their personal relationships demonstrates the transient nature of black mixed-race identity in popular culture.

Affirming, Blurring, and Commodifying Race: The MC of Racial Fluidity

In the film *Precious: Based on the Novel* Push *by Sapphire* (2009), Precious, the main character, asks her social worker (played by Mariah Carey), "So are you Italian or—what color are you? Are you some type of black or Spanish?" Carey, as Ms. Weiss, counters, "What color do you think I am?" This scene, not in Sapphire's novel, symbolizes Carey's seeming identity tease with the media and fans throughout her career. Precious describes Ms. Weiss as a "white bitch" in the novel, someone whose racist, myopic vision prevents her from imagining Precious's possibilities; yet her character changes into a racially and ethnically ambiguous woman in the film (Sapphire 121). Carey's role as a racially ambiguous Ms. Weiss, originally slated for British actress Helen Mirren (who had to drop out because of scheduling conflicts), symbolically speaks to her various "racechanges" throughout her career. Susan Gubar defines "racehange" as "the traversing of race boundaries, racial imitation or impersonation, cross-racial mimicry or mutability, white posing as black or black posing as white, pan-racial mutability" (5). Since Carey's self-titled debut album in 1990, she has crossed racial boundaries and publicly performed various "roles," including white ingénue, biracial outsider, black hip-hopper, and erotic/exotic "Other." Carey's recent self-description as "a black woman who is very light skinned" (interview with Emma Brockes) is a new response for her, as in the past she has responded to the question by answering "person of color," "mixed race," and the glib "I view myself as a human being" (Farley 75). Her image has both deflected and confirmed blackness, creating an "in-between" status that is reinforced via her racialized sexuality. Her persona wears biracial stereotypes like a blackface "costume," allowing audiences to explore racial and sexual fantasies while maintaining racial stereotypes of the sexy mulatta.

Carey's image exploits various manifestations of the mulatta stereotype. On the one hand, she represents the alienated racial outsider, as in her song "Outside," in which she bemoans the difficulties of not belonging. On the other hand, wearing next to nothing in music videos and publicity photos, her image exploits the notion of the racially ambiguous seductress. In "Transatlantic Minstrelsy: Performing Survival Strategies in Slavery and Hip-Hop," Venus Opal Reese argues that "hip hop artists embody the rhetoric, posture, and survival strategies of enslaved people in the southern plantation, which would become the basis for the social types evolved in Atlantic minstrelsy," namely the mammy, jezebel, and sambo (181). She asserts that "unlike their predecessors, who performed these roles as a means of survival, these artists live the roles as if the roles were themselves" (187). Although Reese doesn't focus on the tragic mulatto archetype, she notes that Carey is "hip-hop's 'tragic mulatto'": a "woman of biracial heritage who does not fit into either world. The woman who seems to be desperately confused about her place in the world, willing to pass to ensure a better life" (197). Carey's image speaks to this archetype in direct and subtle ways. For example, in Carey's latest album, *Memoirs of an Imperfect Angel* (2009), one photo of her recalls the infamous images of Jennifer Beals in *Flashdance* (1983): Carey has wet hair and wears black panties and a black T-shirt pulled down off one shoulder, circa 1980s, seemingly mimicking Beals's outfits and sweaty wet hair from the movie, particularly the "Maniac" scene. Like Beals's character, Carey sells racial ambiguity.[5] Magazine and album photos play up her sexuality so that her overall image combines multiple representations: mulatta sex kitten, black performer, and white pin-up. However, Carey and her music are not considered "black" in the same way, for example, that Alicia Keyes represents "blackness." And physically, Carey is too ethnic to be a white sex symbol. The result places Carey in an in-between, mixed-race seductress narrative.

Indeed, Carey's hypersexuality intensifies as she encodes "whiteness" via her album covers and "blackness" via her music, symbolically evoking the "warring" racial divisions and libidinous nature of the mulatta stereotype. For example, the liner for the *Rainbow* CD (1999) opens up to reveal a photo that exploits Carey as a heterosexual male fantasy: she suggestively lies on a bed in white cotton underclothes, wearing stiletto heels and licking a heart-shaped lollipop. A nearby phone lying off the hook may suggest Carey's possible roles as phone-sex operator or prostitute. Magazine photos of Carey are always revealing and "Playboyesque." One 2003 photo from *Vibe* shows Carey in an unzipped miniskirt and unzipped midriff top, suggestively looking downwards at her skirt. Another frames Carey lying on a couch, one hand on her breast, the other suggestively positioned below her stomach. While many pop stars wear skimpy and sexy clothing, Carey's provocative style of dress is coupled with a publicized troubled multiracial identity, making her sexuality fetishized and tragic. Tellingly, Carey cites Marilyn Monroe, a star whose name virtually equaled sex in the 1950s and who began her career as a pin-up, as the person she most admires.[6] Not surprisingly, Barbara Walters likens the two, calling Carey "a soldier's pin-up girl come to life" while describing her Kosovo trip to visit U.S. troops ("Surviving the Glare"). In a 2006 *Marie Claire* article, Carey claims she loves to dress "skimpy," revealing that she "see[s] it as playing dress-up, like Barbies" (qtd. in Evans 98). Thus, Carey's role models are two blond American icons whose image is based on sex and beauty over brains. In many ways, Carey herself has cultivated a multiracial Barbie image, slightly and superficially "Other," yet ultimately a cheap replication of whiteness.

Music reviews and articles have paid close attention to Carey's overt sexuality and racial shifts in a popular-culture context. Vincent Stephens observes: "Along with genre changes, Carey has taken on a more sexualized visual persona and has become more outspoken about her multiracial heritage and struggles for artistic freedom" (rev. of *Rainbow* 234). Caroline Streeter sees Carey "transform[ing] from white to black before our very eyes" (311). Indeed, Carey's album covers trace her shifting racial movements from what Lisa Jones calls "a rainbow body of African descent, skin toasted almond and hair light brown" to her current whitewashed blond pin-up look (*Bulletproof Diva* 200). While other ethnic stars sport blond hair, Carey's hair transformation seems particularly racially motivated, considering initial marketing of Carey that concealed her blackness. In 1990, music critics labeled Carey a "white Whitney Houston" until outside pressures prompted her record company to make a statement. Carey cleared up misconceptions at a press conference where she declared, "My father is black and Venezuelan. My mother is Irish and an opera singer. I am me" (qtd. in *Bulletproof Diva* 197). Following Carey's public disclosure, black publications ran articles such as "Mariah Carey Tells Why She Looks White but Sings Black" and "Mariah Carey: Not Another White Girl Trying to Sing Black," seemingly attempting to assure black audiences that Carey was not trying to pass or disregard her black ancestry. However, Carey's later physical transformation suggests an effort to depart visually from "black" and to reflect white standards of beauty. As Carey's hair turns straighter and blonder, she increasingly signifies "whiteness" while contradictorily maintaining a position as ethnic "other" vis-à-vis her public assertions of biracialism. Richard Dyer suggests that "blondeness is racially unambiguous" and "the ultimate sign of whiteness" (*Heavenly Bodies* 44, 43). Carey represents a racial anomaly because her image simultaneously projects different racial tropes. These competing discourses establish Carey in a biracial narrative that depends on her liminality.

Musically, Carey has moved from pop to hip-hop, in some ways a symbolic shift from white to black. After Carey divorced then–Sony Music president Tommy Mottola, her music and image changed drastically. Carey claims that her *Butterfly* album symbolizes her feelings of personal and professional freedom impelled by her divorce. As she explained in 1997, "I feel more free to put more of myself into my music" (qtd. in Thigpen 113). Since *Butterfly*, Carey has worked with more hip-hop artists and producers to tap into her "broad demographic." As she observes, "I have an audience that's urban and one that's Middle America." She continues, "So I have to really be a little bit conscious of the fact that it's broad, and also it's diverse in terms of the racial thing. I am anyway, being a mixed person racially" (qtd. in Ehrlich 338). Carey has collaborated with hip-hop artists and rappers including Jay-Z, Usher, Da Brat, Missy Elliott, Snoop Dogg, Lil Wayne, and Gucci Mane. Carey's earlier albums *Mariah Carey* (1990), *Emotions* (1991), and *Daydream* (1995) demonstrated her penchant for love ballads and crossover pop songs, save for Carey's "Dreamlover" remix with Ol' Dirty Bastard on *Daydream*. Earlier albums also feature Carey in her pre-blond days, suggesting that Carey's physical transformation heightened after she professionally embraced black culture. In a 2002 MTV interview, Carey revealed, "Most of my friends and most of the music I listen to, and most of my influences are R&B and hip-hop" ("Mariah Carey: Shining through the Rain"). Still, the Carey albums that are most "hip-hop" visually emphasize her whiteness, such as the cover of *Charmbracelet* (2002), which shows her with platinum streaks, or that of *The Emancipation of Mimi* (2005), which features her with flowing blond tresses.

Although Evelyn Alsultany claims that Carey exemplifies how "the media translate multiethnicity and frame it as monoraciality," it is clear that she is frequently viewed as racially ambiguous (150). Writer Joan Morgan writes that Mariah is "a natural mimic, effortlessly assuming the accent of whomever she's with," seemingly confirming her abilities to cross musical, cultural, and racial borders (121). Veronica Chambers notes that *Rainbow* showcases "two Mariahs": "Top-40 Mariah sings octave-soaring mainstream ballads. Hip-hop Mariah records with Master P and Snoop Dogg" (80). Carey's image seems to toy deliberately with binaries: she is classic pop and hip-hop, white and black. Carey's "Heartbreaker" video confirms this paradigm in her portrayal of two characters, "good Mariah" and "bad Mariah," classically differentiated by light and dark hair. The two Mariahs catfight over a man (played by white actor Jerry O'Connell) in a movie theater, symbolically representing her image's racial split. Alex Pappademas interprets the video as a metaphor for Carey's public persona: "Mariah-A is the one who slums glamorously on the

BET network, whereas Mariah-B sings about chasing your dreams on the Disney Channel." The dueling Mariahs also suggest Carey's differing racial representations outside her musical associations, including her physical image, photos, and publicity.

Carey has been noted for her tendency to "champion her multicultural heritage in conversation," constructing a stereotypical mulatta trope (Farley 75). For example, inside the *Rainbow* CD liner Carey writes to fans:

> In a perfect world
> Human beings would co-exist
> Harmoniously, like a rainbow
> A multitude of colors
> Each layer vibrant and clear by itself
> But in unison . . .
> Boundless, breathtaking, celestial.

The message speaks to Carey's desire for racial unity but also reveals why multiracial organizations herald her as an ideal biracial "spokesperson." In "My Saving Grace," Carey positions herself as tragic, describing a difficult childhood in which she felt alienated, self-conscious, and confused because of her mixed-race background. She laments the media's and public's obsession with her racial identity, yet openly discusses her feelings of racial alienation and isolation. She shares feeling always "so separate from everybody, even if I never talked about it" (qtd. in Udovitch 34). She attributes this alienation to various causes—"Because my father's black and my mother's white. Because I'm very ambiguous-looking" (qtd. in Farley 75)—and has claimed multiple racial-identity descriptors. Yet despite Carey's supposed desires to put the issue of her racial background to rest, she often brings it up in interviews and has appeared on national shows like *Oprah* to discuss such issues. "I wish more people would understand that we should be allowed to just be who we are," she told Oprah. "Not just mixed people, not just black, white, you know, Asian, Hispanic, whatever you are. . . . Let's be accepted for ourselves as people rather than so much focus on what color you are" (16). Yet, Carey frequently exploits biracial stereotypes, betraying her role-model status.

Glitter (2001), Carey's semiautobiographical box-office failure, confirms her racialized sexuality despite its attempts to critique mulatta clichés. In one scene of the film, the music video director explains his idea for the main character's video: "She is not black, she is not white, she is exotic, OK?" This same theme follows representations of Carey's public and private life. In July 2001, Carey infamously appeared on MTV's "Total Request Live" pushing an ice-cream cart in a T-shirt emblazoned "Loverboy" (the name of *Glitter*'s first single) and heels. She proceeded to perform a pseudo-striptease, taking off her T-shirt to reveal a hidden skimpy outfit. Entertainment reporters and tabloids ridiculed Carey for her bizarre behavior and incoherent ramblings to *TRL* host Carson Daly. Accordingly, *Ego Trip's Big Book of Racism!* comically named Carey their number one "Tragic Mulatto" for, among other things, "a propensity for 'whorelike attire,' a nervous breakdown, a mocked and derided cinematic debut, and a failed soundtrack" (Jenkins 81). Such descriptions urge the question of what role Carey has in sexualizing her image? Carey reports feeling "constantly amazed" regarding her portrayal as "very loose morally and sexually," an ironic statement considering that Carey invites such readings in nearly all recent publicity photos and public outings ("Mariah Carey Discusses" 58). Though we can never know how much agency stars exert over their image, Carey seems to perpetuate wittingly an over-sexual public persona. Though a 2005 *Essence* article on Carey begins, "This mulatto's hardly tragic. There is no haunting semblance to the 1959 movie classic *Imitation of Life*," her image replicates many characteristics of the archetype (Morgan 121).[7] Overall, she represents a historically comfortable vision of mixed-race women. Carey poses little threat to racial hierarchy because she fits a mold that showcases just enough "blackness" to intrigue but not enough to appear definitive or political.

Carey's public feud with Eminem, a celebrity Harry J. Elam Jr. describes as "trafficking in blackness," complicates and doubles her seeming racial fluidity (384). The feud began after Eminem said he and Mariah dated; in his song "Superman" he briefly mentions his rejection of Carey. Carey has consistently denied a romantic relationship with Eminem, most notably in "Clown," a song *Vibe* calls "a psychological roundhouse . . . Carey isn't publicly fingering Eminem as the 'frail' one but she says, 'Bozo knows exactly who he is'" (Ogunnaike 120). Eminem's response in "Bagpipes from Baghdad" (in which he calls Carey a whore and tells her husband, Nick Cannon, to "back the fuck up") sparked two distinct assertions regarding Carey's racial identity. First, Cannon responded on his blog, attacking Eminem for disrespecting "one of the most notable BLACK females of our time." Using Carey's blackness in his defense of her, Cannon continues, "I thought we moved beyond the days where white men could spew vulgar obscenities at our beautiful queens and get away with in. What's next? Are we going to let this trash say something horrible about our lovely first lady, Mrs. Michelle Obama?" (qtd. in Vozick-Levison). Cannon's statement not only recalls the pre–civil rights era but also harkens back to slavery; his blog post intimates that a white man's sense of sexual entitlement intensifies Carey's "BLACK" identity. In other words, she becomes "more" black when positioned against white racism (imagined or not).[8]

"Bagpipes from Baghdad" also compelled Carey to perform a "racechange" in her video for "Obsessed," a song about a man who lies about his obsession with her.[9] In the video Carey plays both herself and Eminem, who is stalking Mariah-the-star. (In one of the last scenes, Mariah-as-Eminem is run over by a bus when he attempts to take a photo of her). Thus, she is double-passing: passing for white and passing as a man. Race and gender get performed, as Carey goes from sporting a goatee and wearing loose sweats to being glamorous Mariah-the-star in sexy outfits. Viewers understand that Carey is posing as Eminem: his signature hoodie and body posturing make this unmistakable, challenging the fixedness of identity. Elaine Ginsberg writes:

> Cultural associations of the physical body with both race and gender, and the putative visibility of these two identity categories, thus make race and gender passing seem more problematic than other instances of passing. . . . [T]he status and privilege accompanying "whiteness" and "maleness" highlight the similarities of black-to-white race passing and gender passing as sources of cultural anxiety, for both "non-white" and "woman" are sites of difference that affirm the priority of "white" and "man" in the hegemonic ideology. (4–5)

That Carey can convincingly play Eminem (no "whiteface" required) signals her racial mutability, both destabilizing the hypermasculinity inherent in his image (via her performance and her depiction of him) and disrupting race and gender binaries.

Further complicating Carey's "racechange" is Eminem's own celebrity persona, which, as Samuel Craig Watkins argues, "fall[s] somewhat between a bizarre form of twenty-first century minstrelsy . . . and beguiling political commentary" (108). If we read Eminem as symbolically passing for black, then the video presents Carey passing as a cultural passer.[10] As Vincent Stephens writes, "Though Eminem is white, his poor economic background, affiliation with and acceptance by black producers and performers and hypermasculine behavior validate his social-locational and racial 'realness'" (25). Interestingly, following the release of the video, Carey affirmed her blackness in an October 2009 interview in the *Guardian:* "I'm a black woman who is very light skinned" (interview with Emma Brockes). Thus, Carey is at once definitively black, racially ambiguous, transgressing boundary crosser, and passer, both black and mixed race.

The Blacker the Berry, the Clearer the Race

When Halle Berry won the Oscar for best actress in 2002, she became more widely recognized as an accomplished *black* actress. Berry's acceptance speech confirms her racial allegiance: "The moment is so much bigger than me. . . . It's [the Oscar] for every nameless, faceless woman of color that now has a chance because this door tonight has been opened." Despite Berry's claim, competing discourses on her ethnicity consume popular cultural discussions of her. In a 1994 interview with Lisa Jones, Berry makes clear that "I never once announced that I am interracial. I was never the one to bring it up. . . . Yet reporters constantly ask what childhood was like to an interracial person" (60). Berry consistently identifies as African American, evoking an identity grounded in a black politics. Jones asks Berry if mixed-race children should choose a race. Berry replies, "You've got to identify with one group or the other. It is a political choice" (qtd. in Jones 60). Berry learned this, she claims, from her white mother who advised her to "accept being black, embrace it" (qtd. in Kennedy 28). Still, Berry's mixed-race background follows her in her movie roles and public persona, evidenced perhaps in the approval she seems to give to stereotypes of mulatta women. The media's investment in reading Halle Berry within a biracial narrative assures a biracial script both within the movies and in pseudo-liberal discussions of race. She is more easily accepted in a "role," both cinematic and stereotypic, that is familiar to Americans—that of the exotic mixed-race woman.

In an interview with Entertainment Television, Warren Beatty says, "She's a beautiful woman and she's the essence of that biracial thing in America that is so beautiful" ("Halle Berry," *Road to the Red Carpet*). Beatty, who acted with Berry in *Bulworth* (1998), romanticizes mixed-race identity as an American ideal, reducing Berry to the essence of a biracial "thing," no longer an individual but a notion or concept. Praising Berry as a national ideal inadvertently summons the history of black/white mixing in America, namely the sexual abuse of black women by white men during slavery. However, Beatty's comment also suggests a desire to interpret Berry within a "melting pot" framework, one that depoliticizes identity. This rhetoric abounds in multiracial literary interpretations, such as in Maria P. P. Root's assertion that "the accomplishment of complex identities by racially mixed persons gives us the hope that if individuals have been able to resolve conflicting values, claim identities, synthesize multiple heritages, and retain respect for individual heritages . . . perhaps it is possible for us eventually to do this as a nation" ("From Shortcuts to Solutions" 347). Many multiracial activists see a mixed-race Berry in the same way they view Tiger Woods, as an indication of racial harmony or what David L. Andrews and C. L. Cole describe as "racially coded celebrations which deny social problems and promote the idea that America has achieved its multicultural ideal" (70).[11] Reading Berry in a biracial framework falls in line with historical and cinematic representations of mixed-race women and allows a white patriarchal system to prevail under the guise of politically correct rhetoric. In other words, other people define Berry and place her in a category that best satisfies white perceptions of race and mixed race.

The titles of early articles on Berry reveal a tendency to read her as a modern-day tragic mulatto. "Halle Berry, Bruised and Beautiful, Is on a Mission," "The Beautiful and Damned," "Am I Going to Be Happy or Not?" and even an unauthorized biography titled *Halle Berry: A Stormy Life* all highlight Berry's troubled personal life, recalling mixed-race literary characters whose beauty is rivaled only by their ugly misfortunes. Though the media extol Berry's beauty, their accolades always urge references to her tragic life. The media unnecessarily emphasize her racial background in any description of her misfortunes, including an abusive father and ex-boyfriend, two divorces, a suicide attempt, and a recent split with the father of her child. Berry herself claims that the biggest misconception of her is that she is "this brooding, twisted, lovesick person who just can't get it right in life. Every story about me is so heavy and dramatic. That's not how I do life. But that's the impression people have, and that's what keeps getting reiterated" (qtd. in Testino).[12] The authors of *Egotrip's Big Book of Racism!* cite Berry's "emotionally wrenching turn as her troubled role model, Dorothy Dandridge" as partial evidence of her "tragic mulatto" status (Jenkins 81). Berry's life shares eerie similarities with that of Dandridge, whose roles reinforced the stereotype of the exotic in films and who herself lived the stereotype of the tragic mulatta. Yet films other than *Introducing Dorothy Dandridge* (1999)—including *The Flintstones* (1994); *X-Men* (2000) and its sequels, *X2: X-Men United* (2003) and *X-Men: The Last Stand* (2006); *Die Another Day* (2002); *Monster's Ball* (2002); *Catwoman* (2004); and *Frankie and Alice* (2010)—subtly accentuate Berry's image as tragic or exotic. In the miniseries *Queen* (1993), one of Berry's earlier performances, Berry plays Alex Haley's grandmother, daughter of a white master and black slave. The producers stayed "true" to Queen's racial background by choosing Berry for the part and remained loyal to the "tragic mulatress text: Not only does *Queen* drag out mulatto clichés from every B movie and paperback, it luxuriates in them with eerie aplomb" (Jones, *Bulletproof Diva* 50). Yet even Berry's decidedly "monoracial" characters, such as Nina (a pro-black "flygirl") in *Bulworth,* repeat a tragic motif. Patricia Williams writes that Berry's role "never rises above the most ancient of cliches" by bordering "black and white . . . hope and despair . . . good and bad . . . sane and insane; the positive and negative divided by two, multiplied by sex" (11). In the science-fiction comic-book-turned-movie *X-Men,* Berry's character again occupies an "in-between" space. Lynne d Johnson asserts that Berry's role as Storm in *X-Men* did not surprise, given her mixed racial background: "Though not a tragic mulatto in the classic sense of the myth, being mixed in both the racial and genetic mutation sense of the word, Storm is representative of this idea." Like Berry's other films, *Catwoman* also capitalizes on Berry's reputation as exotic, liminal, and hypersexual.[13]

Berry's casting as Leticia Musgrove in *Monster's Ball* prompted diverse reviews from moviegoers and critics. The reaction from the black community was mixed, mostly because of Berry's casting as a stereotypical black woman in a film that "unfolds like something that was written by Simon Legree, the slave owner in *Uncle Tom's Cabin.* Just hours after they meet, the black woman lustfully seduces the startled white man" (Wickham 15A).[14] While many reviews mention the clichés in *Monster's Ball,* most fail to mention the stereotypical image of black women.[15] Actress Angela Bassett declined the role, she claims, because "I wasn't going to be a prostitute on film. . . . I couldn't do that because it's such a stereotype about black women and sexuality" (qtd. in Allison Samuels 54). Bassett does not mention the stereotypes of mixed-race women, implicit in Berry's portrayal of Leticia, a woman who wants Hank to "heal" her through sex. Here the movie recycles nineteenth-century images of black *and* mixed-race women as overly sexual. More specifically, the movie encourages the myth of mixed-race women "as lewd and lascivious as the men are idle, sensual, and dishonest" (Mencke 102). Though the film does not specifically label Leticia mixed race, her characterization urges such readings. Symbolically, the movie recalls the history of miscegenation; yet, more specifically, the movie reinforces general perceptions of Halle Berry as mixed race. One reviewer sarcastically claims that the film suggests that blacks and whites will get along only when "black women are already half white, already measure up to the white beauty standard," like Halle Berry ("Monster Balls"). Berry's role in *Monster's Ball* speaks to Berry's own tragic mulatto image, and her image never strays far from the "biracial" characters she plays.

As so many viewers and audiences have lamented, Hollywood representations of blackness have been limited and narrow. Movies have historically slighted actors who are "too black" and, simultaneously, shunned those who are "not black enough." Like Dorothy Dandridge and Lena Horn, Berry has been hindered by her lighter complexion, sometimes deprived of movie auditions and offers for "black" roles. Berry's manager, Vincent Cirrincione, claims that when Berry auditioned for *Strictly Business* (1991), they told her to "get a tan"; conversely, Cirrincione says other executives have told him that "milk is milk until you add a little Hershey. It doesn't matter if you add a little Hershey or a lot" (qtd. in Kennedy 28). More often than not, Berry does not signify real "blackness." Philip Kerr remarks that in *Monster's Ball*

> I didn't see a black woman who looked, well, black. Am I the only one to have noticed? Halle Berry—who let's face it, is half-white—made a lachrymose, Oscar-winning thing about being a woman of colour, and yet the reality is that she looks no more like a person of colour than I do. Is it just me, or do most of the black women cast in Hollywood films, with their straight hair, thin lips and cappuccino-coloured skins, look just a little bit white? (Kerr 44)

Kerr's offensive statement uses biology to classify Berry, relying on crude physical descriptions like "straight hair" and "thin lips" to declare Berry "not black." Though Kerr's criticism rightly addresses the prejudice against darker actresses, his critique also suggests a restrictive and monolithic view of blackness. Such physical stereotypes of African Americans neglect the wide array of physical characteristics and skin color within black communities. Like *Quicksand*'s Helga Crane or *Caucasia*'s Cole, Berry cannot pass and does not "look" white as Kerr suggests; rather, her physical markings represent those commonly associated with a person of color. That Berry self-identifies as black makes Kerr's statement particularly insulting in terms of his desire to read her as "half-white." The media criminalizes dark skin, associating darkness with poverty, ignorance, and physical ugliness. Cannot Leticia be poor, desperate, downtrodden, and still light-skinned? Aside from presenting narrow-minded views on race, Kerr's description shows that the public and critics invest in Berry's "whiteness."

The media's obsession with Berry's beauty seems to top any fascination they have with that of her white contemporaries, including Julia Roberts, Jennifer Anniston, or Nicole Kidman, not to mention black actresses such as Angela Bassett or Vanessa Williams.[16] Berry's hourglass figure takes on mythic proportions, perhaps only comparable to the infatuation with Jennifer Lopez's derrière. A men's website asserts that Berry was "put on this earth to make men's jaw drop," suggesting a kind of male (white) ownership over Berry's sexuality ("Halle Berry," *Askmen.com*). Best-actor winner Adrian Brody expressed a similar possessiveness with Berry on Oscar night when he took Berry in his arms and passionately kissed her after she presented his award. Brody told *People*, "If you ever have an excuse to do something like that, that was it" ("Kiss Off"). Would Brody have felt the same entitlement with a beautiful white actress? While Brody's actions may not imply a conscious desire to "possess" Berry, they represent not only black women's historic powerlessness but also white male abuse of mixed-race women.

Public discourses about Berry belabor her looks when referring to her celebrity allure. Charlie Kangaris, who directed Berry in *Race the Sun* (1996), compares Berry to "a double espresso machiatto [*sic*], a dollop of shapely foam, a shower of cinnamon and cocoa"; no other actress in "Cinema and the Female Star," a collection of reflections and tributes to actresses on the website *Senses of Cinema,* is so objectified. Warren Beatty claims that people laugh when they first see Berry because "they don't know how else to react. They're not used to someone that beautiful" (qtd. in Hirschberg 26). Literary descriptions of mixed-race women in early American fiction suggest a similar exceptional, almost unreal beauty. In Charles Chesnutt's novel *The House Behind the Cedars* (1900), John, not yet recognizing Rena as his sister, describes her as "striking, handsome, with a stately beauty seldom encountered" (7). These characterizations imply a uniqueness associated with mixed race that persists in popular culture. Lynne Hirschberg claims that Berry's beauty is "actually distracting; the perfection of her face would not seem to allow anything less than a perfect life" (Hirschberg 26). Would people review Berry's beauty in the same way if she were "just black" (and not mixed race)? She represents the supposed mystique of mixed-race people, alluring because they symbolize a social taboo. Her image represents "black" and "not black," which unsettles and entices. A *Time* article that begins "Is it a curse to be beautiful?" continues a familiar rhetoric about Berry's looks, one that intensified after her Oscar win. Descriptions of Berry's beauty intimate what has become a common boasting on numerous multiracial websites—that mixed-race people are "prettier."[17] This notion gets directly and indirectly repeated in advertisements and magazines that use models who physically represent racial mixture. The point here is not to judge or critique Berry's beauty, but rather to examine why it attracts so much attention. Berry cannot be taken out of a historical context of mixed-race beauty images.

From the start of Berry's romance with Gabriel Aubry, the two were viewed as beauty's "it" couple. A *Harper's Bazaar* article notes, "Halle, 42, and her partner, model Gabriel Aubry . . . and baby Nahla are, to quote that great fashion sage Derek Zoolander, 'really really good-looking'" (Laura Brown). However, after they split in 2010, things got ugly. Various gossip websites reported claims that Aubry called Berry a "nigger," and Halle's representative said she had "serious concerns for her daughter's well-being" when her daughter was with her father for long periods (Saad). The ways in which Berry's recent breakup with Aubry played out in the media reveals how racial identity continues to be seen as more than just a personal or individual identity. Much of the media attention focused on Berry's statement that she views her daughter as "black" rather than biracial. While some comments (on the internet and in magazines) celebrate Berry's "loyalty" to blackness, others seem shocked that she relied on archaic race "rules." One of the reasons for this divide can be attributed to a general discomfort with the dual role of Berry's image as both "solely" black and "biracial." Deborah Richards's explanation of her poem "The Halle Berry One Two" speaks to the contradiction: "I suggest that we all want her to slip as well as succeed. I think that's to do with envy" (Richards).[18] Although Richards does not reference Berry's mixed-race background, her observation about envy is telling. With regard to race, the public either wants Berry to "succeed" as mixed race and "fail" as a black woman (or, conversely, succeed as black and "fail" as mixed race). The fact that she solidly affirms her black identity despite public obsession with her mixed-race identity reveals the social pressures people face in terms of racial expectations. Despite people's racial self-identification, there is a public tendency to separate a "black" identity from a biracial identity when it suits public desires. Berry's image reflects back the fantasy that makes Americans both anxious and envious.

Berry's daughter with a white man further complicates her assumed racial "role" in the public eye. Interestingly, invoking Berry's mixed race significantly decreased during the custody battle, especially after she identified her daughter as black. In fact, various celebrity entertainment websites claimed Berry was "playing the race card"; few mentioned that Berry happens to be mixed race herself, a departure from the typical interest in Berry's multiraciality.[19] Much of this backlash toward Berry has to do with the fact that her daughter, Nahla, looks like the future we imagine, with her "light-brown curly hair and green eyes, lighter-than-honey colored skin" (Walker, "Ebony Debate"). In an age of Obama (despite his self-identity as black), we see mixedness as the end of racial tension. It is perhaps not surprising that both Berry and Carey name Obama in their discussion of their children's future. When asked what it meant that she, her daughter, and Obama were "biracial," Berry responded, "Nahla will grow up in a completely different America. Obama is someone who's more like her than not, who shares her history" (Laura Brown). Mariah Carey, mother to twins, also expressed optimism: "Having Obama in office and bringing a child into the world at this point is totally different than me feeling like an outcast when I was growing up and not feeling like it was OK to be ethnically diverse, and I can't believe that we have arrived at this point within society" ("Mariah Carey: I Felt Like an Outcast"). Still, as the images of Carey and Berry reveal, black and mixed-race identities remain contested and slippery in popular culture.

Conclusion

> When your personal multiplicity is printed on your face, in an almost too obviously thematic manner, in your DNA, in your hair and in the neither this nor that beige of your skin—well, anyone can see you come from Dream City. In Dream City everything is doubled, everything is various. You have no choice but to cross borders and speak in tongues. That's how you get from your mother to your father, from talking to one set of folks who think you're not black enough to another who figure you insufficiently white. It's the kind of town where the wise man says "I" cautiously, because "I" feels like too straight and singular a phoneme to represent the true multiplicity of his experience. Instead, citizens of Dream City prefer to use the collective pronoun "we."
>
> —Zadie Smith, "Speaking in Tongues"

In 2008, *Freakonomics* author Steven Levitt, along with three coauthors, wrote a paper titled "The Plight of Mixed Race Adolescents." In addition to finding mixed-race adolescents more attractive than their white or black peers, the study argued that "mixed-race kids manage to be as bad as whites on the white behaviors and as bad as blacks on the black behaviors," essentially arguing that they embody the worst of both "sides" (Levitt).[1] "If we had to pick an explanation that best fits the facts," Levitt admits, "it would be the old sociology model of mixed-race individuals as the 'marginal man': not part of either racial group and therefore torn by inner conflict" (Levitt). Rockquemore, Brunsma, and Delgado categorize the marginal-man theory (developed in 1928) as a "problem approach" based on the idea "that being a mixed-race person in a racially divided world is, in and of itself, a problematic social position that is inevitably marked by tragedy" (16). Levitt and his coauthors' recycling of old stereotypes about mixed race is similar to the reasoning Keith Bardwell, a Louisiana justice of the peace, gave for refusing to perform an interracial marriage ceremony in October 2009. A media firestorm ensued when Bardwell refused to issue a marriage license to a white woman and an African American man, openly admitting that he did not believe in interracial marriages. Bardwell (who has since resigned his position) cited mixed-race children as one reason for his refusal to approve of such unions: "There is a problem with both groups accepting a child from such a marriage. . . . I think these children suffer and I won't help put them through it" ("Interracial Couple Denied Marriage License").

A few weeks after the Louisiana story came out, a less serious incident also received internet and entertainment media buzz when an episode of Tyra Banks's *America's Next Top Model* challenged models to "portray two very different, distinct races" in honor of racial mixedness in Hawaii ("Let's Go Surfing"). Standing in a Hawaiian sugarcane field, Banks and *ANTM* judge Jay Manuel told the models about laborers who migrated to Hawaii to work. Banks then asked, "What happens when men and women from different places come together? Babies! Lots of babies that are from different cultures. A mix" ("Let's Go Surfing"). The model contestants (one Asian, one African American, and four whites) were then dressed in clothes and make-up intended to represent the racial mixtures of Mexican and Greek, Tibetan and Egyptian, Japanese and Malagasy, Botswanan and Polynesian, Native American and East Indian, and Moroccan and Russian. The models were thus wearing (mixed) race as fashion accessory. Various news articles and blogs pointed out that two of the models were essentially wearing blackface, forcing Banks to apologize on her talk show.[2] These two stories, one concerning jurisprudence and the other pop culture, demonstrate that a misunderstanding and misguided celebration of mixed-race individuals continues despite celebrations of what many have called an "Obama post-race" America. As Tavia Nyong'o writes, "The election of Barack Obama certainly stoked a national fantasy of transcending race, or at least, with escaping the divisive and bad feelings that dwelling on racial injustice seems to cause" (6). Banks's photo shoot serves as an example of a national fantasy where we can all put on and take off race, ignoring and/or glossing over painful histories of discrimination and racism. Banks may have naively intended to applaud racial blending, but the decision to shoot the models in a Hawaiian sugarcane field, where many immigrant workers were exploited for their cheap labor, symbolizes a national attempt to escape unsavory stories associated with race and race mixing.[3] Thus, when dangerous racial tropes are not recycled, they are reinvented or extended into new ones that perpetuate naïve views of mixed-race identity.

Research has shown that despite attempts to read mixed-race subjects as embodiments of national fantasies or shame, mixed-race individuals actually identify quite diversely.[4] According to Rockquemore, Brunsma, and Delgado, in terms of identity development for mixed-race individuals, "(a) racial identity varies, (b) racial identity often changes over the life course, (c) racial identity development is not a predictable linear process with a single outcome, and (d) social, cultural, and spatial context are crucial" (21). So why recognize and focus on a black-sentient mixed-race identity? The United States is in a strange place when it comes to how it deals with race or thinks about race relations. The country has made undeniable strides, yet we are clearly not post-race. People are quick to criticize those who supposedly play the "race card"; nevertheless, in general, we live in nation reluctant to admit to an ugly racial past or acknowledge the complexities of our racial present. A black-sentient identity represents the personal and the political, an individual's multiplicities and his/her collective history, cultural memory, and cultural crossings. This identity resists racial scripts; black consciousness does not completely dictate identification. Cultural memory is an important aspect of a black-sentient identity because it shapes black awareness. It is not surprising, for example, that both *Quicksand*'s Helga Crane and *Caucasia*'s Birdie Lee feel an affinity with blackness when that cultural memory is evoked. Before Helga Crane leaves Denmark, her decision is confirmed when she hears a spiritual: "Those wailing undertones of 'Swing Low, Sweet Chariot' were too poignantly familiar. They struck into her longing heart and cut away her weakening defenses." She then admits to herself that she is "homesick, not for America, but for Negroes" (Larsen 92). Larsen's choice of "Swing Low, Sweet Chariot" has a cultural and subversive significance. Eric J. Sundquist explains that the spiritual "was transparently available to being coded with the ideology of resistance to and escape from slavery—the slave carried home to freedom in the North, where others had gone before him" (519). While Helga may not recognize the song as a symbol of resistance, her being moved by the song symbolizes her black-sentient identity—she has an undeniable connection to her black heritage and a history of racial struggle despite the fact that one page later she expresses her desire to "have two lives," a seeming reference to a desire for racial fluidity (Larsen, *Quicksand* 93). Birdie Lee's reaction to hearing black music produces a similar effect. During her trip to New York City, Birdie and Mona are sitting at a park bench when she hears "some kind of talking music" (Senna, *Caucasia* 220). Enchanted by the music and dancing teenagers, Birdie notes that "the underlying tune was somehow familiar, something I had known once, long ago" (220). Like Helga, Birdie feels a sense of familiarity and cannot ignore the music; this moment reaffirms her connection to her blackness and prompts a "lump of disappointment and envy" (221). That Birdie is witness to the beginnings of hip-hop is equally important: like Helga, she is privy to a black cultural form aligned with resistance. Music fittingly represents the impulse for these characters' connections to blackness. Guthrie P. Ramsey suggests:

> Cultural forms such as tales, stories, and music (especially *performative* aspects of such) function as reservoirs in which cultural memories reside. These memories allow social identities to be knowable, teachable, and learnable. . . . [T]he cultural, communal, and family memories associated with forms like music . . . often become standards against which many explore and create alternative and highly personal identities for themselves. (32–33)

Indeed, both Helga and Birdie "create alternative . . . identities" based on their affinity to blackness and their understanding of themselves as mixed-race subjects. In this project, a black-sentient mixed-race identity recognizes the importance of the role of cultural memory for mixed-race subjects for whom white (or closer-to-white) privilege does not negate a black awareness.

A black-sentient identity is a useful point of departure in analyzing a range of other literary and social texts, including television, cinema, and celebrity images. In the now-cancelled CW Television Network sitcom *Girlfriends* (2001–8), character Lynn Searcy (played by Persia White) is proudly biracial and black.[5] While some episodes focus on Lynn's relationship with her interracial family (including her search to find her black father and her relationship with her white biological mother), others simply make reference to her racial identity. In a season-one episode, "Hip-ocracy," one of the four girlfriends, Toni, talks about rejecting a man for being too dark skinned. When Lynn advocates celebrating all hues of African American skin, Toni responds, "That's really easy for you to say" because Lynn is "half white." Lynn responds, "Then half of me is pissed off"—a retort that humorously speaks to the common compartmentalizing of race that causes people to ascribe certain characteristics or behavior to one part or the other of a mixed-race person's racial make-up. Rebecca Walker recalls this kind of racial "halfing" when she recounts episodes with her high school boyfriend, who sees in Rebecca a racial split: "[H]e says my white comes out when I'm at Urban [High School], when I slip and say *like* every other word or when I ask him if he's heard the new Police record, or if I analyze a movie for too long or with too much intensity" (266). While Walker resents this joking, Lynn's comment plays with racial expectations, critiquing the notion that she is excluded from reacting to Toni's colorism issues (or "black" issues more generally) simply because she is "half white."

Much like the character Freddie Brooks (played by Cree Summer) in *A Different World* (1987–1993), Lynn seems to embrace both her black and mixed-race identity, never abandoning either.[6] In fact, even while expressing an affinity for racial fluidity, Lynn usually claims a black identity. In the last season, Lynn pursues a singing career as Indigo Skye, a name that speaks to her bohemian sensibilities. The problem is that her record label finds her too bohemian and not black enough. In the episode "What's Black A-Lackin'?" Lynn confronts her A&R executive, Jason, about another singer (played by R&B artist Chrisette Michele) who has received studio time before her. Jason admits that the record company "didn't know what to do with you" because they "don't think you're black enough" to sell albums. Lynn is shocked by his suggestion that the label needs to "find" her an identity. Later, she vents to her friends about the pressures she has felt all her life to prove her blackness to both whites and blacks: "I'm just sick of people trying to force me to check a box so they have a category to put me in. Why can't there be a box for none of your damn business? Why do you want to know?" ("What's Black A-Lackin'?"). Her questions repeat a familiar reaction to the "What are you?" question, and her reaction to her record company suggests that racial categories are illogical and blackness cannot be confined to one form of cultural production. Still, later she refers to herself as a black woman, suggesting that she seemingly views herself as both black and mixed race; thus, she is perhaps best analyzed as representing a black-sentient identity.

In many ways, the celebrity image of actress Rashida Jones, daughter of music producer Quincy Jones and actress Peggy Lipton, symbolizes a black-sentient identity in a contemporary context where blackness is still seen as fixed and unchanging. Though Jones proudly asserts that she is "lucky . . . [to] have so many clashing cultural, racial things going on: black, Jewish, Irish, Portuguese, Cherokee," she asserts, "The thing is, I do identify with being black, and if people don't identify me that way, that's their issue. I'm happy to challenge people's understanding of what it looks like to be biracial" (Barden). Jones's image is particularly interesting to analyze, given her racially ambiguous television and movie roles. Like actor Vin Diesel, her characters are often racially vague: when she is not marked as Italian (as character Karen Scarfolli on *Freaks and Geeks,* Karen Filippelli on *The Office,* or Ann Perkins on *Parks and Recreation*), she is "raceless," as in her breakout movie role as the fiancé of Peter Kalven (played by Paul Rudd) in the comedy *I Love You, Man* (2009). In the film, Jones's character, Zooey Rice, encourages her (white) fiancé to develop male friendships so that he can have a best man for their wedding. While viewers are introduced to Peter's family, Zooey's family remains absent from the film, even, strangely, during the wedding scene. In fact, Zooey walks down the aisle with her best friends, blatantly excluding Zooey's family and by extension her race and cultural heritage. One blogger writes, "It was as if some executive said, 'Mmm . . . if we give Rashida a father, or mother, then her ambiguity becomes specific and ethnic specificity is too much of a downer in a comedy about white guys'" (Adkins). Such roles, perhaps in conjunction with other aspects of Jones's image, has prompted surprise and speculation about Jones's race on the web, suggesting she doesn't follow expected (or accepted) racial scripts. I use Jones as an example of how a black-sentient identity can expand how we think about mixed-race identity and blackness. When asked if she felt like she was a "symbol for this new 'post-racial age' we're supposedly living in," Jones replied, "Kinda! I remember doing an article like six years ago where I was like, 'You watch. All the questions about, "What are you? Why don't you look like this?" are gonna start to fade away.' And more and more, every single day you're seeing it" (interview with Sean O'Neal). Jones intimates that the future will bring about less restrictive views on race, perhaps when identifying as black and claiming a mixed-race identity will not be seen as mutually exclusive.

Jones's optimism about the future is echoed in *Caucasia* when Deck Lee tries to soothe his daughter Cole by focusing on the future. When she complains about how her white grandmother treats her, Deck responds, "Baby, don't pay that old lady any mind. She'll be gone soon. She's a dying breed. You're the future" (Senna 265). Deck's assurances allude to his optimism for a more enlightened society and his expectations that his daughter will represent the end of racial strife and the emergence of a more liberal social order. Liberals and conservatives alike have repeatedly placed idealistic expectations on mixed-race individuals in discussions of racism and multiculturalism. A black-sentient mixed-race identity defies stereotypic or idealistic expectations of mixed-race identity without abandoning personal identity. Certainly, class privilege allows individuals to ponder the convergence and disjunction of their social, political, and personal identities. James McBride recalls not having "time or money or inclination to look beyond my own poverty to discover what identity was" (261). Like McBride, not everyone has the social option or ability to claim multiracial. Senna reminds us, "Racial fluidity, ambiguity, comes with privilege." She continues, "Take away Tiger Wood's money, his sports affiliations (put him on a basketball court in Harlem), take away his Stanford education, and let's see how fluid his racial identity is" (Arias 448). Still, questioning what it means to be black or "part-black" allows one to be critical of traditional assumptions about racial identification and realize the urgency of racial responsibility in a society built upon racial inequality. Helga Crane grapples with these overlapping identities in *Quicksand* as she searches for acceptance and "home." Helga resents her blackness in Harlem, where she finds hypocrisy and contradiction among racial uplifters. She is equally unhappy as the prized multiracial pet of her Danish aunt and uncle. Throughout she remains loyal to her blackness, aware of a black consciousness. While Helga may succumb to racial expectations, she never stays satisfied with them. Such characters not only break free from literary and historic stereotypes but also offer possibilities for mixed-race identification.

James McBride asserts that he doesn't want to be known as "Mr. Mulatto, whose children try to be every race in the world," a comment that seems to ridicule overly enthusiastic mixed-race-pride supporters who advertise a mixed-race "nationalism" undermining blackness ("What Color Is Jesus?" 196). Until power relations equalize, any celebration of mixed race needs to recognize those who are not celebrating or benefiting from America's longtime fascination. A black-sentient identity does not privilege mixed race, but rather establishes a space that balances historic memory with personal (mixed-race) retrospection.

Notes

1. What's Old Is New Again

1. For a succinct overview of the multiracial movement, see Melissa Nobles's *Shades of Citizenship: Race and the Census in Modern Politics,* 129–45.
2. Sentience is a term frequently used in discussions of animal ethics, philosophy, and morality.
3. http://www.merriam-webster.com/dictionary/sentient.
4. It should be noted that the "multiracial movement" and multiracial organizations include a diverse group of mixed-race advocates who represent an array of racial blending, some of whom are not "mixed" in the contemporary sense in which we use the term and many others who do not have black as a part of their identity makeup. For the purposes of this book's focus, unless specified, my discussion of mixed race particularly speaks to black/white mixed-race identity.
5. For example, on February 25, 2004, *The John Walsh Show* (since canceled) aired "Multiracial: Where Do I Belong?" which centers on the tensions between black and biracial. The show's guests included biracial "experts" such as Brooke Kroeger, author of *Passing: When People Can't Be Who They Are,* and Rebecca Walker. Other guests represented a black/biracial dichotomy (for example, a black activist who opposes interracial marriage and biracial teenagers who claim to have the best of both worlds). More recently, an episode of *The Tyra Banks Show,* "Biracial Women Who Hate Their Other Side," featured one black/white mixed-race women who hated her blackness, fueling animosity from the audience.
6. I use *black-sentient* over *black-identified* because the mixed-race subjects in this study do not necessarily claim a black identity.
7. Homi Bhabha argues that vernacular cosmopolitanism "is to be on the border, *in between,* introducing the global-cosmopolitan 'action at a distance' into the very grounds—now displaced—of the domestic" ("Unsatisfied" 48).
8. Georgiana Banita argues, "Obama's autobiographical writings blur the distinction between a transnational perspective of the United States seen as one global player among others and an exceptionalist view of America as the core from which a universally shared global humanity emanates" (25–26). As opposed

to scholars who examine his biracial or bicultural identity, Banita argues that Obama's writing "reject[s] the paradigm of multiethnic life writing as the mapping of mutable, hybrid subjectivities in favor of an investment in the self as both local . . . and avidly transnational" (26).

9. Other examples of such views include Stanley Crouch's "What Obama Isn't: Black Like Me," published in the *New York Daily News.*

10. Mariah Carey echoed this sentiment, claiming "that her racial ambiguity is something that naturally attracts her to Barack Obama as a presidential candidate: 'I can relate a lot to so many of the stories he tells. Clearly I am not the political analyst of the ages, but this is something that hits me on a deeper level than anything I've ever experienced growing up'" (qtd. in Crane, "She Owns the Night").

11. Several scholars have made comparisons between Obama and Ellison, including M. Cooper Harris, "'Let Us Not Falter Before Our Complexity': Barack Obama and the Legacy of Ralph Ellison," and chapter 7 of Gene Andrew Jarrett, *Representing the Race: A New Political History of African American Literature.*

12. The *Daily Kos,* a liberal political blog, even accused the Clinton campaign of manipulating photos of Obama to make him appear blacker. See Kos, "Clinton Campaign Making Obama 'Blacker.'"

13. There are, of course, exceptions, including two public figures, Ralph Nader and Jesse Jackson, who questioned Obama's blackness in June 2008. In a *Rocky Mountain News* interview, Nader said that Obama talked white and suggested he was out of touch with the black masses. Jesse Jackson, in a live-microphone, off-camera comment, said Obama was "talking down to black people." See Sprengelmeyer, "Nader: Obama Trying to 'Talk White'" and Zeleny, "Jesse Jackson Apologizes for Remarks on Obama" for further discussion of these controversial statements.

14. See Jesse Washington, "Obama's True Colors: Black, White . . . or Neither?"

15. Such views are common on the internet and in articles in popular-culture publications, such as Carl Campanile and George A. King, "Biracial Voters Take Pride in Obama's 'Milestone,'" in the *New York Post.*

16. Rainer Spencer argues that the mixed ancestry of African Americans problematizes the way some scholars and multiracial activists separate "first-generation" multiracial individuals from African Americans. He maintains that the "historical erasure of Afro-Americans' mixed ancestry" allows "the meaningless distinction of black/white multiracial identity [to] be erected and maintained" (99).

17. This term, "post-race," has been frequently used with reference to Barack Obama. In a *New York Times* article, Janny Scott describes Obama as having a "postracial style." David Mendell, who wrote *Obama: From Promise to Power,* also suggests Obama has been looked at as a "'post-racial' candidate" (Carroll). For further discussion of "post-race," see Suki Ali's *Mixed-Race, Post-Race: Gender, New Ethnicities, and Cultural Practices.*

18. West's sentiments about liking "mutts" are reflected in hip hop videos and advertisements for hip hop clothing. In *Pimps Up, Ho's Down: Hip Hop's Hold on Young Black Women,* T. Denean Sharpley maintains, "That the vast majority of the young women in these videos are either fairer-skinned, ethnically mixed, or of indeterminate ethnic/racial origins, with long, straight, or curly hair would suggest along with the stereotype of hypersexuality and sexual accessibility, a particular type of beauty is offered up as ideal" (27). See her chapter "Video Vixens, Beauty Culture, and Diasporic Sex Tourism" for further discussion of how mixed race gets fetishized in hip hop videos.

19. See Kimberly McClain DaCosta, "Selling Mixedness: Marketing with Multiracial Identities."

20. It should be noted that similar discussions and debates over terminology have engaged scholars and activists in the United Kingdom (where multiracial organizations such as MOSAIC, est. 1990, and Intermix, est. 1999, mirror American multiracial organizations). See Peter J. Aspinall's "'Mixed Race,' 'Mixed Origins' or What?: Generic Terminology for the Multiple Racial/Ethnic Group Population."

21. See Roediger, *The Wages of Whiteness: Race and the Making of the American Working Class* and *Working Towards Whiteness: How Immigrants Became White*; Harris, "Whiteness as Property"; and Allen, *The Invention of the White Race.*

22. The "Fancy Trade" or "sale of light-skinned black women for the exclusive purpose of prostitution and concubinage" also capitalized on the sexual allure of mixed-race women (Gray 37). See Deborah Gray White, *Ar'n't I a Woman?: Female Slaves in the Plantation South.*

23. An *Ebony* magazine article (Normant, "Am I Black, White Or In Between?") sets up a similar "test." The bottom of the first page asks, "Which box would you check?" and offers three possibilities (black, white, in between) under the photos of Mariah Carey, Halle Berry, Tiger Woods, and Chelsi Smith (Miss USA 1995).

24. Haurykiewicz suggests that the image of the mule represents the silencing of black women. While recognizing the racial connection between the representation of the mule and Janie's mixed ancestry, Haurykiewicz writes, "The sexual sterility of mules may represent a form of silencing, as we see that Janie's ability and desire to communicate is frequently linked to sexual satisfaction while her silence is an indication that her sexual desires are missing or thwarted" (46).

25. I use the term "mulatto" as a historic term, recognizing its limitations, inconsistencies, and offensive connotations. See Berzon, p. 9, for further discussion of the origin and first uses of the word.

26. For further discussion, see Ira Berlin, *Slaves without Masters: The Free Negro in the Antebellum South.*

27. For example, in an 1815 letter from Thomas Jefferson to Francis Gray, Jefferson responds to Gray's questions about what constitutes "mulatto" and what makes

a black man legally white. Jefferson cites Virginia law and provides a series of mathematic equations, demonstrating the legal complexities associated with racial taxonomy. See appendix C, *Sally Hemings and Thomas Jefferson: History, Memory, and Civic Culture,* ed. Jan Ellen Lewis and Peter S. Onuf.

28. See Michael A. Elliott, "Telling the Difference: Nineteenth-Century Legal Narratives of Racial Taxonomy."

29. The ruling was not overturned until *Brown v. Board of Education* (1954), which deemed "separate but equal" unconstitutional.

30. Though much scholarship on the *Plessy* case focuses on the actual ruling, Mark Golub's essay "*Plessy* as 'Passing': Judicial Responses to Ambiguously Raced Bodies in *Plessy v. Ferguson,*" "situates the issue of racial ambiguity within a comprehensive legal strategy to challenge segregation" (563). See also Thomas J. Davis, "Race, Identity, and the Law: *Plessy v. Ferguson*" (1896).

31. See John G. Mencke, pp. 125–27, and Frederick L. Hoffman, pp. 177–208, for further discussion of the supposed inferiority of the mulatto.

32. These beliefs persisted into the twentieth century. In the 1930s, George and Josephine Schuyler considered their biracial daughter, Philippa Duke Schuyler, something of a biological experiment. Josephine, a white Texas heiress, believed her daughter was a gifted child, partly because of her interracial genes. She claimed it was "hybrid vigor resulting from their miscegenation that had afforded Philippa the potential for high achievement" (Talalay 56).

33. For further discussion about the Rhinelander case, see Mark J. Madigan, "Miscegenation and the Diction of Race and Class in the Rhinelander Case and Nella Larsen's *Passing.*"

34. For further discussion see Peter Wallenstein, "Interracial Marriage on Trial: *Loving v. Virginia* (1967)."

35. For early discussions that debate the social construction of race, see Barbara J. Fields, "Ideology and Race in American History"; K. Anthony Appiah and Amy Guttman, *Color Conscious: The Political Morality of Race*; and Lucius Outlaw, "Toward a Critical Theory of Race."

36. For other examples, see Rainer Spencer, *Challenging Multiracial Identity* and George Yancy, "Racial Justice in a Black/Nonblack Society."

37. See Kerry Ann Rockquemore and David L. Brunsma, *Beyond Black: Biracial Identity in America,* and Maria P. P. Root, "From Exotic to a Dime a Dozen."

38. See Sollors, 223.

39. See Susan Bost, *Mulattas and Mestizas: Representing Mixed Identities in the America, 1850–2000.*

40. *Imitation of Life* (1934), *Show Boat* (1936), *God's Step Children* (1937), *Pinky* (1949), and *Lost Boundaries* (1949) all expose the multiple dilemmas associated with trying to pass for white. In many ways, the lives of the mulatto characters

in these movies epitomize the sad fate of the tragic mulatto, for a trace of black blood somehow dooms the happiness of each of them. The film roles played by lighter-skinned actresses with "café au lait" complexions (notably Dorothy Dandridge, Lena Horne, and Eartha Kitt) perpetuated the image of the mulatta as sex object in films through the 1940s and 1950s.

41. Another film is *Mixing Nia* (1998).

42. Mixed-race autobiographies and memoirs published within the last fifteen years include Shirlee Taylor Haizlip, *The Sweeter the Juice: A Family Memoir in Black and White*; Hans J. Massaquoi, *Destined to Witness: Growing Up Black in Nazi Germany*; Scott Minerbrook, *Divided to the Vein: A Journey into Race and Family*; Barack Obama, *Dreams from My Father: A Story of Race and Inheritance*; Gregory Williams, *Life on the Color Line: The True Story of a White Boy Who Discovered He Was Black*; Angela Nissel, *Mixed: My Life in Black and White*; Kym Ragusa, *The Skin between Us: A Memoir of Race, Beauty, and Belonging*; June Cross, *Secret Daughter: A Mixed-Race Daughter and the Mother Who Gave Her Away*; and Danzy Senna, *Where Did You Sleep Last Night? A Personal History.*

2. From Naxos to Copenhagen

1. "Mulatto" first appeared on U.S. census forms in 1850. It disappeared in the 1900 census and then reappeared in 1910 and 1920. In 1930, the census recognized "White," "Negro," "Indian," and several Asian nationalities. For further discussion of race and the census, see Hochschild and Powell, "Racial Reorganization and the United States Census 1850–1930: Mulattoes, Half-Breeds, Mixed Parentage, Hindoos, and the Mexican Race," and Melissa Nobles, *Shades of Citizenship: Race and the Census in Modern Politics.*

2. The years 1920–30 also signal an important time in Larsen's adult life, namely her literary career. Larsen began writing in 1925, and her only novels were published in the late 1920s. The year 1930 also marks an end for Larsen, her literary death. After being falsely accused of plagiarizing her short story "Sanctuary" (1930), Larsen never published again.

3. For representative examples, see Thadious Davis and Charles L. Larson.

4. Hutchinson writes, "At critical junctures the evidence seemed lacking and the conclusions unwarranted" (3).

5. Durrow is the author of *The Girl Who Fell from the Sky* (2010), a novel whose protagonist is the daughter of a Danish mother (named Nella) and African American father.

6. For criticism that focuses on Helga as a tragic mulatto, see Berzon, Sato, and Singh. An exception is Ross Posnock, who argues that "Helga is as ambivalent about black people as she is about everything else" (79).

7. For criticism that focuses on Helga's sexuality, see Hostetler, Monda, and Bettye Williams.
8. For psychoanalytic criticism on *Quicksand,* see Johnson and Hardwig.
9. Garvey and the UNIA are briefly mentioned at the end of chapter 9 when Helga attends a tea: "The aimless talk glanced from John Wellinger's lawsuit for discrimination because of race against a downtown restaurant and the advantages of living in Europe, especially France, to the significance, if any, of the Garvey movement" (Larsen 51).
10. In the same essay, "Loving Blackness as Political Resistance," hooks discusses Larsen's *Passing,* suggesting the possibility that Clare "is the only character in the novel who truly desires 'blackness' and that it is this desire that leads to her murder" (146).
11. Some scholars have viewed Helga's clothing as an extension of her limited agency. For essays that examine Helga's obsession with fashion and shopping, see Kimberly Monda, "Self-delusion and Self-sacrifice in Nella Larsen's *Quicksand*"; Meredith Goldstein, "Shopping to Pass, Passing to Shop: Bodily Self-Fashioning in the Fiction of Nella Larsen"; and Kaley Joyes, "The 'Highly Important Matter of Clothes': Apparel and Identity in Nella Larsen's *Quicksand.*"
12. Deborah McDowell writes, "Like so many novels by women, *Quicksand* likens marriage to death" (xxi). For similar readings, see Barnett and Bettye Williams.

3. Homeward Bound

1. In "Mixed Metaphors: Positioning 'Mixed Race' Identity," Minelle Mahtani describes stereotypical metaphors used to characterize the mixed-race experience. These include feeling "'out of place' or having 'no place to call home'" (77). My intent is not to reinscribe the marginal status of mixed-race individuals but rather to elucidate how a sense of homelessness that often pervades the postcolonial experience mirrors the mixed-race experience with regard to displacement.
2. Other instances in which Jacinta correlates a black Briton and African American experience include when she reflects on her personal racial struggles. After Jacinta's mother dies, she will return to her home in the United States and must teach John Edgar Wideman's *Philadelphia Fire* (1990) to her college class. She dreads teaching the class because "Wideman's novel [is] about urban chaos and the repercussions of racism. . . . It is too close to the pain I have known" (242).
3. See Mark Christian, *Multiracial Identity: An International Perspective,* chap. 1.
4. Shame is often associated with the mixed-race experience: "Historically, multiraciality in the United States has been a mark of shame and ignominy. The need to establish and sustain firm categories of race as a way to maintain White dominance in America left no place for the multiracial. Thus the mixed blood, who

threatens these categories, was either monoracialized or represented as 'deviant' and 'pathological'" (Kwan and Speirs 1). While Jacinta is British, her experience with the public (such as at the hospital) suggest she is placed in a similar dichotomy.

5. Jacinta's romanticization of Africa mirrors Helga Crane who initially idealizes each place she lives. When Helga visits Alabama, for example, "[t]here was a recurrence of the feeling that now, at last, she had found a place for herself, that she was really living" (Larsen 118).
6. In some ways this parallels Jacinta's statement to her classmates that she was from "Bohemia" after her mother explains "we weren't plebian or working-class even though we were as poor as church mice; we were classless because we were Bohemian, on account of the fact that my father was a genius and she was a failed actress" (Roy, *Lady Moses* 8). Both Jacinta's Bohemia and Birdie and Cole's Elemeno are imaginary places that are either classless or raceless.
7. It is important to note that Deck lies outside societal definitions of an "authentic" black identity, given his education, social standing, and newly discovered black pride. For example, Birdie notes that he speaks differently depending on his company, leading Sandy to assert he has a "'jive turkey act.'" Birdie reveals, "In the past year, he had discovered Black Pride (just a few years later than everyone else), and my mother said he was trying to purge himself of his 'honkified past'" (Senna, *Caucasia* 9).
8. See Kenneth Robert Janken, *White: The Biography of Walter White, Mr. NAACP.*
9. Here, Senna signifies on Guinier and Torres, who contend: "Those who are racially marginalized are like the miner's canary: their distress is the first sign of a danger that threatens us all" (11).
10. See Daniel Grassian, "Passing into Post-ethnicity: A Study of Danzy Senna's *Caucasia,*" and Kathryn Rummell, "Rewriting the Passing Novel: Danzy Senna's *Caucasia.*"

4. "This Is How Memory Works"

1. See Walter Benn Michaels for further discussion of Toomer's American identity.
2. The largest multiracial organizations in America include AMEA and Project Race. *Interracial Voice,* an online magazine, frequently publishes editorials advocating multirace options on forms.
3. From "Beliefs and Oppositions" in *The Multiracial Activist,* a "libertarian oriented activist journal."
4. Online organizations and websites that seem to privilege mixed race over "monorace" include *The Mulatto People* and *Mixed Folks.com,* a website that dedicates much space to mixed-race celebrities, especially those assumed to be

white. See Lisa Nakamura's "Mixedfolks.com: 'Ethnic Ambiguity,' Celebrity Outing, and the Internet," in which she discusses *Mixed Folks.com* and asserts that it "subordinates star gossip to a specific political goal: that of promoting the visibility and rights of mixed race folks who are not necessarily stars" (72).

5. For example, Obama occasionally thinks of the various communities he has been associated with similarly. Wondering how Indonesian workers will fare ten to twenty years in the future, he imagines obstacles they will face in the "new order. Some would move to America. And the others, the millions left behind in Djakarta, or Lagos, or the West Bank, they would settle into their own Altgeld Gardens, into a deeper despair" (183–84). Such thoughts suggest the subtle connections he makes between the African American community he serves (Altgeld) and other ethnic/racial communities in which he has lived.
6. Incidentally, Walker's sense of homelessness mirrors Danzy Senna's description of lacking a "homeland" in her memoir, *Where Did You Sleep Last Night: A Personal History* (2009): "For us [her siblings], there is no before—no nostalgic moment of purity to harken back to, no motherland in Africa and Europe to shift our gaze away. There is only, always and already, the failure of this nation and of their union, from which we three emerge, bruised and battered but still breathing. This is our only homeland" (198).
7. "Transverse" is also an anatomical plane of motion that theoretically divides the body into superior (top) and inferior (bottom) parts. Instead of dividing the body into right/left or front/back, the transverse splits into upper/lower, inscribing an imaginary hierarchy. Passing invokes this hierarchy between black and white.
8. For discussion of Booker T. Washington's political power brokering and his role as political middleman between whites and blacks from 1895 after his famous "Atlanta Compromise" speech until his death in 1915, especially his relationship with Theodore Roosevelt, see Louis R. Harlan.
9. The classic example of using white readership to garner support is Harriet Beecher Stowe, *Uncle Tom's Cabin* (1852).
10. For further discussion of reverse racial passing, see Phillip Brian Harper and Baz Dreisinger. Harper also discusses Ruth McBride's passing for black.
11. McBride was born in 1957, Obama in 1961, and Walker in 1969.
12. Interestingly, when defending black anger to his white girlfriend, Obama recalls saying, "[I]t was a matter of remembering—nobody asks why Jews remember the Holocaust." Obama then rejects his girlfriend's claim that Jewish remembering is "different" from African American memory (211).
13. The problem with this belief emanates from what Lisa Jones refers to as a "nationalist vibe" in her essay "Is Biracial Enough? (Or, What's This about a Multiracial Category on the Census?: A Conversation)."

14. Tanya Kateri Hernandez writes: "[T]he census' race question is a mechanism for monitoring the extent to which socioeconomic opportunities are stratified by race, it is nonsensical to divvy up the racial classification response into shares . . . when the social experience of race is not perceived in shares" (158).
15. See Deborah Ramirez for a more thorough examination of these arguments.
16. From the U.S. Bureau of the Census, *Overview of Race and Hispanic Origin* regarding the 2000 census.
17. See Nobles, chap. 2.

5. B(l)ack to Last Drop?

1. As I mention later, Lopez purposely uses the language "What color are you?" because it is the same question Carey's movie character, Ms. Weiss, is asked in *Precious: Based on the Novel* Push *by Sapphire.*
2. At the end of the interview, Lopez has Carey read his DNA-ethnicity-testing results (the show had been asking various celebrity guests to participate in the testing, including Larry David, Jessica Alba, and Snoop Dogg). When he tells Carey he has a swab for her, should she care to be tested, Carey declines, explaining she will stick to what she knows.
3. For an in-depth analysis of this episode, see Michele Elam, "'They's mo' to being' black than meets the eye!': Performing Mixed Race in Dave Chappelle's 'The Racial Draft' and Carl Hancock Rux's *Talk,*" chap. 5, *The Souls of Mixed Folks: Race, Politics, and Aesthetics in the New Millennium.*
4. In "The 'One Drop' Rule Through a Multiracial Lens: Examining the Roles of Race and Class in the Racial Classification of the Children of Partially Black Parents," Jenifer Bratter's research shows that multiracial families most likely to classify their child as black are those in which one parent is multiracial and the other parent is black. She writes, "The high prevalence of the 'one drop' rule among Black-multiracial parent families suggest that 'multiracial' and 'Black' identities do not necessarily exist on opposite sides of the social spectrum. They often exists within the same household and many multiracial parents report their children as 'Black'" (191–92).
5. Donald Bogle writes, "Beals . . . went without any racial identity whatsoever in her features. In *Flashdance* (1983)—a drama about a beautiful young welder in Pittsburgh, who aspires to be a dancer—Beals is clearly the tan Other" (291).
6. In fact, Carey named her daughter Monroe after Marilyn Monroe.
7. Interestingly, the magazine cover reads, "Mariah Carey: America's Most Misunderstood Black Woman."
8. This reasoning in some ways mirrors the position of some mixed-race individuals who claim blackness because of racial oppression. Kerry Ann Rockquemore

and David L. Brunsma cite "experiencing negative treatment from whites" as one of the factors that contribute to mixed-race individuals claiming a "singular identity" (mixed-race individuals who identify themselves as either solely white or black) (67).

9. A preview of the video debuted on "America's Got Talent," a primetime show hosted by Carey's husband. The single debuted at number 11 on the Billboard Hot 100, making it Carey's highest chart debut since 1998.

10. See Eric King Watt, "Border Patrolling and 'Passing' in Eminem's *8 Mile,*" and Baz Dreisinger, *Near Black: White to Black Passing in American Culture.*

11. Such perceptions abound in websites such as *The Mulatto People* and often show up in online discussions, particularly following Berry's Oscar speech, which angered many people who self-identify as multiracial. For example, responding to a post in a "Moms of Biracial Children" forum, one woman writes, "I didn't watch the awards but it's pretty sad that she had to put a label on the [Black] community she was thanking. . . . It's comments like that [that] continues [*sic*] the separatism of races" ("Did Halle Berry Forget Her Mom Is White?"). Another respondent writes, "My daughter a beautiful little girl loves Halle Berry and couldn't understand why she only said she was black. I think it was a very confusing statement." See "Did Halle Berry Forget Her Mom Is White?" for other postings.

12. In a 2008 interview, Berry also admitted she is "drawn to tortured women" because "unconsciously, she has always chosen to play women who are experiencing the issues she's working out in her own life" (Newman 89).

13. Ironically, in the television adaptation of *Their Eyes Were Watching God* (2005), in which Berry plays Janie Crawford, the filmmakers leave out Janie's mixed ancestry, including her grandmother's rape by her white master.

14. See, for example, discussions of Berry within the online discussion "Bassett: 'Monster' Role Was Demeaning."

15. For a sample of reviews on *Monster's Ball,* see Roger Ebert, Leslie Felperin, Lisa Schwarzbaum, and Stephanie Zacharek.

16. Berry has talked extensively about being perceived as "too beautiful" in Hollywood. She admits, "[F]ighting against my looks has become a large part of my career as an actress. I mean, everyone should have such problems, but producers never consider me for anything that isn't glamorous" (Hirschberg 26).

17. See, for example, *The Mulatto People.*

18. Rowell explains, "The premise is that Halle Berry makes a Faustian deal with Grace Jones that promises her lifestyle to Grace, if she wins an Academy Award for Best Actress. The poem/play is about the payback" (1006).

19. See, for example, Gina Serpe, "Halle Berry Turns Daughter's Race Into, Well, a Race Thing"; Chris Jancelewicz, "Quips & Quotes: Things Get Ugly—Really Ugly—in Halle Berry Custody Battle"; and Nadra Kareem Nittle, "Race Card: The Racial Divide in the Reaction to Halle Berry's Custody Battle."

Conclusion

1. In the appendix, the writers explain their "scientific" method of evaluating attractiveness: "At the end of the in-home interview in Wave I the interviewer was asked to rate the physical attractiveness of the respondent on a scale from 1 to 5, where 0 indicates 'very unattractive', and 5 indicates 'very attractive'" (29).
2. See "Tyra Banks Finally Addresses 'Top Model' Bi-Racial Photo Shoot Controversy."
3. See Edward D. Beechert, *Working in Hawaii: A Labor History,* and Gary Y. Okihiro, *Cane Fires: The Anti-Japanese Movement in Hawaii 1865–1965.*
4. See Kerry Ann Rockquemore and David L. Brunsma, *Beyond Black: Biracial Identity in America.*
5. The CBS website describes the character as a "free spirited, bi-racial woman with a unique outlook on life" ("Persia White").
6. In *Watching Race: Television and the Struggle for Blackness,* Herman Gray describes Freddie as "the politically correct neo-urban hippie" (99).

Bibliography

Adkins, Keith Josef. "Rashida Jones and the Hollywood Shuffle." *Root.com* 14 May 2009. Accessed 1 May 2011 <http://www.theroot.com/blogs/biracial/rashida-jones-and-hollywood-shuffle>.

Alcoff, Linda Martin. *Visible Identities: Race, Gender, and the Self.* New York: Oxford UP, 2006.

Alexander, Donnell. "Cool Like Me." *Seeing and Writing.* Ed. Donald and Christine McQuade. Boston: Bedford, 2000. 367–70.

Ali, Suki. *Mixed-Race, Post-Race: Gender, New Ethnicities, and Cultural Practices.* Oxford, UK: Berg, 2003.

Alsultany, Evelyn. "Toward a Multiethnic Cartography: Multiethnic Identity, Monoracial Cultural Logic, and Popular Culture." *Mixing It Up: Multiracial Subjects.* Ed. SanSan Kwan and Kenneth Speirs. Austin: U of Texas P, 2004. 141–62.

AMEA: Association of Multi-Ethnic Americans. Accessed 19 Feb. 2003 <http://www.ameasite.org>.

Andrews, David L., and C. L. Coles. "America's New Son: Tiger Woods and America's Multiculturalism." *Sport Stars: The Cultural Politics of Sporting Celebrity.* Ed. David L. Andrews and Steven J. Jackson. New York: Routledge, 2001. 70–86.

Anzaldua, Gloria. *Borderlands/La Frontera: The New Mestiza.* San Francisco: Aunt Lute, 1987.

Appiah, K. Anthony, and Amy Guttman. *Color Conscious: The Political Morality of Race.* Princeton, NJ: Princeton UP, 1996.

Ashe, Bertram. "Post-Soul President: *Dreams from My Father* and the Post-Soul Aesthetic." *The Obama Effect: Multidisciplinary Renderings of the 2008 Campaign.* Ed. Heather E. Harris, Kimberly R. Moffit, and Catherine R. Squires. Albany: State U of New York P, 2010. 103–15.

Aspinall, Peter J. "'Mixed Race,' 'Mixed Origins' or What?: Generic Terminology for the Multiple Racial/Ethnic Group Population." *Anthropology Today* 25.2 (Apr. 2009): 3–8.

Associated Press. "Interracial Couple Denied Marriage License by Louisiana Justice of the Peace." *HuffingtonPost.com* 16 Oct. 2009. Accessed 1 Nov. 2009 <http://www.huffingtonpost.com/2009/10/15/interracial-couple-denied_n_322784.html>.

Azoulay, Katya Gibel. *Black, Jewish, and Interracial: It's Not the Color of Your Skin, but the Race of Your Kin, and Other Myths of Identity.* Durham, NC: Duke UP, 1997.

Banita, Georgiana. "'Home Squared': Barack Obama's Transnational Self-Reliance." *Biography* 33.1 (Winter 2010): 24–45.

Bardin, Brantley. "Meet Karen from *The Office:* Interview with Rashida Jones." *Women's Health* Apr. 2008. Accessed 1 Dec. 2009 <http://www.womenshealthmag.com/life/rashida-jones-interview>.

Barnett, Amy DuBois. "On the Very Solid, Fantastically Full Life of Halle Berry." *Ebony* Mar. 2011. LexisNexis Academic Easy Search. Accessed 1 June 2011 <http://www.lexisnexis.com/hottopics/lnacademic/>.

Barnett, Pamela E. "'My Picture of You Is, After All, the True Helga Crane': Portraiture and Identity in Nella Larsen's *Quicksand.*" *Signs: Journal of Women in Culture and Society* 20.3 (Spring 1995): 575–600.

"Bassett: 'Monster' Role Was Demeaning." Online discussion forum. *The Black Web* Portal Forum. Accessed 28 Mar. 2004 <http://www.blackwebportal.com/forums/viewmessages.cfm?Forum=5&Topic=1872>.

Beechert, Edward D. *Working in Hawaii: A Labor History.* Honolulu: U of Hawaii P, 1985.

Beland, Nicole. "Meet the Parents." *Mademoiselle* Apr. 2001: 61–66.

Berlant, Lauren. "The Face of America and the State of Emergency." *Disciplinarity and Dissent in Cultural Studies.* Ed. Carey Nelson and Dilip Parameshwar Gaonkar. New York: Routledge, 1996. 397–439.

Berlin, Ira. *Slaves without Masters: The Free Negro in the Antebellum South.* New York: Pantheon, 1974.

Berzon, Judith. *Neither White nor Black: The Mulatto Character in American Fiction.* New York: New York UP, 1978.

Bhabha, Homi K. "Culture's in between." *Multicultural States: Rethinking Difference and Identity.* Ed. David Bennett. London: Routledge, 1998. 29–36.

———. *The Location of Culture.* New York: Routledge, 1994.

———. "Unsatisfied: Notes on Vernacular Cosmopolitanism." *Postcolonial Discourses: An Anthology.* Ed. Gregory Castle. Malden, MA: Blackwell, 2001. 38–52.

The Birth of a Nation. Dir. D. W. Griffith. David W. Griffith Corp., 1915.

Black, White, Other: Biracial Americans Talk about Race and Identity. Ed. Lise Funderburg. New York: Morrow, 1994.

Bogle, Donald. *Toms, Coons, Mulattoes, Mammies, and Bucks: An Interpretive History of Blacks in American Films.* New York: Continuum, 2001.

Bost, Suzanne. *Mulattas and Mestizas: Representing Mixed Identities in the Americas, 1850–2000.* Athens: U of Georgia P, 2003.

Bowman, Elizabeth Atkins. "Black Like Who?" *Black Issues* 3.1 (Jan.–Feb. 2001): 24–27.

Brady, Owen E., and Derek C. Maus. "Introduction." *Finding a Way Home: A Critical Assessment of Walter Mosley's Fiction.* Ed. Owen E. Brady and Derek C. Maus. Jackson: UP of Mississippi, 2008. ix–xxiv.

Bratter, Jenifer. "The 'One Drop' Rule through a Multiracial Lens: Examining the Roles of Race and Class in the Racial Classification of Partially Black Parents." *Multiracial Americans and Social Class: The Influence of Social Class on Racial Identity.* Ed Kathleen Odell Kogan. New York: Routledge, 2010. 184–204.

Brown, Laura. "HALLELUJAH." *Harper's Bazaar* May 2009. Accessed 15 May 2011 <http:www.harpersbazaar.com/magazine/cover/halle-berry-0509>.

Brown, Sterling A. "Negro Character as Seen by White Authors." *Journal of Negro Education* 2.2 (Apr. 1933): 179–203.

Brown, William Wells. *Clotel, or the President's Daughter.* 1853. Armonk, NY: Sharpe, 1996.

Brunsma, David L. "Mixed Messages: Doing Race in the Color-Blind Era." *Mixed Messages: Multiracial Identities in the "Color-Blind" Era.* Ed. David L. Brunsma. Boulder, CO: Lynne Rienner, 2006. 1–11.

Butterfield, Stephen. *Black Autobiography in America.* Amherst: U of Massachusetts P, 1974.

"Can Barack Win the Black Vote?" *Talk of the Nation.* Natl. Public Radio. 14 Feb. 2007. Transcript.

Carey, Mariah. "Clown." *Charmbracelet.* Island Def Jam, 2002.

———. *The Emancipation of Mimi.* Island Def Jam, 2005.

———. Interview with Dimitri Ehrlich. *Interview.* Oct. 1999: 338–39.

———. Interview with Emma Brockes. *The Guardian.* 3 Oct. 2009: 14.

———. *Memoirs of an Imperfect Angel.* Island Def Jam, 2009.

———. "My Saving Grace." *Charmbracelet.* Island Def Jam, 2002.

———. "Obsessed." *Memoirs of an Imperfect Angel.* Island Def Jam, 2009.

———. "Outside." *Butterfly.* Columbia, 1997.

———. *Rainbow.* Columbia, 1999.

Carroll, Jason. "Behind the Scenes: Is Barack Obama Black or Biracial?" *CNN.com* 9 June 2008. Accessed 10 June 2008 <http://www.cnn.com/2008/POLITICS/06/09/btsc.obama.race/>.

Chambers, Veronica. "Mariah on Fire." *Newsweek* 15 Nov. 1999: 80–81.

Chesnutt, Charles. *The House Behind the Cedars.* 1900. Athens: U of Georgia P, 1988.

Chideya, Farai. "In Character: Who Would You Talk To?" Natl. Public Radio. 2 Jan. 2008. Accessed 22 July 2008 <http://www.npr.org/blogs/newsandviews/2008/01/in_character_who_would_you_tal.html>.

Child, Lydia Maria. "The Quadroons." *Fact and Fiction: A Collection of Stories.* 1842. New York: C. S. Francis, 1846.

Christian, Mark. *Multiracial Identity: An International Perspective.* Houndmills, UK: Macmillan, 2000.

Conway, Moncure Daniel. *Testimonies Concerning Slavery.* London: Chapman & Hall, 1864.

Crane, Dan. "She Owns the Night." *Elle.com* 7 July 2008. Accessed 9 March 2012 <http://www.elle.com/Pop-Culture/Cover-Shoots/She-Owns-the-Night>.

Cross, June. *Secret Daughter: A Mixed-Race Daughter and the Mother Who Gave Her Away.* New York: Penguin, 2006.

DaCosta, Kimberly McClain. "Selling Mixedness: Marketing with Multiracial Identities." *Mixed Messages: Multiracial Identities in the "Color-Blind" Era.* Ed. David L. Brunsma. Boulder, CO: Lynne Rienner, 2006. 183–99.

Dalmage, Heather W. *Tripping on the Color Line: Black-White Multiracial Families in a Racially Divided World.* New Brunswick, NJ: Rutgers UP, 2000.

Daniel, G. Reginald. "Black and White Identity in the Millennium: Unsevering the Ties That Bind." *The Multiracial Experience: Racial Borders as the New Frontier.* Ed. Maria P. P. Root. Thousand Oaks, CA: Sage, 1996. 121–39.

———. *More Than Black? Multiracial Identity and the New Racial Order.* Philadelphia: Temple UP, 2002.

Davis, James. *Who Is Black? One Nation's Definition.* University Park: Pennsylvania State UP, 1991.

Davis, Thadious. *Nella Larsen, Novelist of the Harlem Renaissance: A Woman's Life Unveiled.* Baton Rouge: Louisiana State UP, 1994.

Davis, Thomas J. "Race, Identity, and the Law: *Plessy v. Ferguson* (1896)." *Race on Trial: Law and Justice in American History.* Ed. Annette Gordon-Reed. New York: Oxford UP, 2002. 61–76.

Defalco, Amelia. "Jungle Creatures and Dancing Apes: Modern Primitivism and Nella Larsen's *Quicksand.*" *Mosaic* 38.2 (June 2005): 19–35.

Derricotte, Toi. *The Black Notebooks: An Interior Journey.* New York: Norton, 1997.

"Did Halle Berry Forget Her Mom is White?" Online posting. 11 Sept. 2000. "Moms of Biracial Children." *Commitment.com.* Accessed 23 Feb. 2004 <http://www.commitment.com/boards/boardMB/MBbrmsgs/142.html>.

Dreisinger, Baz. *Near Black: White to Black Passing in American Culture.* Amherst: U of Massachusetts P, 2008.

Du Bois, W. E. B. *The Souls of Black Folk.* 1903. New York: Dover, 1994.

Dunbar, Paul Laurence. *Selected Poems.* Introduction by Herbert Woodward Martin. New York: Penguin, 2004.

Durrow, Heidi W. "Dear Ms. Larsen, There's a Mirror Looking Back." *Poemmemoirstory* 3 (2008): 101–9.

———. *The Girl Who Fell from the Sky.* Chapel Hill: Algonquin, 2010.

Dyer, Richard. *Heavenly Bodies: Film Stars and Society.* New York: St. Martin's, 1986.

———. *Stars.* London: BFI, 1979.

Ebert, Roger. Rev. of *Monster's Ball,* dir. Marc Forster. *Chicago Sun-Times Online* 1 Feb. 2002. Accessed 1 Mar. 2004 <http://rogerebert.suntimes.com/apps/pbcs.dll/article?AID=/20020201/REVIEWS/202010304/1023 >.

Elam, Michele. *The Souls of Mixed Folks: Race, Politics, and Aesthetics in the New Millennium.* Stanford, CA: Stanford UP, 2011.

Elam, Harry J., Jr. "Change Clothes and Go: A Postscript to Postblackness." *Black Cultural Traffic: Crossroads in Global Performance and Popular Culture.* Ed. Harry J. Elam Jr. and Kennell Jackson. Ann Arbor: U of Michigan P, 2005. 379–88.

Elliott, Michael A. "Telling the Difference: Nineteenth-Century Legal Narratives of Racial Taxonomy." *Mixed Race America and the Law: A Reader.* Ed. Kevin R. Johnson. New York: New York UP, 2003. 116–17.

Ellison, Ralph. *Invisible Man.* 1952. New York: Vintage, 1980.

Eminem. "Bagpipes from Baghdad." *Relapse.* Interscope Records, 2009.

———. "Superman." *The Eminem Show.* Interscope Records, 2002.

Evans, Rory. "Mariah Carey's Emancipation." *Marie Claire* Mar. 2005: 94–98.

Fanon, Frantz. *Black Skin, White Masks.* New York: Grove, 1967.

Farley, Christopher John. "Pop's Princess Grows Up." *Time* 25 Sept. 1995: 75.

Felperin, Leslie. Rev. of *Monster's Ball,* dir. Marc Forster. *Sight and Sound* 12.6 (June 2002): 46.

Fields, Barbara J. "Ideology and Race in American History." *Region, Race and Reconstruction: Essays in Honor of C. Vann Woodward.* Ed. J. Morgan Kousser and James M. McPherson. New York: Oxford UP, 1982. 143–77.

Fisher, Tracy. "Sex in the Nation: White Women, Brown Babies, and the Politics of Belonging." *Gendered Citizenships: Transnational Perspectives on Knowledge Production, Political Activism, and Culture.* Ed. Kia Lilly Caldwell, Kathleen Coll, Tracy Fisher, Renya K. Ramirez, and Lol Siu. New York: Palgrave, 2009. 173–90.

Foley, Barbara. "Rhetoric and Silence in Barack Obama's *Dreams from My Father.*" *Cultural Logic* (2009): 1–46. Accessed 21 Dec. 2011 <http://clogic.eserver.org/2009/Foley.pdf>.

Foucault, Michel. *The History of Sexuality: An Introduction.* New York: Vintage, 1978.

Fredrickson, George M. *The Black Image in the White Mind: The Debate on Afro-American Character and Destiny, 1817–1914.* New York: Harper & Row, 1971.

Frucht, Abby. "Continental Divide." *New York Times Book Review* 15 Mar. 1998: 35.

Funderburg, Lise. *Black, White, Other: Biracial Americans Talk about Race and Identity.* New York: Morrow, 1994.

Fusco, Coco. "Sacred Naked Nature Girls." *BOMB* 52 (Summer 1995). Accessed 4 Jan. 2010 <http://bombsite.com/issues/52/articles/1884>.

Gilroy, Paul. *Against Race: Imagining Political Culture beyond the Color Line.* Cambridge, MA: Harvard UP, 2000.

———. *The Black Atlantic: Modernity and Double Consciousness.* Cambridge, MA: Harvard UP, 1993.

Ginsberg, Elaine K. "Introduction: The Politics of Passing." *Passing and the Fictions of Identity.* Ed. Elaine K. Ginsberg. Durham, NC: Duke UP, 1996. 1–18.

Giroux, Henry A. "The Politics of National Identity and the Pedagogy of Multiculturalism in the USA." *Multicultural States: Rethinking Difference and Identity.* Ed. David Bennett. London: Routledge, 1998. 178–94.

Gladwell, Malcolm. "Lost in the Middle." *Half and Half: Writers on Growing Up Biracial and Bicultural.* Ed. Claudine Chiawei O'Hearn. New York: Pantheon, 1998. 112–24.

Glissant, Edouard. *Caribbean Discourse: Selected Essays.* Charlottesville: UP of Virginia, 1989.

Glitter. Dir. Vondie Curtis-Hall. Twentieth Century Fox, 2001.

Gloster, Hugh M. *Negro Voices in American Fiction.* Chapel Hill: U of North Carolina P, 1948.

Goldsmith, Meredith. "Shopping to Pass, Passing to Shop: Consumer Self-Fashioning in the Fiction of Nella Larsen." *Recovering the Black Female Body.* Ed. Michael Bennett and Vanessa Dickerson. New Brunswick, N.J.: Rutgers UP, 2001. 97–120.

Golub, Mark. "Plessy as 'Passing': Judicial Responses to Ambiguously Raced Bodies in *Plessy v. Ferguson.*" *Law and Society Review* 39.3: 563–600.

Gordan, Lewis. *Her Majesty's Other Children: Sketches of Racism from a Neocolonial Age.* Oxford, UK: Rowman & Littlefield, 1997.

Gossett, Thomas F. *Race: The History of an Idea in America.* New York: Oxford UP, 1997.

Grassian, Daniel. "Passing into Post-ethnicity: A Study of Danzy Senna's *Caucasia.*" *Midwest Quarterly* 47.4 (Summer 2006): 317–55.

Gray, Herman. *Watching Race: Television and the Struggle for Blackness.* Minneapolis: U of Minnesota P, 2004.

Green, Tara. *A Fatherless Child: Autobiographical Perspectives on African American Men.* Columbia: U of Missouri P, 2009.

Greenfield-Sanders, Timothy, and Elvis Mitchell. *The Black List.* New York: Atria, 2008.

Grill, Trina. "Anti-Essentialism and Intersectionality: Tools to Dismantle the Master's House." *Mixed Race America and the Law: A Reader.* Ed. Kevin R. Johnson. New York: New York UP, 2003. 123–24.

Gubar, Susan. *Racechanges: White Skin, Black Face in American Culture.* New York: Oxford UP, 1997.

Guinier, Lani, and Gerald Torres. *The Miner's Canary: Enlisting Race, Resisting Power, Transforming Democracy.* Cambridge, MA: Harvard UP, 1992.

Haizlip, Shirlee Taylor. *The Sweeter the Juice: A Family Memoir in Black and White.* New York: Simon & Schuster, 1994.

Hall, Ronald, Kathy Russell, and Midge Wilson. *The Color Complex: The Politics of Skin Color among African Americans.* New York: Anchor, 1992.

Hall, Stuart. "The Spectacle of the 'Other.'" *Representation: Cultural Representations and Signifying Practices.* Ed. Stuart Hall. London: Sage, 1997.

"Halle Berry." *Askmen.com.* Accessed 1 Mar. 2004 <http://www.askmen.com/women/actress/22b_halle.berry.html>.

"Halle Berry." *Road to the Red Carpet.* Entertainment Television. 3 May 2003.

Hardwig, Bill. "'A Lack Somewhere': Lacan, Psychoanalysis, and *Quicksand.*" *Soundings* 80.4 (Winter 1997): 573–89.

"Harmonic Convergences." *O, the Oprah Magazine.* Apr. 2006: 270–73.

Harper, Frances E. W. *Iola Leroy.* 1893. Boston: Beacon, 1987.

Harper, Phillip Brian. "Passing For What? Racial Masquerade and the Demands of Upward Mobility." *Callaloo* 21.2 (1998): 381–97.

Harlan, Louis R. *Booker T. Washington: The Wizard of Tuskegee, 1901–1915.* New York: Oxford UP, 1983.

Harris, Cheryl L. "Whiteness as Property." *Harvard Law Review* 106.8 (1993): 1709–91.

Harris, M. Cooper. "'Let Us Not Falter before Our Complexity': Barack Obama and the Legacy of Ralph Ellison." *The Obama Effect: Multidisciplinary Renderings of the 2008 Campaign.* Ed. Heather E. Harris, Kimberly R. Moffit, and Catherine R. Squires. Albany: State U of New York P, 2010. 116–30.

Harrison-Kahan, Lori. "Passing for White, Passing for Jewish: Mixed Race Identity in Danzy Senna and Rebecca Walker." *MELUS* 30.1 (Spring 2005): 19–48.

Haurykiewicz, Julie A. "From Mules to Muliebrity: Speech and Silence in *Their Eyes Were Watching God.*" Southern Literary Journal 29.2 (Spring 1997): 45–60.

Haynes, Esther. "Am I Going to Be Happy or Not?" *Jane* Dec. 2003: 126–28.

Hernandez, Tanya Kateri. "'Multiracial Discourse': Racial Classifications in an Era of Color-Blind Jurisprudence." *Maryland Law Review* 57.1 (1998): 97–173.

Hernandez-Ramdwar, Camille. "Ms. Edge Innate." *Miscegenation Blues: Voices of Mixed Race Women.* Ed. Carol Camper. Toronto: Sister Vision, 1994. 2–7.

"Hip-ocracy." *Girlfriends: The Complete First Season.* Writ. Regina Y. Hicks. Dir. Leonard R. Garner Jr. CW, 2000. DVD.

Hirschberg, Lynn. "The Beautiful and Damned." *New York Times Magazine* 23 Dec. 2001: 26.

Hochschild, Jennifer L., and Brenna Marea Powell. "Racial Reorganization and the United States Census 1850–1930: Mulattoes, Half-Breeds, Mixed Parentage, Hindoos, and the Mexican Race." *Studies in American Political Development* 22 (Spring 2008): 59–96.

Hoffman, Frederick L. *Race Traits and Tendencies of the American Negro.* New York: Macmillan, 1896.

hooks, bell. *Killing Rage: Ending Racism.* New York: Henry Holt, 1995.

Horton, Hayward Derrick. "Racism, Whitespace, and the Rise of the Neo-Mulattoes." *Mixed Messages: Multiracial Identities in the "Color-Blind" Era.* Ed. David L. Brunsma. Boulder, CO: Lynne Rienner, 2006. 117–21.

Hostetler, Ann E. "The Aesthetics of Race and Gender in Nella Larsen's *Quicksand.*" *PMLA* 105 (1990): 35–46.

Hunter, Michele. "Revisiting the Third Space: Reading Danzy Senna's *Caucasia.*" *Literature and Racial Ambiguity.* Ed. Tera Hubel and Neil Brookes. New York: Randopi, 2002. 297–316.

Hurston, Zora Neale. "How It Feels To Be Colored Me." *I Love Myself When I Am Laughing . . . and Then Again When I Am Looking Mean and Impressive.* Ed. Alice Walker. New York: Feminist P, 1979. 152–55.

———. *Their Eyes Were Watching God.* 1937. Urbana: U of Illinois P, 1978.

Hutchinson, George. *In Search of Nella Larsen: A Biography of the Color Line.* Cambridge, MA: Belknap P of Harvard UP, 2006.

———. "Nella Larsen and the Veil of Race." *American Literary History* 9.2 (Summer 1997): 329–49.

I Love You, Man. Dir. John Hamburg. DreamWorks, 2009.

Ifekwunigwe, Jayne O, ed. *'Mixed Race' Studies: A Reader.* London: Routledge, 2004.

Interracial Voice. Ed. Charles Michael Byrd. Accessed 8 Apr. 1999 <http://www.interracialvoice.com>.

Jancelewicz, Chris. "Quips & Quotes: Things Get Ugly—Really Ugly—in Halle Berry Custody Battle." *Popeater.com* 12 Feb. 2011. Accessed 1 May 2011 <http://www.popeater.com/2011/02/12/quips-quotes-halle-berry/>.

Janken, Kenneth Robert. *White: The Biography of Walter White, Mr. NAACP.* New York: New P, 2003.

Jarrett, Gene Andrew. *Representing the Race: A New Political History of African American Literature.* New York: New York UP, 2011.

Jeffries, Dexter. *Triple Exposure: Black, Jewish and Red in the 1950s.* New York: Dafina, 2003.

Jenkins, Sacha, et al. *Ego Trip's Big Book of Racism!* New York: Regan, 2002.

Johnson, Barbara. *The Feminist Difference: Literature, Psychoanalysis, Race, and Gender.* Cambridge: Harvard UP, 1998.

Johnson, James Weldon. *The Autobiography of an Ex-Colored Man.* 1912. New York: Penguin, 1990.

Johnson, Kevin R. Ed. *Mixed Race America and the Law: A Reader.* New York: New York UP, 2003.

Johnson, Lynne d. "Bearing the Black Female Body as Witness in Sci-Fi." *PopMatters.com* 1 Dec. 2003. Accessed 1 Mar. 2004 <http://www.popmatters.com/pm/column/johnson031218/ >.

Jones, Lisa. "The Blacker the Berry." *Essence* June 1994: 60+.

———. *Bulletproof Diva: Tales of Race, Sex, and Hair.* New York: Doubleday, 1994.

Jones, Rashida. Interview with Sean O'Neal. *AV Club.* Apr. 8 2009. Accessed 1 Dec. 2009 <http://www.avclub.com/articles/rashida-jones,26240/.>

Jones, Suzanne W. "The Obama Effect on American Discourse about Racial Identity: *Dreams from My Father* (and Mother), Barack Obama's Search for Self." *The Obama Effect: Multidisciplinary Renderings of the 2008 Campaign.* Ed. Heather E. Harris, Kimberly R. Moffitt, and Catherine E. Squires. Albany: State U of New York P, 2010. 131–52.

Joyes, Kaley. "The 'Highly Important Matter of Clothes': Apparel and Identity in Nella Larsen's *Quicksand.*" *Fringe* 19 July 2009. Accessed 21 Dec. 2011 <http://www.fringemagazine.org/lit/criticism/the-highly-important-matter-of-clothes"-apparel-and-identity-in-nella-larsens-quicksand/>.

Kangaris, Charlie. "Cinema and the Female Star—A Symposium Part 1: Halle Berry." *Senses of Cinema* 23 (Nov.–Dec. 2002). *Senses of Cinema Inc.* Accessed 1 Mar. 2004 <http://www.sensesofcinema.com/2002/23/symposium1/#berry>.

Kellogg, Cristin. "Identifying the Future." *Insight on the News.* 1 May 2000. Accessed 23 Feb. 2004 <http://www.findarticles.com/cf_dls/m1571/16_16/61934316/p1/article.jhtml>.

Kennedy, Dana. "Halle Berry, Bruised and Beautiful, Is on a Mission." *New York Times* 10 Mar. 2002: 2A+.

Kerr, Philip. "A Shocking Cheek." *New Statesmen* 17 June 2002: 44.

Kirkland, Bruce. "Word's Out: Vin's In." *Toronto Sun* 4 Aug. 2004. Accessed 4 Mar. 2004 <http://www.canoe.ca/JamMoviesArtistsD/diesel_vin.html>.

"Kiss Off." *People* 29 Dec. 2003: 150–51.

Knox, Robert. "Do Races Ever Amalgamate?" *'Mixed Race' Studies: A Reader.* Ed. Jayne O. Ifekwunigwe. London: Routledge, 2004. 37–38.

Kos. "Clinton Campaign Making Obama 'Blacker.'" *DailyKos.com* 5 Mar. 2008. Accessed 24 July 2008 <http://www.dailykos.com/storyonly/2008/3/5/131156/5021>.

Kroeger, Brooke. *Passing: When People Can't Be Who They Are.* New York: Public Affairs, 2003.

Kwan, SanSan, and Kenneth Speirs. "Introduction." *Mixing It Up: Multiracial Subjects.* Eds. SanSan Kwan and Kenneth Speirs. Austin: U of Texas P, 2004. 1–10.

La Ferla, Ruth. "Generation E.A.: Ethically Ambiguous." *New York Times* 28 Dec. 2003, sec 9: 1+.

Larsen, Nella. *Quicksand and Passing.* 1928, 1929. Ed. Deborah McDowell. New Brunswick, NJ: Rutgers UP, 1986.

Larson, Charles. *Invisible Darkness: Jean Toomer and Nella Larsen.* Iowa City: U of Iowa P, 1993.

Lee, Wanda M. L. "Therapeutic Considerations in Work with Biracial Girls." *Biracial Women in Therapy: Between the Rock of Gender and the Hard Place of Race.* Ed. Angela R. Gillem and Cathy A. Thompson. New York: Haworth, 2004. 203–16.

Levitt, Steven. "The Plight of Mixed-Race Children." *New York Times.com* 12 Aug. 2008. Accessed 1 Dec. 2009 <http://freakonomics.blogs.nytimes.com/2008/08/12/the-plight-of-mixed-race-children/>.

Lewis, Jan Ellen, and Peter S. Onuf, eds. *Sally Hemings and Thomas Jefferson: History, Memory, and Civic Culture.* Charlottesville: UP of Virginia, 1999.

"Limbaugh on Obama: 'Halfrican American.'" *Media Matters for America.org* 24 Jan. 2007. Accessed 1 Feb. 2007 <http://mediamatters.org/items/200701240010>.

Lopez Tonight. TBS network. 16 Dec. 2009.

Mahtani, Minelle. "Mixed Metaphors: Positioning 'Mixed Race' Identity." *Situating 'Race' and Racisms in Time, Space, and Theory: Critical Essays for Activists and Scholars.* Ed. Jo-Anne Lee and John Lutz. Montreal: McGill-Queen's UP: 2005. 77–93.

"Mariah Carey Discusses Her Sex Life, Race, Career." *Jet* 31 May 1999: 56–60.

"Mariah Carey: I Felt Like an Outcast." *Musicrooms.net* 30 Nov. 2010. Accessed 1 May 2011 <http://www.musicrooms.net/showbiz/20968-mariah-carey-i-felt-like-an-outcast.html>.

"Mariah Carey: Shining through the Rain." Interview with John Norris. MTV. 3 Dec. 2002.

"Mariah Carey Talks to Biracial Teens." *Oprah.* ABC. 27 Dec. 1999. Transcript.

"Mariah Carey Tells Why She Looks White but Sings Black." *Jet* 3 Apr. 1991: 56–57.

Massaquoi, Hans J. *Destined to Witness: Growing Up Black in Nazi Germany.* New York: Morrow, 1999.

MAVIN. Accessed 18 July 2003 < http://www.mavinfoundation.org/new/ >.

McBride, James. *The Color of Water: A Black Man's Tribute to His White Mother.* New York: Riverhead, 1996.

———. Interview with Bill Zimmerman. 25 Aug. 2001. Oberlin College. Accessed 27 Mar. 2002 <http://www.sunysb.edu/writrhet/instruct/mcbrideinterview.html>.

———. "What Color Is Jesus?" *Half and Half: Writers on Growing Up Biracial and Bicultural.* Ed. Claudine Chiawei O'Hearn. New York: Pantheon, 1998. 181–96.

McCarroll, Meredith. "'Claiming': White Ambition, Multiracial Identity, and the New American Racial Passing." *At Home and Abroad: Historicizing Twentieth-Century Whiteness in Literature and Performance.* Ed. La Vinia Delois Jennings. Knoxville: U of Tennessee P, 2009. 197–220.

McDowell, Deborah E. "Introduction." *Quicksand and Passing* by Nella Larsen. Ed. Deborah E. McDowell. New Brunswick, NJ: Rutgers UP, 1986. ix–xxxi.

Mencke, John G. *Mulattoes and Race Mixture: American Attitudes and Images, 1865–1918.* Ann Arbor, MI: UMI Research P, 1979.

Michaels, Walter Benn. *Our America: Nativism, Modernism, and Pluralism.* Durham, NC: Duke UP, 1995.

Minerbrook, Scott. *Divided to the Vein: A Journey into Race and Family.* New York: Harcourt, 1996.

"Miss Illinois Crowned Miss America." *Jet* 7 Oct. 2002: 8–10.

"Mix It Up!" *O, the Oprah Magazine* Apr. 2006: 270–73.

MixedFolks.com. Accessed 19 Feb. 2003 <http://www.mixedfolks.com/mfc/Welcome.html >.

Monda, Kimberly. "Self-Delusion and Self-Sacrifice in Nella Larsen's *Quicksand.*" *African American Review* 31.1 (Spring 1997): 23–29.

"Monster Balls." Rev. of *Monster's Ball,* dir. Marc Forster. *Metaphilm.* Accessed 29 Feb. 2004 <http://www.metaphilm.com/philms/monstersball.html>.

Morgan, Joan. "Free At Last." *Essence* Apr. 2005: 118–24.

Morrison, Toni. "Home." *The House That Race Built.* Ed. Wahneema Lubiano. New York: Vintage, 1998. 3–12.

The Mulatto People. Ed. Richard Miller. Accessed 19 Feb. 2003 <http://www.mulatto.cjb.net>.

The Multiracial Activist. Ed. James A. Landrith Jr. Accessed 19 Feb. 2003 <http://www.multiracial.com>.

"Multiracial: Where Do I Belong?" *The John Walsh Show.* NBC (syndicated series). 25 Feb. 2004.

Mumford, Kevin J. *Interzones: Black/White Sex Districts in Chicago and New York in the Early Twentieth Century.* New York: Columbia UP, 1997.

Nakamura, Lisa. "Mixedfolks.com: 'Ethnic Ambiguity,' Celebrity Outing, and the Internet." *Mixed Race Hollywood.* Ed. Mary Beltran and Camilla Fojas. New York: New York UP, 2008. 64–83.

Nakashima, Cynthia L. "Voices From the Movement: Approaches to Multiraciality." *The Multiracial Experience: Racial Borders as the New Frontier.* Ed. Maria P. P. Root. Thousand Oaks, CA: Sage, 1996. 79–97.

Nakazawa, Donna Jackson. "A New Generation Is Leading the Way." *Parade* 6 July 2003: 4–5.

Newman, Judith. "Halle Breaks It Down." *InStyle* Feb. 2008: 82–89.

Nipps, Emily. "Disconnected Community." *St. Petersburg Times Online* 5 Oct. 2003. Accessed 23 Feb. 2004 <http:///www.sptimes.com/2003/10/05/news_pf/Sports/Disconnected_Community.shtml>.

Nissel, Angela. *Mixed: My Life in Black and White.* New York: Villard, 2006.

Nittle, Nadra Kareem. "Race Card: The Racial Divide in the Reaction to Halle Berry's Custody Battle." *BitchMagazine.org.* Accessed 4 Feb. 2011 <http://bitchmagazine.org/post/race-card-the-racial-divide-in-the-public's-reaction-to-halle-berry's-custody-battle>.

Njeri, Itabari. "The Last Plantation." *'Mixed Race' Studies: A Reader.* Ed. Jayne O. Ifekwunigwe. London: Routledge, 2004. 295–302.

———. "Sushi and Grits: Ethnic Identity and Conflict in a Newly Multicultural America." *Lure and Loathing: Essays on Race, Identity, and the Ambivalence of Assimilation.* Ed. Gerald Early. New York: Penguin, 1993. 13–40.

Nobles, Melissa. *Shades of Citizenship: Race and the Census in Modern Politics.* Stanford: Stanford UP, 2000.

Normant, Lynn. "Am I Black, White Or In Between?" *Ebony.* Aug. 1995: 108–12.

Nyong'o, Tavia. *The Amalgamation Waltz: Race, Performance, and the Ruses of Memory.* Minneapolis: U of Minnesota P, 2009.

Obama, Barack. *Dreams from My Father: A Story of Race and Inheritance.* New York: Kodansha Globe, 1995.

———. Interview with Paula Zahn. *Paula Zahn Now.* CNN. 13 Sept. 2004. Transcript.

"Obamapalooza." *On the Media.* Natl. Public Radio. 27 Oct. 2006. Transcript.

Ogunnaike, Lola. "Through the Fire." *Vibe* Mar. 2003: 113–20.

Okihiro, Gary Y. *Cane Fires: The Anti-Japanese Movement in Hawaii 1865–1965.* Philadelphia: Temple UP, 1991.

Olney, James. *Memory and Narrative: The Weave of Life-Writing.* Chicago: U of Chicago P, 1999.

Omi, Michael and Howard Winant. *Racial Formations in the United States.* New York: Routledge, 1994.

Outlaw, Lucius. "Toward a Critical Theory of Race." *Anatomy of Racism.* Ed. David T. Goldberg. Minneapolis: U of Minnesota P, 1990. 58–82.

Pabst, Naomi. "Blackness/Mixedness: Contestations Over Crossing Signs." *Cultural Critique* Spring 2003: 178–212.

Pappademas, Alex. "Over the 'Rainbow': A Tale of Two Mariahs." *Boston Phoenix* 22 Nov. 1999. Accessed 24 Mar. 2004 <http://weeklywire.com/ww/11-22-99/boston_music_ 2.html>.

"Persia White." *CBS Television Studios.* 2007. Accessed 5 May 2011 <http://www.cbspressexpress.com/div.php/paramount_network/original/bio?id=605&bid=762&dpid=70>

Piper, Adrian. "Passing for White, Passing for Black." *Passing and the Fictions of Identity.* Ed. Elaine K. Ginsberg. Durham, NC: Duke UP, 1996. 234–69.

Pires-Hester, Laura. "The Emergence of Bilateral Diaspora Ethnicity among Cape Verdean-Americans." *The African Diaspora: African Origins and New World Identities.* Ed. Isidore Okpewho, Carole Boyce Davies, and Ali A. Mazrui. Bloomington: Indiana UP, 1998. 485–503.

Posnock, Ross. *Color & Culture: Black Writers and the Making of the Modern Intellectual.* Cambridge: Harvard UP, 1998.

Prasad, Chandra, ed. *Mixed: An Anthology of Short Fiction on the Multiracial Experience.* New York: Norton, 2006.

Precious: Based on the Novel Push *by Sapphire.* Dir. Lee Daniels. Lionsgate, 2008.

PROJECT RACE: Reclassify All Children Equally. Accessed 19 Feb. 2003 <http://www.projectrace.com>.

Raboteau, Emily. *The Professor's Daughter.* New York: Henry Holt, 2005.

"The Racial Draft." *Chappelle's Show.* Comedy Central Network, 2004.

Raguasa, Kym. *The Skin Between Us: A Memoir of Race, Beauty, and Belonging.* New York: Norton, 2006.

Ramirez, Deborah. "Multicultural Empowerment: It's Not Just Black and White Anymore." *Stanford Law Review* 47.5 (1995): 957–92.

Ramsey, Guthrie P. *Race Music: Black Cultures from Bebop to Hip-Hop.* Berkeley: U of California P, 2004.

Reese, Venus Opal. "Transatlantic Minstrelsy: Performing Survival Strategies in Slavery and Hip-Hop." *Recharting the Black Atlantic: Modern Cultures, Local Communities, Global Connections.* Ed. Annalisa Oboe. New York: Routledge, 2008. 181–96.

Rhee, Foon. "Chewing over Obama's 'Mutt' Reference." *Boston.com* 10 Nov. 2008. Accessed 15 Nov. 2008 <http://www.boston.com/news/politics/politicalintelligence/2008/11/chewing_over_ob.html>.

Richards, Deborah. "'An Accumulation of Things Happening': An Interview with Deborah Richards." *Callaloo* 27.4 (Fall 2004): 998–1008.

Ritz, David. "Heart to Heart." *Essence* Dec. 2002: 128+.

Robertson, Gil. "The Chameleon." *Savoy* Sept. 2002: 56+. ProQuest. Accessed 9 Sept. 2006 <http://proquest.umi.com>.

Rockquemore, Kerry Ann, and David L. Brunsma. *Beyond Black: Biracial Identity in America.* 2nd ed. Lanham, MD: Rowman & Littlefield, 2008.

Rockquemore, Kerry Ann, David L. Brunsma, and Daniel J. Delgado. "Racing to Theory or Retheorizing Race?: Understanding the Struggle to Build a Multiracial Identity Theory." *Journal of Social Issues* 65.1 (2009): 13–34.

Roediger, David R. *The Wages of Whiteness: Race and the Making of the American Working Class.* London: Verso, 1991.

———. *Working Towards Whiteness: How Immigrants Became White.* New York: Basic, 2005.

Root, Maria P. P. "A Bill of Rights for Racially Mixed People." *The Multiracial Experience: Racial Borders as the New Frontier.* Ed. Maria P. P. Root. Thousand Oaks, CA: Sage, 1996. 3–14.

———. "Five Mixed-Race Identities: From Relic to Revolution." *New Faces in a Changing America: Multiracial Identity in the 21st Century.* Ed. Loretta I. Winters and Herman L. DeBose. Thousand Oaks, CA: Sage, 2003. 3–20.

———. "From Exotic to a Dime a Dozen." *Biracial Women in Therapy: Between the Rock of Gender and the Hard Place of Race.* Ed. Angela R. Gillem and Cathy A. Thompson. New York: Haworth, 2004. 19–31.

———. "From Shortcuts to Solutions." *Racially Mixed People in America.* Ed. Maria P. P. Root. Newbury Park, CA: Sage, 1992. 342–47.

———. "The Multiracial Experience: Racial Borders as a Significant Frontier in Race Relations." *The Multiracial Experience: Racial Borders as the New Frontier.* Ed. Maria P. P. Root. Thousand Oaks, CA: Sage, 1996. xiii–xxviii.

———, ed. *Racially Mixed People in America.* Thousand Oaks, CA: Sage, 1992.

Romano, Renee C. *Race Mixing: Black-White Marriage in Postwar America.* Cambridge, MA: Harvard UP, 2003.

Roy, Lucinda. *Lady Moses.* New York: HarperCollins, 1998.

———. "Searching for Belonging: Contemporary Expressions of Home, Hybridity, and Identity in Lucinda Roy's *Lady Moses.*" Interview with Laura Dunn. *Black British Literature: The Lucinda Roy Page.* Accessed 25 Jan. 2007 <http://www.english.tamu.edu/pers/fac/muana/lucindaroy.htm>.

Rubin, Jessica G. *Surviving the Color Line: (Im)migration, Ethnicity, and Gender in Willa Cather, Gertrude Stein, and Nella Larsen.* New York: Routledge, 2004.

Rummell, Kathryn. "Rewriting the Passing Novel: Danzy Senna's *Caucasia*." *Griot* 26.2 (Fall 2007): 1–12.

Saad, Nardine. "Halle Berry, Gabriel Aubry Battle for Custody of Daughter Nahla." *LATimes.com* 3 Feb. 2011. Accessed 1 June 2011 <http://latimesblogs.latimes.com/gossip/2011/02/halle-barry-gabriel-aubry-custody-battle-daughter-nahla.html>.

Saks, Eva. "Representing Miscegenation Law." *Mixed Race America and the Law: A Reader.* Ed. Kevin R. Johnson. New York: New York UP, 2003. 11–12.

Salgado, Raquel Scherr. "Misceg-narrations." *Mixing It Up: Multiracial Subjects.* Ed. SanSan Kwan and Kenneth Speirs. Austin: U of Texas P, 2004. 31–70.

Samuels, Allison. "Angela's Fire." *Newsweek* 1 July 2002: 54.

Samuels, David. "Invisible Man: How Ralph Ellison Explains Barack Obama." *New Republic* 22 Oct. 2008: 22–27.

Sapphire. *Push.* New York: Vintage, 1996.

Sato, Hiroko. "Under the Harlem Shadow: A Study of Jessie Fauset and Nella Larsen." *The Harlem Renaissance Remembered.* Ed. Arna Bontemps. New York: Dodd, Mead, 1972.

Savishinsky, Neil J. "African Dimensions of the Jamaican Rastafarian Movement." *Chanting Down Babylon: The Rastafari Reader.* Ed. Nathaniel Samuel Murrell, William D. Spencer, and Adrian Anthony McFarlane. Philadelphia: Temple UP, 1998. 125–44.

"Say *What?*" Comp. Charreah Jackson. *Essence* Dec. 2006: 72.

Scheper, Jeann. "The New Negro Flaneuse in Nella Larsen's *Quicksand*." *African American Review* 42.3–4 (Fall/Winter 2008): 679–95.

Schwarzbaum, Lisa. Rev. of *Monster's Ball. EW.com* 16 Jan. 2002. Accessed 22 Mar. 2005. <http://www.ew.com/ew/article/0,,194330,00.html>.

Scott, Janny. "A Biracial Candidate Walks His Own Fine Line." *New York Times.com* 29 Dec. 2007. Accessed 19 Apr. 2012 <http://www.nytimes.com/2007/12/29/us/politics/29obama.html?ref=jena>.

Selzer, Linda F. "Barack Obama, the 2008 Presidential Election, and the New Cosmopolitanism: Figuring the Black Body." *MELUS* 35.4 (Winter 2010): 15–37.

Senna, Danzy. "The Africana QA: Danzy Senna." Interview. *Africana.com* 6 July 2004. Accessed 2 Apr. 2012 <http://www.rebeccalweber.com/danzy.html>.

———. *Caucasia.* New York: Riverhead, 1998.

———. "The Mulatto Millennium." *Half and Half: Writers on Growing Up Biracial and Bicultural.* Ed. Claudine Chiawei O'Hearn. New York: Pantheon, 1998. 12–27.

———. "Passing and the Problematic of Multiracial Pride (or, Why One Mixed Girl Still Answers to Black)." *Black Cultural Traffic: Crossroads in Global*

Performance and Popular Culture. Ed. Harry J. Elam Jr. and Kennell Jackson. Ann Arbor: U of Michigan P, 2005. 83–87.

———. "Race and Other Flammable Topics: A Conversation between Danzy Senna and Porochista Khakpour." Interview. *Poets & Writers* Mar./Apr. 2010. 36–44.

———. *Symptomatic*. New York: Riverhead, 2004.

———. "To Be Real." *To Be Real: Telling the Truth and Changing the Face of Feminism*. Ed. Rebecca Walker. New York: Anchor, 1995. 5–20.

———. *Where Did You Sleep Last Night? A Personal History*. New York: Farrar, 2009.

Serpe, Gina. "Halle Berry Turns Daughter's Race Into, Well, a Race Thing." *EOnline.com* 8 Feb. 2011. Accessed 1 May 2009 <http://www.eonline.com/uberblog/b224846_halle_berry_turns_daughters_race_into.html#ixzz1QFFVNgKQ>.

Sharpley-Whiting, T. Denean. *Pimps Up, Ho's Down: Hip Hop's Hold on Young Black Women*. New York: New York UP, 2007.

Shohat, Ella. *Unthinking Eurocentrism: Multiculturalism and the Media*. London: Routledge, 1995.

Singh, Amritjit. *The Novels of the Harlem Renaissance*. University Park: Pennsylvania State UP, 1976.

Smith, John David. *Black Judas: William Hannibal Thomas and the American Negro*. Athens: U of Georgia P, 2000.

Smith, Valerie. *Self-Discovery and Authority in Afro-American Narrative*. Cambridge: Harvard UP, 1991.

Smith, Zadie. "Speaking in Tongues." *New York Review of Books* 26 Feb. 2009. Accessed 1 Dec. 2009 <http://www.nybooks.com/articles/22334>.

Sollors, Werner. *Neither Black nor White yet Both: Thematic Explorations of Interracial Literature*. New York: Oxford UP, 1997.

Spencer, Rainer. *Challenging Multiracial Identity*. Boulder, CO: Lynne Rienner, 2006.

Spillers, Hortense J. "Notes on an Alternative Model: Neither/Nor." *The Year Left 2: An American Socialist Yearbook*. Ed. Mike Davis, Manning Marable, Fred Pfeil, and Michael Sprinker. London: Verso, 1987.

Sprengelmeyer, M. E. "Nader: Obama Trying to 'Talk White.'" *Rocky Mountain News* 25 June 2008. Accessed 14 July 2008 <http://www.rockymountainnews.com/news/2008/jun/25/nader-critical-of-obama-for-trying-to-talk-white/>.

Stowe, Harriet Beecher. *Uncle Tom's Cabin*. 1852. New York: Penguin, 1986.

Stephens, Vincent. "Pop Goes the Rapper: A Close Reading of Eminem's Genderphobia." *Popular Music* 24.1 (Jan. 2005): 21–36.

———. Rev. of *Rainbow*. *Popular Music and Society* 26.2 (Summer 2003): 234–35.

Streeter, Caroline A. "Faking the Funk?: Mariah Carey, Alicia Keys, and (Hybrid) Black Celebrity." *Black Cultural Traffic: Crossroads in Global Performance and*

Popular Culture. Ed. Harry J. Elam Jr. and Kennell Jackson. Ann Arbor: U of Michigan P, 2005. 185–207.

———. "The Hazards of Visibility: 'Biracial' Women, Media Images, and Narratives of Identity." *New Faces in a Changing America: Multiracial Identity in the 21st Century.* Ed. Loretta I. Winters and Herman L. DeBose. Thousand Oaks, CA: Sage, 2003. 301–22.

Sundquist, Eric J. *To Wake the Nations: Race in the Making of American Literature.* Cambridge, MA: Harvard UP, 1993.

"Surviving the Glare: Celebrities Who Prevailed After Scandal." Interviews by Barbara Walters with Mariah Carey and others. *20/20.* ABC. 9 May 2002.

Svetkey, Benjamin. "Vin at All Costs." *EW.com* 26 July 2002. Accessed 22 Mar. 2012 <http://www.ew.com/ew/article/0,,330344,00.html>.

Talalay, Kathryn. *Composition in Black and White: The Life of Philippa Schuyler.* New York: Oxford UP, 1995.

Tate, Claudia. *Psychoanalysis and Black Novels: Desire and Protocols of Race.* New York: Anchor, 1995.

Terborg-Penn, Rosalyn. "African Feminism: A Theoretical Approach to the History of Women in the African Diaspora." *Women in Africa and the African Diaspora.* Ed. Rosalyn Terborg-Penn and Andrea Benton Rushing. Washington, DC: Howard UP, 1996. 23–41.

Terry, Don. "The Skin Game: Do White Voters Like Barack Obama Because 'He's Not Really Black?'" *Chicago Tribune.com* 24 Oct. 2004. Accessed 7 Oct. 2006 <http://www.chicagotribune.com/features/magazine/chi-0410240530oct24,1,3154871.story>.

Testino, Mario. "Halle's Hollywood." *Vogue* Sept. 2010. Mariotestino.com. Accessed 22 Mar. 2011 <http://www.mariotestino.com/page/686>.

Thigpen, David E. Rev. of *Butterfly. Time* 15 Sept. 1997: 113.

"Thomas Odhiambo." *Practicing Science, Living Faith: Interviews with Twelve Leading Scientists.* Ed. Philip Clayton and Jim Schaal. New York: Columbia UP, 2007. 109–20.

Thomas, William Hannibal. *The American Negro: What He Was, What He Is, and What He May Become.* New York: Macmillan, 1901.

Toomer, Jean. "The Cane Years." *The Wayward and the Seeking: A Collection of Writings by Jean Toomer.* Ed. Darwin T. Turner. Washington, DC: Howard UP, 1982. 116–27.

———. "The Crock of Problems." *Jean Toomer: Selected Essays and Literary Criticism.* Ed. Robert B. Jones. Knoxville: U of Tennessee P, 1996. 55–59.

"Tyra Banks Finally Addresses 'Top Model' Bi-Racial Photo Shoot Controversy." *Oxygen.com* Accessed 1 Dec. 2009 <http://features.oxygen.com/celebrity-news/tyra-banks-finally-addresses-top-model-bi-racial-photo-shoot-controversy>.

Udovitch, Mim. "An Unmarried Woman." *Rolling Stone* 5 Feb. 1998: 30–32.

United States Bureau of the Census. "Overview of Race and Hispanic Origin." *Census 2000.* Brief 5. Washington: GPO, Mar. 2001.

Vozick-Levison, Simon. "Nick Cannon Calls Out Eminem for Insulting Mariah Carey: Pick a Side!" *EW.com* 11 May 2009. Accessed 1 May 2011 <http://music-mix.ew.com/2009/05/11/cannon-eminem/>.

Wald, Gayle. *Crossing the Line: Racial Passing in Twentieth-Century U.S. Literature and Culture.* Durham, NC: Duke UP, 2000.

Walker, Rebecca. *Black, White, and Jewish: Autobiography of a Shifting Self.* New York: Riverhead, 2001.

———. "Black, White and Jewish." *Glamour* Mar. 2001: 174, 181–84.

———. "Double Blood." *Are We Born Racist?: New Insights from Neuroscience and Positive Psychology.* Ed. Jason Marsh, Rodolfo Mendoza-Denton, and Jeremy Adam Smith. Boston: Beacon, 2010. 130–35.

———. "Ebony Debate: One-Drop Rule." *Ebony.* May 2011: 90.

———. "Higher Yellow." *Giant Steps: The New Generation of African American Writers.* Ed. Kevin Young. New York: HarperCollins, 2000. 244–49.

———. Interview. "Border Talk." *PBS Online.* Accessed 17 Oct. 2003 <http://www.pbs.org/pov/pov2002/borders/talk/dialogue009_rw.html>.

———. "Introduction." *Mixed: An Anthology of Short Fiction on the Multiracial Experience.* Ed. Chandra Prasad. New York: Norton, 2006.

———. "Pale As I Am." *Essence* June 2002: 119+.

Wallenstein, Peter. "Interracial Marriage on Trial: *Loving v. Virginia* (1967)." *Race on Trial: Law and Justice in American History.* Ed. Annette Gordon-Reed. New York: Oxford UP, 2002. 177–96.

Washington, Jesse. "Obama's True Colors: Black, White . . . or Neither?" *Newsweek.com* 14 Dec. 2008. Accessed 15 Dec. 2008 <http://www.newsweek.com/id/174404/page/1>.

Washington, Mary Helen. "Nella Larsen: Mystery Woman of the Harlem Renaissance" *Ms.* Dec. 1980: 44–50.

Watkins, S. Craig. *Hip Hop Matters: Politics, Popular Culture, and the Struggle for the Soul of a Movement.* Boston: Beacon, 2006.

Watts, Eric King. "Border Patrolling and 'Passing' in Eminem's *8 Mile.*" *Critical Studies in Media Communications* 22.3 (Aug. 2005): 187–205.

Werbner, Pnina. "Vernacular Cosmopolitanism." *Theory, Culture & Society* 23.2–3 (May 2006): 496–98.

"What's Black-A-Lackin'?" *Girlfriends: The Final Season.* Writ. Kevin and Michele Marburger. Dir. Tracee Ellis Ross. CW, 2010. DVD.

White, Deborah Gray. *Ar'n't I a Woman?: Female Slaves in the Plantation South.* New York: Norton, 1999.

"Why Obama Chooses 'Black' Over 'Biracial.'" Natl. Public Radio 9 Jan. 2008. Accessed 14 July 2008 <http://www.npr.org/templates/story/story.php?storyId=17958438>.

Wickham, DeWayne. "Bassett Criticism Has Its Merit." *USA Today* 8 July 2002: 15A.

Wieder, Tamara. "Saving Race." *The Boston Phoenix.Com* 14–20 May. Accessed 11 June 2005 <http://www.bostonphoenix.com/boston/news_features/qa/multi_1/documents/03827943.asp>

Williams, Bettye J. "Nella Larsen: Early Twentieth Century Novelist of Afrocentric Feminist Thought." *College Language Association Journal* 39.2 (1995): 165–78.

Williams, Gregory. *Life on the Color Line: The True Story of a White Boy Who Discovered He Was Black.* New York: Dutton, 1995.

Williams, Patricia. "Bulworth Agonistes." *The Nation* 7 June 1998: 11.

Williamson, Joel. *New People: Miscegenation and Mulattoes in the United States.* 1980. Baton Rouge: Louisiana State UP, 1995.

Willie, Sarah. "Playing the Devil's Advocate: Defending a Multiracial Identity in Fractured Community." *Names We Call Home: Autobiography of Racial Identity.* Ed. Becky Thompson and Sangeeta Tyagi. New York: Routledge, 1996. 275–81.

"Woods Calls Obama's Election 'Absolutely Incredible.'" *ESPN.com* 11 Nov. 2008. Accessed 22 Dec. 2011 <http://sports.espn.go.com/golf/news/story?id=3695226 >.

Yancy, George. "Racial Justice in a Black/Nonblack Society." *Mixed Messages: Multiracial Identities in the "Color-Blind" Era.* Ed. David L. Brunsma. Boulder, CO: Lynne Rienner, 2006. 49–62.

Young, Robert J. C. *Colonial Desire: Hybridity in Theory, Culture, and Race.* New York: Routledge, 1995.

Zacharek, Stephanie. Rev. of *Monster's Ball,* dir. Marc Forster. Salon.com 4 Jan. 2002. Accessed 28 Mar. 2004 <http://www.salon.com/2002/01/04/monsters_ball/ >.

Zack, Naomi. *Race and Mixed Race.* Philadelphia: Temple UP, 1994.

———, ed. *American Mixed Race: The Culture of MicroDiversity.* Lanham: Rowman & Littlefield, 1995.

Zeleny, Jeff. "Jesse Jackson Apologizes for Remarks on Obama." *New York Times* 10 July 2008. Accessed 14 July 2008 <http://www.nytimes.com/2008/07/10/us/politics/10jackson.html>.

Index

An Account of the Regular Gradation in Man (White), 14
Africa, 56, 60–61, 135n5
African Americans, 9, 18, 53, 61–62, 130n16
Africana worldview, 60
Alabama, Pace v. (1882), 15
Alcott, Linda, 56
Alexander, Donnell, 11
Ali, Suki, 94
Allen, Theodore, 11
Allure magazine, 2
Alsutany, Evelyn, 111
American Mixed Race: The Culture of Diversity (1995), 19
The American Negro (Thomas), 14
America's Next Top Model, 122
"Am I Black, White, or In Between?" (*Ebony* magazine), 101
Andrews, David L., 116
anthologies discussing mixed race, 19, 100. *See also specific works*
"Anti-Essentialism and Intersectionality: Tools to Dismantle the Master's House" (Grill), 3
Anzaldua, Gloria, 19, 56
Ashe, Bertram, 95–96
Association of Multiethnic Americans (AMEA), 11, 77–78, 101
attractiveness survey, 139n1
Aubry, Gabriel, 119–120
Aubry, Nahla, 119, 120
The Autobiography of an Ex-Colored Man, 21
Azoulay, Katya Gibel, 99
Baniana, Georgiana, 129–30n8
Banks, Tyra, 122
Bardwell, Keith, 121–22
Bassett, Angela, 117
Beatty, Warren, 115, 119
"To Be Real," 40–41
Berry, Halle: "black enough" v. "not black enough," 118; black identification, 106; blackness and "mixedness" alternative representations, 25; black racial loyalty, 115, 119; black-sentient mixed-race identity, 107–8; black woman stereotype manifestations, 119; exotic mixed-race woman, 115, 116; filmography, 116, 138n13; media beauty focus, 118–120n16; mulatta stereotype manifestations, 115–17; as "multiracial heroine," 107; mystique of mixed race, 119; on Obama, 120; one-drop rule evocation, 105, 106; optimism about multiracial/ multicultural/ future, 120; as racial harmony indicator, 115–16, 120, 138n11; on racial identification as political choice, 115; stereotypes, 115–18; tragic mulatto archetype, 107, 116–17, 138n12
Berzon, Julia, 20
Bhabha, Homi, 52, 88–89
biracial identity, 5, 75–76, 78
Black, Jewish and Interracial: It's Not the Color of Your Skin, but the Race of Your Kin, and Other Myths of Identity (Azoulay), 99

Black, White and Jewish: Autobiography of a Shifting Self (Walker), 10, 24, 78, 79, 85–94. *See also* Walker, Rebecca
Black, White, Other: Biracial Americans Talk about Race and Identity, 100
The Black Atlantic (Gilroy), 18
black culture as initial "home," 52, 54
"black enough" v. "not black enough": Berry, Halle, 118; "cool" character, 11; Moses, Jacinta *(Lady Moses)*, 54–55; Obama, Barack, 8, 9, 130nn12–13; Senna, Danzy, 6; Walker, Rebecca, 90–91
black-Jewish connection: Lee, Birdie (*Caucasia*), 70–71, 99; McBride, James, 98, 99, 102–3; Moses, Jacinta *(Lady Moses)*, 98, 99; Obama, Barack, 134n12; Walker, Rebecca, 98–99, 102–3
blackness affinity, 123–24
blackness as "cool," 11
blackness responsibility, 84–85, 98. *See also* black racial loyalty
black racial loyalty: Berry, Halle, 115, 119, 120; Crane, Helga (*Quicksand*), 33, 34, 40, 127, 134n10; Walker, Rebecca, 92, 93. *See also* blackness as initial "home"; blackness responsibility
black-sentient mixed-race identity: Berry, Halle, 107–8; black consciousness understanding, 10; blackness connections, 78–79; black politics privileging, 84; Carey, Mariah, 107–8; celebrity images, 124–26; Crane, Helga (*Quicksand*), 32, 38, 44–45; cultural memory, 123–24; explained, 2–4, 5, 20, 129n2, 129n6; focus on pertinent racial issues, 85; framework for mixed-race identity, 38; Jones, Rashida, 125–26; Lee, Birdie (*Caucasia*), 68, 69–70, 72–76; McBride, James, 78–79, 81–82, 85; memory and legacy importance, 85–86; Moses, Jacinta *(Lady Moses)*, 59; multilayered racial identity view, 101–3; multiplicity of characteristics, 123; Obama, Barack, 7–8, 78–79; political slant, 99; reliance on the past, 81–82, 90; as visceral, 82; Walker, Rebecca, 78–79, 94
black v. biracial identity, 3, 129n5
"black/white," 5
Bodies That Matter (Butler), 39
Bogle, Donald, 137n5
border crossing metaphor: Carey, Mariah, 108; Lee, Birdie (*Caucasia*), 58; Moses, Jacinta *(Lady Moses)*, 58; Obama, Barack, 96; Walker, Rebecca, 87, 88, 91–92, 94
Borderlands/La Frontera (Anzaldua), 19
"*border patrolling*," 37
Brady, Owen E., 56
Bratter, Jennifer, 137n5
British blackness experience, 53, 61–62
Brody, Adrian, 118–19
Brooks, Freddie (*A Different World*), 124, 139n6
Brown, Sterling, 20
Brown, William Wells, 21
Brunsma, David L., 3, 19, 32, 121, 123
Burnin' Down The House: Home in African American Literature (Prince), 51
Butler, Judith, 39
Butterfield, Stephen, 81

Campanile, Carl, 130n15
"Can Barack Obama Win the Black Vote?," 6
Cane, 21
Cannon, Nick, 113
Cape Verdeans, 71

Carey, Mariah: as biracial "spokesperson," 112; blackness and "mixedness" alternative representations, 25; black-sentient mixed-race identity, 107–8, 114; blondeness, 110; career activity and physical transformations, 111–12; hypersexuality, 109–11, 113; mulatta stereotype manifestations, 108–11, 112–13; multicultural heritage championship, 112; multiple cultural and racial manifestations, 114; multiracial Barbie, 110; "multiracial heroine," 107; on Obama, 120; one-drop rule evocation, 105, 106; optimism about multiracial/multicultural/ future, 120; "racechanges," 108; racial ambiguity, 108–9, 137n5; as racial harmony indicator, 120; shifting racial movements, 110–12; "in-between" status and stereotypes, 108–9; tragic mulatto archetype, 107, 109
Caucasia (Senna), 24, 64, 69. *See also* Lee, Birdie (*Caucasia*); Senna, Danzy
Chambers, Veronica, 111
"The Changing Face of America" (*Parade* magazine cover), 1–2
Chappelle, Dave, 106
chapter summaries, 23–25
Chesnutt, Charles, 21, 119
Chicano mestizos, 56
Child, Lydia Maria, 20–21
childhood desire for borders (racial identity), 86–87
childhood racial difference consciousness, 80–82, 83, 87–91
Cirrincione, Vincent, 117–18
"'Claiming': White Ambition, Multiracial Identity, and the New American Racial Passing" (McCarroll), 105
Clotel: Or, the President's Daughter, a Narrative of Slave Life in the United States (Brown), 21
Cohen, Alex, 8
Cole, C.L., 116
Cole, John, 7
Collins, Patricia Hill, 59–60
colonial mimicry, 88–89
The Color Line: A Brief in Behalf of the Unborn" (Ellwood), 16
The Color of Water: A Black Man's Tribute to His White Mother (McBride), 4, 24, 25, 37, 78–85. *See also* McBride, James
Commonwealth of Virginia, Loving v. (1967), 17
concepts of race: American history, 13–17; black-sentient mixed-race identity, 2–4, 129n2, 129n6; characterization in literature and film, 20–23; contemporary fascination and confusion, 10–13; "home" concept and mixed race, 25; interracial marriages, 10–11, 16–17; mixed-race as "other," 14; mixed-race movement, 18–20; music, 23; "nation"-"race" interconnectedness, 8–9; Obama, 5–10; overview, 1–4; racial ambiguity, 23; racial contradictions, 15, 131–32n27; racism underpinnings, 19–20; as remix, 23; scholarly discourse, 17–20; stereotypes, 20–23; terminology, 2–4, 13–20. *See also* one-drop rule; *specific individuals and literary works*
contradictions inherent in blackness, 84
Conway, Moncure Daniel, 16
"coolness" as black, 11
The Corndog Man (1999 movie), 23
cosmopolitanism, 3–4, 5, 129n7
Crane, Helga (*Quicksand*): biological background, 36, 37; biracial identity, 32; bird metaphor, 41–42;

Crane, Helga (*Quicksand*) (cont.)
blackness affinity, 123–24; blackness limitations, 48–49; black racial loyalty, 33, 34, 40, 127, 134n10; black-sentient mixed-race identity, 28, 32, 38, 44–45; closet metaphor, 38–39; clothing as limited agency symbol, 38–39, 134n11; colors, 33; contradictions inherent in blackness, 84; contradictory beliefs, 40; creolization, 29; discriminatory behavior from both blacks and whites, 37–38; evolution of self-identity, 48; geographical changes and identity changes, 28–29, 34–35; identity flexibility, 36–37; limitations of racelessness goal, 28–30, 43, 49; loneliness and mixed-race individuals, 46; monoracial identity resistance, 35–36, 39–40, 41, 45; mulatto classification and U.S. Census, 29, 133n1; multiplicity of black identity, 41; overview, 23–24; power of black racial ties, 42, 44, 45; psychological interpretation, 32; "queer" references, 33–34; racial dilemma, 32; racial fetishization, 42; racial identity agency, 42, 45–48, 49, 50; racial identity flexibility, 36; racial stereotyping, 42–43; rebellion against racial rules and classifications, 33–34, 47; religious conversion, 45–47; romanticization of Africa, 135n5; search for racial "home," 34–35, 44–50, 126–27; self-formation process, 28, 36–37; shame element of mixed-race identity, 37–38; social expectations adherence struggle, 44, 48, 49, 134n12; social status, 37, 38–39; tragic mulatto archetype, 43, 49–50
creolization, 29
cultural memory, 10
current fascination with mixed race, 10–11, 10–13, 131n18

Daley, Carson, 113
Dalmage, Heather M., 37
Dandridge, Dorothy, 116, 117
Dash, Julie, 23
Davis, James, 90
"Dear Ms. Larsen, There's a Mirror Looking Back" (Durrow), 30
Dear Senator: A Memoir by the Daughter of Strom Thurmond, 24
defense mechanism, 57
Delgado, Daniel J., 19, 121, 123
Derricote, Toi, 92
Devil in a Blue Dress (Mosley novel and 1995 movie), 22–23
Dickerson, Deborah, 6
Diesel, Vin, 125
A Different World, 124
"diluted" black identity, 6
displacement, 69–70, 72. *See* search for racial "home"
"doing v. being," 85
Dreams from My Father: A Story of Race and Inheritance (Obama), 9, 24, 95–100. *See also* Obama, Barack
Du Bois, W.E.B., 87
Dunbar, Paul Laurence, 41
Durrow, Heidi W., 21, 30
Durrow, Mark, 100
Dyer, Richard, 106–7, 110

Ebony magazine, 101
Ego Trip's Big Book of Racism! 113, 116
Elemeno, 62–63
Ellison, Ralph, 7, 63
Ellwood, Charles A., 16
Eminem, 113
Essence magazine, 10, 113
ethnicity testing, 105–6, 137n2

Fanon, Franz, 42, 64, 65, 69, 84–85
fatherlessness, 66–67, 72
Ferguson, Plessy v. (1896), 15, 132n20
fetishization of biracial women, 11–12, 131n22
flesh memory, 72–73
focus on pertinent racial issues, 85
Foley, Barbara, 95
Foucault, Michel, 12
Freakonomics, 121
Frucht, Abby, 58–59

Garvey, Marcus, 33
gender identity and mixed race, 58
"Generation E.A. Ethnically Ambiguous" (*New York Times*), 23
geographical changes and identity changes, 28–29, 34–35, 62, 64. *See also* border crossing metaphor; search for racial "home"
Gilroy, Paul, 18, 51
Ginsberg, Elaine, 114
Girlfriends, 124–25
The Girl Who Fell from the Sky (Durrow), 21
Gladwell, Malcolm, 34
Glissant, Edouard, 29
Gloster, Hugh M., 31–32
Goldsmith, Meredith, 33
Golub, Mark, 132n30
Gordon, Lewis, 19
Gossett, Thomas, 14
Grill, Tina, 3
the *Guardian*, 114
Gubar, Susan, 108
Guns 'n Roses, 23

"halfing," 124
Hall, Stuart, 12, 81–82
Halle Berry: A Stormy Life, 116
Harlem Renaissance, 21
Harold, Erika, 12
Harpers Bazaar, 119
Harris, Cheryl, 11
Haurykiewicz, Julie, 13
Hernandez, Tanya Kateri, 19, 137n14
Hershel, Helena Jia, 57
"Higher Yellow" (Walker), 66
Hirschberg, Lynne, 119
homelessness. *See* search for racial "home"
hooks, bell, 34, 134n10
Horne, Lena, 117
Horton, Hayward Derrick, 6
The House Behind the Cedars (Chesnutt), 21, 119
"How It Feels To Be Colored Me" (Hurston), 67
Hunter, Michele, 74
Hurston, Zora Neale, 13, 67
Hutchinson, George, 28, 28–29, 30, 32
"hybridity"-homosexuality association, 58
"hybrid" nature of African Americans, 9, 130n16
hyperawareness of race, 53. *See also* childhood desire for borders; childhood racial difference consciousness; self-identity formation complexity

Ifekwunigwe, Jayne O., 53, 54
Illusions (1983 movie), 23
I Love You, Man, 125
Imitation of Life (1934 movie), 113, 132–33n40
Imitation of Life (1959 movie), 113
interracial marriages, 10–11
Invisible Man (Ellison), 7, 63, 64, 69
invisibleness, 62–66, 68. *See also* passing
"Is There A Plot To Create A 'Colored' Buffer Race in America?" (*Ebony* magazine), 101

Jackson, Jesse, 130n13
Jefferson, Thomas, 131–32n27
Jewish-black connection. *See* black-Jewish connection
Jewish-mixed race connection, 70, 71
Johnson, James Weldon, 80
Johnson, Lynne D., 117
Johnson, Mat, 102
Jones, Alice, 16
Jones, Grace, 138n18
Jones, Lisa, 18, 102–3, 110, 115
Jones, Rashida, 125–26
Jones, Suzanne W., 4

Kangaris, Charlie, 119
Kelley, Matt, 2
Kerr, Philip, 118
King, George A., 130n15
Know, Robert, 14
Kroeger, Brooke, 129n5

Lady Moses (Roy), 24, 53–62. *See also* Moses, Jacinta *(Lady Moses)*; Roy, Lucinda
Larsen, Nella, 21, 23–24, 27, 30, 133n2. *See also* Crane, Helga (*Quicksand*); *Quicksand* (Larsen)
Lee, Birdie (*Caucasia*): black culture as initial "home," 52; black-Jewish connection, 70–71, 99; blackness affinity, 123–24; black-sentient mixed-race identity, 68, 69–70, 72–76; border crossing metaphor, 58; contradictions inherent in blackness, 84; corporeality, 72–73; displacement, 69–70, 72; fatherlessness, 66–67, 72; flesh memory, 72–73; geographical changes and identity changes, 62, 64; home as imagined space, 62–63; hyperawareness of race, 53; invisibleness, 62–66, 68; Jewish identity, 70, 71; limitations of racelessness goal, 75; mixed race-Jewish connection, 70, 71; monoracial identity resistance, 69; passing, 70–72; passing and invisibility, 64–65, 67–69; passing as locale, 52; passing for black, 71–72; psychological defense mechanism, 57; racial identity formation, 52–53; racial root recognition, 4; search for father, 73; search for racial "home," 52, 62, 65, 68; self-awareness as other than black, 80; spirituality of color, 73; tragic mulatto archetype, 67–68, 73–74; as transnational, 4
Lee, Cole (*Caucasia*), 66, 126
Lee, Deck (*Caucasia*), 66, 126
Lee, Wanda M., 105
Levitt, Steven, 121
Light in August, 21
Limbaugh, Rush, 6
limitations of racelessness goal, 28–30, 43, 49, 75
Lopez, George, 105–6, 137nn1–2
Lost Boundaries (1949 movie), 132–33n40
Loving v. Commonwealth of Virginia (1967), 17

Mademoiselle magazine, 11–12, 12–13
Maus, Derek C., 56
MAVIN Foundation, 2, 102
McBride, James: biracial identity, 78; birth, 136n11; black-Jewish connection, 98; blackness responsibility, 98; black-sentient mixed-race identity, 78–79, 81–82, 85; childhood desire for borders (racial identity), 86–87; childhood racial difference consciousness, 80–82, 83; closeness to blackness with connection to Jewishness, 99; complexity of

self-identification, 100; fluidity of identity choices, 37; frustration of racial/political reality, 4; identity formation complexity, 79–82; on mixed race "nationalism," 127; Orthodox Jewish practice of mourning, 102–3; outsider race labeling reaction, 100; political slant, 99; on poverty vs. identity discovery, 126; racial identification as choice, 84; racial responsibility, 84–85; racial truth evasion by parent, 82; responsibility to both sides of ancestry, 96; search for racial "home," 93–94; visceral feeling of black sentient mixed-race identity, 82; as writer-activist, 78–79
McCarroll, Meredith, 105
McDowell, Deborah E., 32
"Meet the Parents" (*Mademoiselle* magazine), 12–13
memory and legacy importance, 85–86
miner's canary and racial marginalization, 73, 135n9
Misceg-narrations (Scherr Salgado), 77
Mixed: An Anthology of Short Fiction on the Multiracial Experience, 21, 25
MixedFolks.com, 11
mixed marriage legalization, 17
Mixed: My Life in Black and White (Nissel), 24
"mixed race," 5
"mixed-race beauty," 12
mixed-race experience of Africa, 60–61
mixed race-Jewish connection, 71
mixed-race "nationalism," 99, 127
mixed-race organizations. *See* multiracial organizations
monoracial identity resistance, 35–36, 39–40, 41, 45, 57, 60, 69
Monroe, Marilyn, 110, 137n6
Monster's Ball, 117
Morgan, Joan, 110
Morrison, Toni, 51
Moses, Jacinta *(Lady Moses)*: African American v. black Briton experience, 53, 61–62; binary thinking, 59–60; black culture as initial "home," 54; "black enough" v. "not black enough," 54–55; black-Jewish connection, 99; black-sentient mixed-race identity, 59; border crossing metaphor, 58; "coloured" identification, 53; contradictions inherent in blackness, 84; fluid borders, 59; hybridity-homosexuality association, 58; hyperawareness of race, 53; mixed-race experience of Africa, 60–61; monoracial identity resistance, 57, 60; overall estrangement, 55; passing as locale, 52; psychological defense mechanism, 57; racial identity formation, 52–53; romanticization of Africa, 56, 61, 135n5; same-sex desire, 58; search for racial "home," 52–57, 62; shame element of mixed-race identity, 55–56, 134–35n3; split into two selves, 57
Mosley, Walter, 22–23
Movement Child, 87, 89
mulatto, 13–14, 16, 29, 131nn24–25, 133n1. *See also* tragic mulatto archetype
The Mulatto People, 78
"mule" imagery, 13–14, 131n24
multicultural movement, 2, 101, 102, 103, 129n4
multilayered view of racial identity, 101–3
"Multiple Discourse: Racial Classifications in an Era of Color-Blind Jurisprudence" (Hernandez), 19
The Multiracial Activist, 78
The Multiracial Experience: Racial Borders as the New Frontier (1996), 19

multiracial organizations: Association of Multiethnic Americans (AMEA), 77–78, 101, 135n2, Project RACE; explained, 129n4, 131n20; MAVIN Foundation, 2, 102; Project RACE, 11, 101, 135n2
Mumford, Kevin, 11
"mutt" identity, 10

Nader, Ralph, 130n13
Nakazawa, Donna, 13
"nation"-"race" interconnectedness, 8–9
need for community v. desire for personal freedom, 87
Negro Poetry and Drama (*Brown*), 20
"neo-mulatto," 6
"The New Face of America" (*Time* magazine cover), 2, 8
New Republic magazine, 7
Newsweek magazine, 2
New York Times, 23
Nissel, Angela, 24
Njeri, Itabari, 75
Noble, Melissa, 102
Nuyorican, 90
Nyong'o, Tavia, 122

O, the Oprah Magazine, 1, 2
Obama, Barack: biracial identity, 78, 96; birth, 136n11; black acceptance struggle, 96; on black anger, 99; "black enough" v. "not black enough," 8, 9, 130nn12–13; blackness and political aspirations, 8, 130nn12–13; blackness connections, 78–79; black-sentient mixed-race identity, 7–8, 78–79; border crossing metaphor, 96; community organizing with multiracial and multicultural connections, 79, 136n5; contradictions of racial perceptions of others, 5–8; cosmopolitanism variations, 4, 129–130n8; Ellison comparison, 7, 130n11; individualism v. racial identity, 95–96; mixed-race identification, 7, 130n10; "mutt" identity, 10; as racial harmony indicator, 125; racial identity v. authenticity, 9; on racial inheritance and family, 97–98; racial utopian vision, 8; responsibility to both sides of ancestry, 96; as transnational, 129–130n8
Odhiambo, Thomas, 60
Oliver, Akilah, 72–73
Olney, James, 9–10
Omi, Michael, 18
one-drop rule, 15, 84, 105–6, 137n4
optimism about multiracial/multicultural future, 120, 125–26
Orthodox Jewish practice of mourning, 102–3
otherness, 92

Pace v. Alabama (1882), 15
Page, Clarence, 6
Pappademas, Alex, 111–12
Parade magazine, 1–2, 12
passing, 67–69, 70–72, 132–33n40. *See also* invisibleness
Passing (Larsen), 21, 27, 30–31. *See also* Larsen, Nella
"Passing and the Problematic of Multiracial Pride (or, Why One Mixed Girl Still Answers to Black)" (Senna), 6
passing for black, 71–72
"Passing for White, Passing for Jewish: Mixed Race Identity in Danzy Senna and Alice Walker" (Harrison-Kahn, Lori), 71
Philadelphia Fire (Wideman), 134n2
Pinky (1949 movie), 132–33n40

Plessy v. Ferguson (1896), 15, 132n30
"The Plight of Mixed Race Adolescents" (Levitt), 121
Posnock, Ross, 5
"post-race," 9, 130n12
power of black racial ties, 42, 44, 45. *See also* black racial loyalty
Powers, William, 7
Precious: Based on the Novel Push *by Sapphire*, 108, 137n1
Prince, Valerie Sweeney, 51
Production Administrative Code, 22
The Professor's Daughter (Raboteau), 21
Project RACE, 11, 101, 135n2
psychological defense mechanism, 57

"The Quadroons" (Child), 20–21
Quicksand (Larsen), 27–50. *See also* Crane, Helga (*Quicksand*); Larsen, Nella

Raboteau, Emily, 21
Against Race (Gilroy), 51
"Race, Biraciality, and Mixed Race - In Theory" *(Gordon)*, 19
Race and Mixed Race (1993), 19
"racechanges," 108, 114
race concepts. *See* concepts of race
race definitions. *See* concepts of race
racelessness goal limitations, 28–30, 43, 49, 75
Race-Mixing: Black-White Marriage in Postwar America (Romano), 75
The Races of Men (Knox), 14
racial ambiguity, 108–9, 137n5
racial and cultural memory personalization, 93–94
"The Racial Draft" (Chappelle skit), 106
racial fetishization, 42
Racial Formations in the United States (Omi and Winant), 18
racial identification as choice, 83, 84
racial identity agency, 36, 45–48, 49, 50
racial identity formation. *See* self-identity formation complexity
racial identity switching, 88–94
Racially Mixed People in America (1992), 19
racial truth evasion, 80
racism, 19
Ramsey, Guthrie P., 124
rebellion against racial rules and classifications, 33–34, 47. *See also* monoracial identity resistance
Reese, Venus Opal, 109
Rhinelander, Alice, 16
Rhinelander, Leonard, 16
Rockquemore, Kerry Ann, 19, 32, 121, 123
Roediger, David, 11
Romano, Renee C., 75
romanticization of Africa, 61
Root, Maria P.P., 19, 83–84, 115
Roy, Lucinda, 24, 61. *See also Lady Moses* (Roy)
Rummell, Kathryn, 75

Sacred Naked Nature Girls (Oliver), 72–73
Samuels, David, 7
Savishinsky, Neil J., 33
Scheper, Jeanne, 41
Scherr Salgado, Raquel, 77
search for father, 66–67, 72, 73
search for racial "home": African Americans, 51–52; Crane, Helga (*Quicksand*), 28, 34–35, 36, 44–50, 51, 126–27; displacement of mixed-race individuals, 134n1; Lee, Birdie (*Caucasia*), 52, 62, 65, 68; McBride, James, 93–94; Morrison, Toni, 51; Moses, Jacinta *(Lady Moses)*, 52–57, 54–57, 62; Senna, Danzy, 52; Walker, Rebecca, 93–94

In Search of Nella Larsen: A Biography of the Color Line (Hutchinson), 30
Searcy, Lynn (*Girlfriends*), 124–25
segregation of races, 17
self-awareness as other than black, 80
self-identity formation complexity: Berry, Halle, 25, 108–9, 112, 114, 137n5; Carey, Mariah, 25, 108–9, 110–12, 112, 114, 137n25; Crane, Helga (*Quicksand*), 28, 32, 36–37, 40, 41, 48, 84; Lee, Birdie (*Caucasia*), 52–53, 80, 84; McBride, James, 4, 37, 79–82, 96, 100; Moses, Jacinta (*Lady Moses*), 52–53, 57, 58, 60–61, 84; Obama, Barack, 5–8, 10, 78, 95–96; Senna, Danzy, 126; Walker, Rebecca, 4–5, 84–85, 87–91, 92, 94
Selzer, Linda, 4
Senna, Danzy: on "black enough" v. "not black enough," 6; on blackness and multiplicity, 9; on current fascination with mixed race, 10; engagement with black-sentient mixed race subjectivity, 24; on mixed race "homelessness," 52; multiplicity of black identity, 40–41; on racial identity, 79; on racial self-identity and privilege, 126; *Symptomaniac*, 21–22; "transverse passing," 90. *See also Caucasia* (Senna)
separatist racial philosophy, 78, 101
Shades of Citizenship: Race and the Census in Modern Policy (Noble), 102
shame element of mixed-race identity, 37–38, 55–56, 134–35n3, 139n1
Showboat (1936 movie), 132–33n40
Show Me the Miscegenation! 10
Slash, 23
Smith, John David, 14
Smith, Zadie, 121
social expectations adherence struggle, 44, 48, 49, 134n12
social status, 37, 38–39
Sollors, Werner, 20, 49–50
The Souls of Black Folk (Du Bois), 87
"Speaking in Tongues" (Smith), 121
Spencer, Rainier, 130n16
spirituality of color, 73
split into two selves, 57
Stars (Dyer), 106–7
Stephens, Vincent, 110, 114
stereotypes, 92, 108–11, 115–18. *See also* tragic mulatto archetype
Story-Jacinta (*Lady Moses*), 60–61
Stowe, Harriet Beecher, 136n9
Streeter, Carolyn, 110
Strictly Business, 117–18
Summer, Cree, 124
Sundquist, Eric J., 123
"Sympathy" (Dunbar), 41
Symptomaniac, 21–22

Talk of the Nation (NPR), 6
Testimonies Concerning Slavery (Conway), 16
Their Eyes Were Watching God (Hurston), 13
"Therapeutic Considerations in Work with Biracial Girls" (Lee), 105
"Therapeutic Perspectives on Biracial Identity Formation and Internalized Oppression" (Hershel), 57
Thomas, William Hannibal, 14
Time magazine, 2, 8
tragic mulatto archetype: Berry, Halle, 107, 116–17, 138n12; Carey, Mariah, 107, 109; Crane, Helga (*Quicksand*), 43, 49–50; Lee, Birdie (*Caucasia*), 67–68, 73–74; as literary and popular culture cliché, 103; in literature, 21–22; in movies, 22–23, 132–33n40; origins, 20
"Transatlantic Minstrelsy: Performing Survival Strategies in Slavery and Hip-Hop" (Reese), 109

"transverse passing," 90–91, 136n7
The Tyra Banks Show, 129n5

Uncle Tom's Cabin (Stowe), 117, 136n9
"unhomeliness," 52. *See also* displacement; search for racial "home"
Universal Negro Improvement Association, 33
U.S. Census form classification, 101–2, 106, 137n14

Vibe, 113
visceral black-sentient mixed-race identity, 82

Wald, Gayle: invisibleness, 68
Walker, Rebecca: on alienation, 66; anonymity, 92; on Berry and one-drop rule, 106; biracial identity, 78; birth, 136n11; "black enough" v. "not black enough," 90–91; blackness responsibility, 98; black racial loyalty, 92, 93; black-sentient mixed-race identity, 78–79, 94; black v. biracial identity, 129n5; border crossing metaphor, 87, 88, 92, 94; childhood desire for borders (racial identity), 86–87; childhood displacement, 86–87; childhood racial contradiction and conflict, 87–91; closeness to blackness with connection to Jewishness, 98–99; colonial mimicry, 88–89; complexity of self-identification, 100; on embracing complexities of black-sentient mixed-race identity, 84–85; on familial and communal ties, 40; frustration of mixed race allegiance demands, 4–5; memory and legacy importance, 10, 85–86; need to belong v. desire for personal freedom, 87; on Obama, 9; Orthodox Jewish practice of Mourning, 102–3; otherness, 92; on pliability of racial and cultural identity, 4; political slant, 99; racial and cultural memory personalization, 93–94; racial and cultural translator role, 91–92; on racial "halfing," 124; racial identity switching, 88–94; racial neutrality with black identity, 94; on relevance of being "mixed," 1; search for racial "home," 93–94; as writer-activist, 78–79
Walters, Barbara, 110
Washington, Booker T., 91, 136n8
Watkins, Samuel Craig, 114
Werbner, Prima, 3–4
West, Kanye, 10
"What Are You? Voices of Mixed Race Young People (1999), 19, 100
White, Charles, 13–14
White, Persia, 124–25
"whitespace," 6
Who is Black (Davis), 90
"Why Obama Chooses 'Black' over Biracial" (Cohen), 8, 9
Wideman, John, 134n2
Williams, Patricia, 116–17
Williamson, Joel, 14
Willie, Sarah, 75
Winant, Howard, 18
Woods, Tiger, 6–7, 11, 116
writer-activists, 78–79

Young, Robert J.C., 58

Zahn, Paula, 7
Zarembka, Joy, 8–9

Crossing B(l)ack was designed and typeset on a Macintosh OS 10.4 computer system using InDesign software. The body text is set in 10/13 Minion Pro and display type is set in Formata. This book was designed and typeset by Stephanie Thompson and manufactured by Thomson-Shore, Inc.